The Sandhill Crane State
A Naturalist's Guide to Nebraska

Paul A. Johnsgard

The Sandhill Crane State

A Naturalist's Guide to Nebraska

Paul A. Johnsgard

School of Biological Sciences
University of Nebraska–Lincoln

Zea Books
Lincoln, Nebraska
2021

Copyright © 2021 Paul A. Johnsgard

ISBN: 978-1-60962-210-7 paperback
ISBN: 978-1-60962-211-4 e-book

doi: 10.32873/unl.dc.zea.1305

Composed in Cabin types.

Zea Books are published by the University of Nebraska–Lincoln Libraries.

Electronic (pdf) edition available online at
https://digitalcommons.unl.edu/zeabook/

Print edition available from Lulu.com at
http://www.lulu.com/spotlight/unllib

UNL does not discriminate based upon any protected status.
Please go to http://www.unl.edu/equity/notice-nondiscrimination

Abstract
This book includes the locations, descriptions, and points of biological, historical, geological, or paleontological interest of nearly 350 sites in Nebraska, most of which are free to access. Its 53,000 words include accounts of 9 state historical parks, 8 state parks, 2 national forests, 2 national monuments, and 7 national wildlife refuges as well as 181 wildlife management areas, 56 waterfowl production areas, and 54 state recreation areas. It also includes 48 state and county maps, 18 drawings, 33 photographs, and nearly 200 literature citations.

Page 1: Sandhill cranes in flight
Page 2: Sandhill cranes, dancing
Page 5 (opposite): Sandhill crane family
Page 6: Sunset with cranes

Dedicated to Paul Royster and Linnea Fredrickson,
who transformed an anticipated retirement life of increasing boredom
to one of repeated delight and self-fulfillment

Contents

List of Maps 8

List of Figures 9

List of Photographs 9

Introduction 11

Introduction to Nebraska's Natural Heritage 17

A Sampling of Nebraska's Greatest Natural and Historic Treasures 18

I. The Far Western Region 29

II. The West-Central Region 39

III. The East-Central Region 56

IV. The Eastern Region 77

Tallgrass Prairie Ecology 140

Some Remnant Tallgrass Prairies of Nebraska 152

References 158

Index 164

Maps

State Maps

S1. Nebraska's Landforms. 12
S2. Nebraska's Original Vegetation 13
S3. Nebraska Counties 14
S4. Nebraska Regions and County Description
    Sequence by Region 15

County Maps

Note: Not all county maps cover the entire county. To help with locating sites, the location of one town or city per map is shown in large type.

1. Sioux County. 96
2. Dawes County. 97
3. Sheridan and Garden Counties. 98
4. Scotts Bluff County. 99
5. Kimball County 100
6. Morrill County. 101
7. Garden and Deuel Counties. 102
8. Cherry County. 103
9. Keya Paha County 104
10. Brown County. 105
11. Thomas and Blaine Counties. 106
12. Arthur County. 107
13. Keith County 108
14. Lincoln County. 109
15. Dawson County 110
16. Chase County. 111
17. Frontier County. 112
18. Gosper and Phelps Counties 113
19. Hitchcock County 114
20. Harlan County 115
21. Knox County 116
22. Antelope County 117
23. Pierce and Madison Counties 118
24. Platte, Nance, and Merrick Counties. 119
25. Sherman County 120
26. Buffalo County. 121
27. Hall County 122
28. Hamilton and Clay Counties 123
29. York, Fillmore, and Seward Counties 124
30. Kearney and Franklin Counties. 125
31. Adams County 126
32. Dixon and Dakota Counties 127
33. Dodge County 128
34. Washington County 129
35. Saunders and Lancaster Counties 130
36. Douglas and Sarpy Counties 131
37. Seward County. .132
38. Lancaster County 133
39. Cass County 134
40. Otoe County. 135
41. Gage County 136
42. Johnson County .137
43. Nemaha and Richardson Counties. 138
44. Pawnee County .139

Figures and Photographs

Figures

Sandhill cranes in flight. 1
Sandhill crane family 5
Sandhill crane, male calling 16
Incubating upland sandpiper 23
Burrowing owl family 38
Prairie falcon and chick with green-winged teal . . . 72
American tree sparrow in winter 76
Detailed structure of big bluestem 141
Detailed structure of little bluestem 143
Detailed structure of Indiangrass 145
Western prairie fringed orchid and a visiting
    white-lined sphinx moth 147
Detailed structure of switchgrass 149
Greater prairie-chicken, male in display 150
Ferruginous hawk with rattlesnake 151
Locations of remnant tallgrass prairies in
    southeastern Nebraska 155
Loggerhead shrike on yucca stalk with seed pods. . 157
Burrowing owl, defensive threat 162
Long-billed curlew in flight. 163

Photographs

Sandhill cranes, dancing 2
Sunset with cranes 6
Platte River landscape 10
Chimney Rock 17
Cranes on the Platte River 19
Agate Fossil Beds National Monument 28
Pronghorn male, Oglala National Grassland 31
Bull elk, Pine Ridge area 33
Scotts Bluff National Monument 35
Western grebes, Crescent Lake NWR 37
Burrowing owls, young and adult 38
Bison and calf, Fort Niobrara NWR 40
Niobrara River valley, Cherry County 42
Cherry County sandhills 44
Loup River valley sandhills 47
Coyote eating a cottontail rabbit 48
Long-billed curlew, female incubating. 50
Sharp-tailed grouse, male on lek 53
Great horned owl, on nest in Cherry County 54
Sandhill crane roost, Lillian Annette Rowe
    Sanctuary 57
Greater prairie-chicken males displaying
    to a female 63
Sandhill cranes, landing on a Platte River roost . . . 65
Sandhill crane roost, Crane Trust 67
Whooping crane, adult foraging 71
Trumpeter swan family, Missouri River
    valley wetland 77
Young raccoon, Missouri River valley woods 79
White-tailed deer, doe 81
Migrating snow geese, Lancaster County 82
White-tailed deer, fawn in native prairie 84
Prairie coneflowers, Spring Creek Prairie
    Audubon Center 88
Tallgrass prairie, Spring Creek Prairie
    Audubon Center 90
Greater prairie-chicken, Pawnee County 93
Fall color, Indian Cave State Park 94, 95

Introduction

I suppose I mentally began writing this book the first day I arrived in Lincoln. I received my introduction to Nebraska on a hot day in July 1961, about a month prior to starting my initial teaching job as an instructor in the University of Nebraska's Zoology Department. I had just returned from two years of research in England and was eager to begin life again in the United States.

I spent that month investigating the university's facilities, especially its library and art gallery, and seeing Lincoln's parks and other municipal attractions. I soon discovered that remnants of tallgrass prairie were not far from town and that relict saline marshlands bordered Little Salt Creek north of town. Furthermore, there was a gorgeous prairie river nearby, the Platte, that was far more fascinating than the muddy and sluggish Red River that flowed lazily past the tiny village where I had grown up in southeastern North Dakota. As time permitted during my first year of teaching, I also visited Omaha's great Joslyn Art Museum, its then-fledgling zoo, and the spectacular floodplain hardwood forest along the Missouri River at Fontenelle Forest.

At that time I was only vaguely aware of the more distant and vast Nebraska Sandhills region, the pine-covered canyons and bluffs of the Pine Ridge region in northwestern Nebraska, and the stunning Niobrara River valley along their northern edge. All of these wonders—the Platte, the Sandhills, and the Niobrara—would eventually beguile me to the point that I felt obligated to write books about each of them. By the end of my first year in Nebraska I had decided that this was the place I wanted to spend the rest of my life, and during my remaining years to explore it and try to understand some of its physical beauties and its biological complexities.

Now, sixty years later, I feel as if I have come full circle, having traveled tens of thousands of miles over the state's highways, roads, and sandy trails; waded its rivers and marshes; and reclined silently among its grasses, wildflowers, and grassland birds, surrounded by some of the most beautiful prairies left in the country.

As a means of partial repayment for my wonderful life in Nebraska, I recently decided that I should describe most of the state's natural attractions for others who might like to take similar journeys of discovery. I think people can benefit from information about what these sites are like, where they are located, and why they are worth visiting. With a few exceptions, these are rural rather than city sites, and most are free to access rather than being commercial enterprises.

Biological features are constantly changing, and what I have described here may be quite different a year or decade hence. In 1961 perhaps 100,000 sandhill cranes migrated through Nebraska along with about a million snow geese, whereas now there are about a million cranes and 12 million snow geese. On the other hand, prairie-adapted birds have declined drastically over the past few decades, as have most insect-eating songbirds.

Ninety percent of the state's temporary wetlands that were present a century ago are now gone, and some long-standing creeks have not held water for decades. Several of our rivers are now variously polluted and their waters diverted for agriculture. Nebraska ranks second in the American states (behind California) in terms of total land acreage under irrigation. Fertilizer-caused nitrate levels in the central Platte River region are a serious human health concern. Some of our city water sources are now in real jeopardy from pollution accidents, and our rivers are increasingly in danger of flooding or drying up, mostly because of climate change and overuse.

Looking down from a jet at nearly 40,000 feet, the surface of Nebraska looks like a wholly flat tableland, and its pollution problems are not evident, although the land is often pockmarked with the evidence of center-pivot irrigation systems. Yet, it is tilted slightly downward from west to east, at an average rate of about nine feet per mile. As a result, most of the state's rivers flow eastwardly at a moderate rate until they reach the fairly deep Missouri River valley, where they are deflected southward (Map S1).

Bluffs and escarpments are mostly characteristic of the Pine Ridge region in the northwestern corner of the state, the Niobrara valley from the northern edge of the Sandhills east to the Missouri River valley, the North Platte valley, and the Wildcat Hills (directly south of the North Platte valley and north of the long, but now mostly

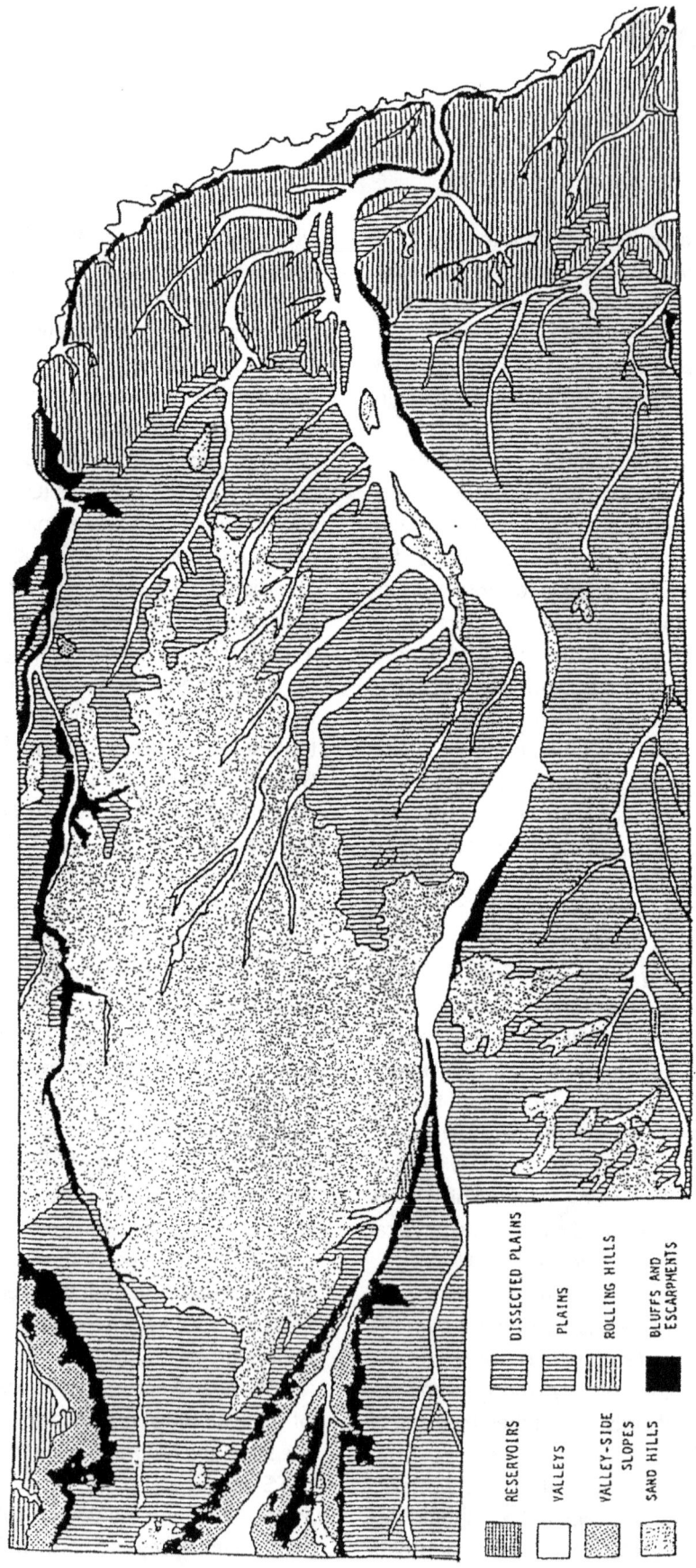

S1. Map of Nebraska's Landforms. After a map by the University of Nebraska Conservation and Survey Division.

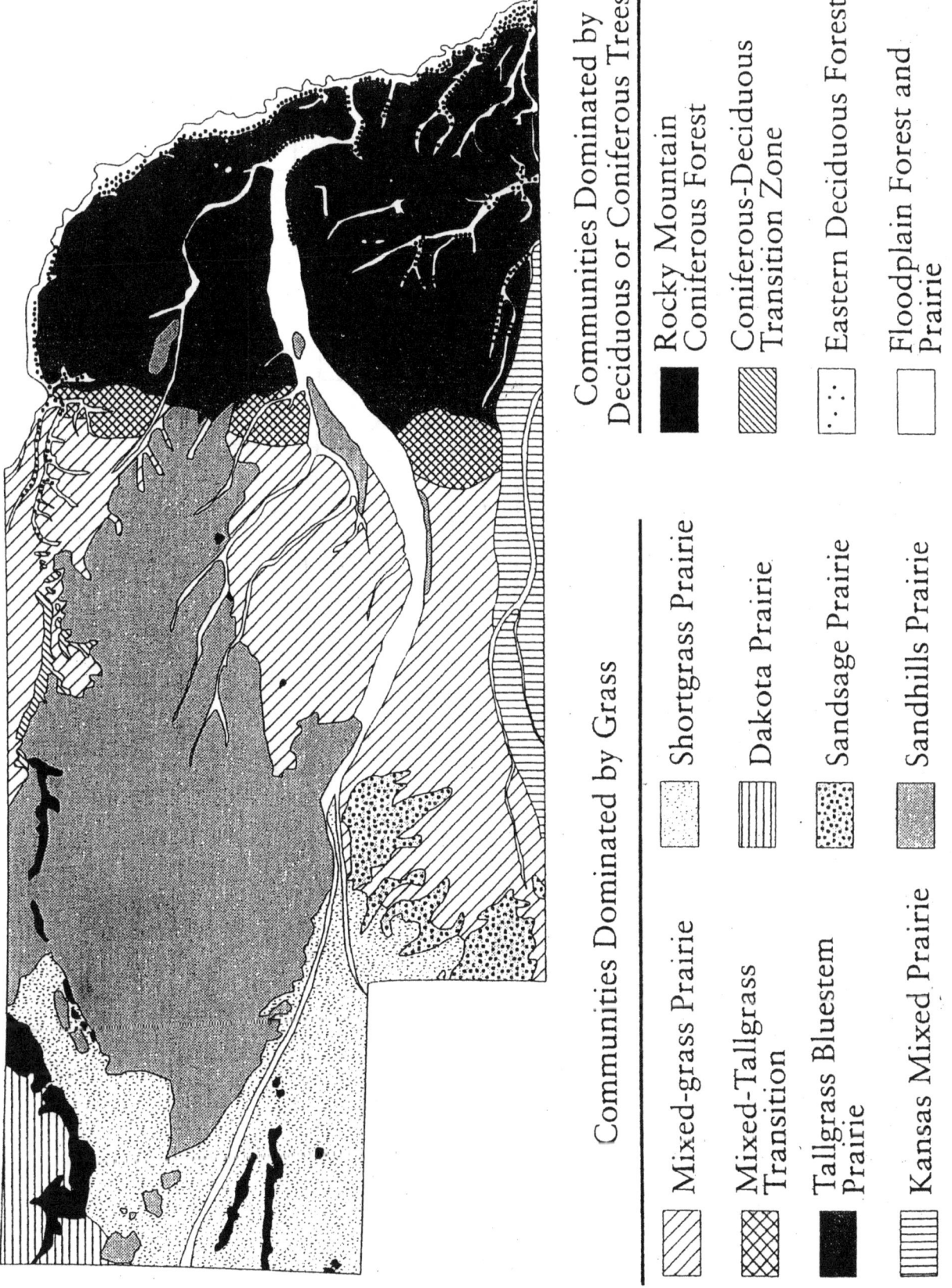

S2. Map of Nebraska's Original Vegetation. After a map by Robert Kaul.

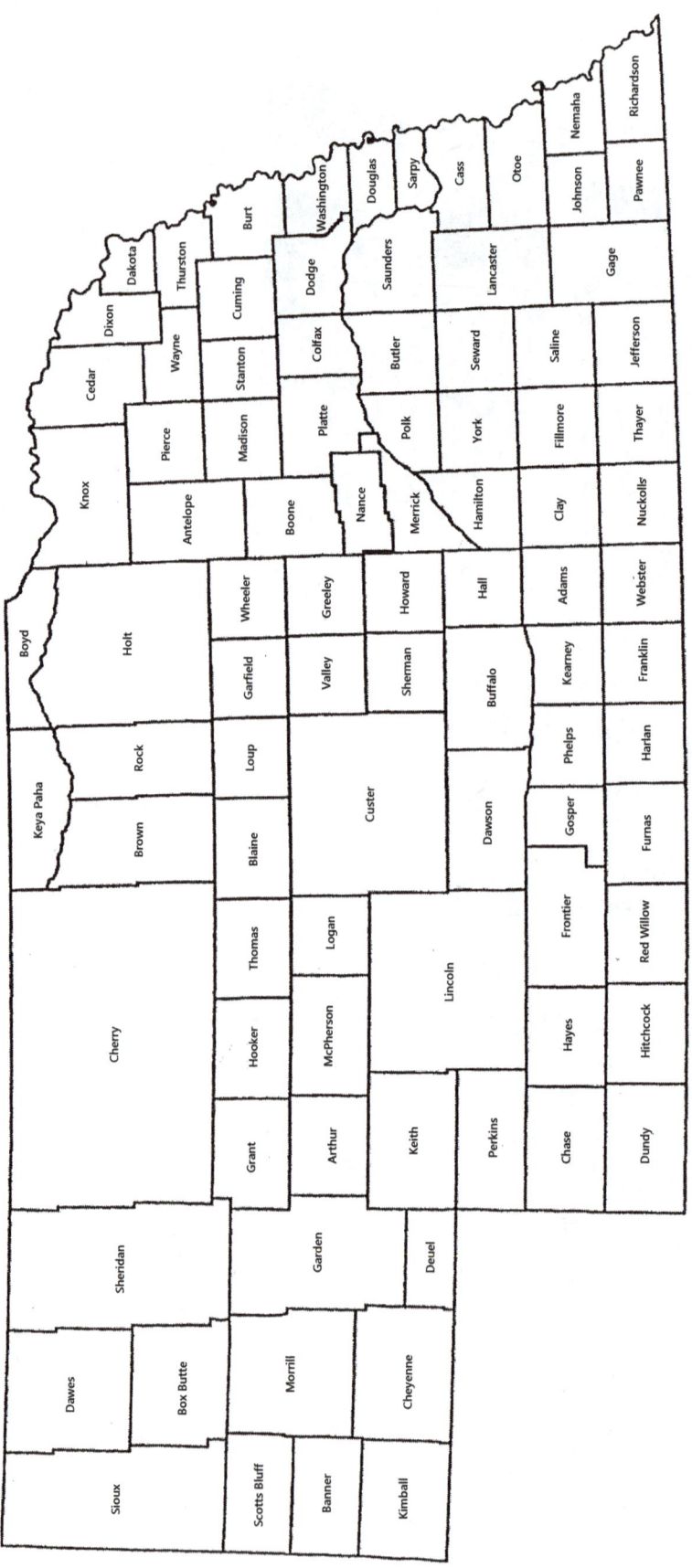

S3. Map of Nebraska Counties

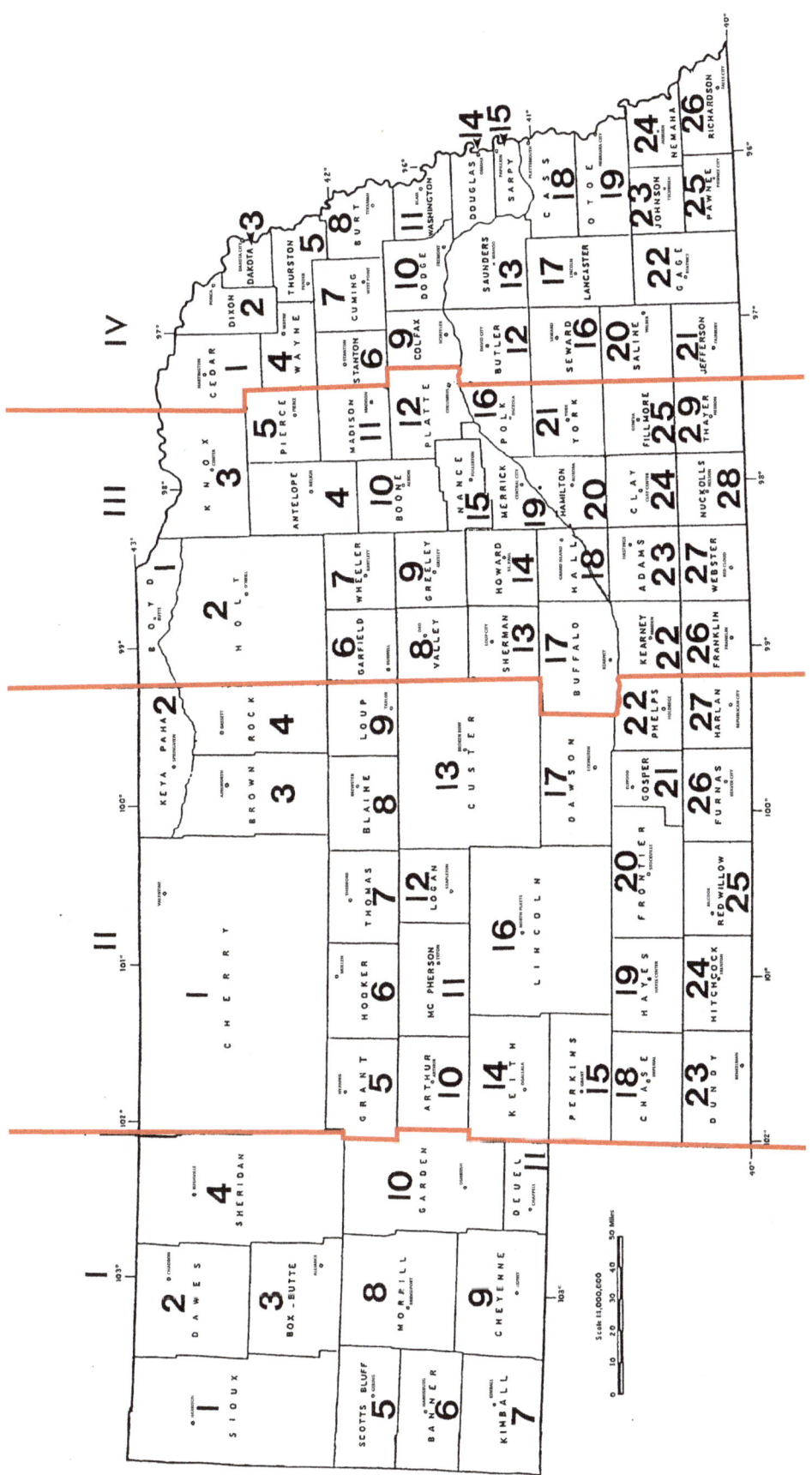

S4. Map of Nebraska Regions and County Description Sequence by Region

dry, Pumpkin Creek). Bluffs also occur to a limited degree along the southern bank of the Platte River and the western bank of the Missouri River.

The unique Nebraska Sandhills occupy a vast area of deep sand deposited by post-glacial rivers from the Rocky Mountains and cover about 19,000 square miles between the Niobrara and Platte Rivers, with a few extensions south of the Platte River. Beneath the Sandhills is an even greater region of water-saturated sands, the Ogallala aquifer, which extends from southernmost South Dakota to Texas.

Otherwise, the surface of Nebraska is almost entirely composed of plains and dissected (wind- and water-eroded) plains. Additionally, in eastern Nebraska gently rolling hills are largely covered by soils ("till") and huge rounded boulders (glacial "erratics") that were carried in fairly recently by Pleistocene glaciers from much farther north. As recently as 175 years ago, these boulders served as convenient rubbing posts for bison in their great herds that migrated through Nebraska.

The original vegetation pattern of Nebraska (Map S2) shows many geographic similarities to its landforms, especially in the case of the Nebraska Sandhills prairie. Generally the western "panhandle" was once covered by shortgrass prairie, the middle third with mixed-grass prairie, and the eastern third with tallgrass prairie. This vegetation pattern reflects the fact that the west-to-east winds typical of the state arrive in western Nebraska in a water-depleted condition, owing to rain-shadow effects from mountains farther west that extract most of their moisture. Moving east, the winds gradually pick up moisture from the more moisture-rich air masses moving north from the Gulf Coast, especially in the form of spring and summer storms. The eastern region's associated tallgrass prairies and its deep organic-rich and highly fertile soils have resulted in the nearly total destruction of these prairies, as they have been gradually plowed and replaced by agricultural cropland.

Farther west in Nebraska, many large areas of relatively unmodified prairie still remain, although much of it has been highly overgrazed. Most of our few riverine hardwood forests also still survive, at least as second-growth stands, although recent forest fires have decimated some of the best examples. Likewise, the coniferous forests of western Nebraska are still present, although they too have had a serious recent fire history.

Nebraska has a total of 93 counties (Map S3), with those in the west more sparsely populated and generally larger than the other counties. Cherry County is by far the largest. In it and in many western counties, the cattle population easily outnumbers the human population, and until recent decades and the advent of mass poisoning programs by state and federal agencies (Johnsgard, 2005), the prairie dog population probably greatly outnumbered both.

This book is divided into four broad geographic regions, numbered west to east (I to IV). Within each region as many as 29 counties are described. They are organized sequentially from north to south and secondarily from west to east (Map S4). Nearly 350 publicly and privately owned sites of possible interest to naturalists are described. Major site abbreviations are **NWR**s (national wildlife refuges, 7 described), **WMA**s (wildlife management areas, 181 described), **WPA**s (waterfowl production areas, 56 described), and **SRA**s (state recreation areas, 54 described). Because detailed information on them can be easily found elsewhere, I have generally not included city zoos in my descriptions, and because few of the state's smaller municipal parks support any rare species of special biological interest, I have also generally not provided separate descriptions of these sites.

Sandhill crane, male calling

Introduction to Nebraska's Natural Heritage

Nebraska has an abundance of natural habitats and associated wildlife, including 7 national wildlife refuges totaling 174,000 acres, 2 national forests totaling 257,000 acres, 2 national monuments totaling 5,900 acres, and 1 national grassland totaling 94,000 acres. Nebraska also has 8 state parks, 9 state historical parks, more than 60 state recreation areas, and about 300 wildlife management areas. About 800,000 acres are public-access state and federal lands in the state. Nebraska's state and federal public lands represent about 2 percent of the state's total area.

Among land vertebrate species, the current state species lists for Nebraska include 89 species of mammals and 463 birds (Johnsgard, 2020a) as well as 14 amphibians and 48 reptiles (Ballinger, Lynch, and Smith, 2010). County checklists of the birds of any of the state's 93 counties can be downloaded at www.noubirds.org/Birds/CountyChecklists.aspx. An online source to locating more than 300 birding sites in Nebraska can be found at http://nebraskabirdingtrails.com/, and a county-by-county online guide to birding in Nebraska ("Birds of Nebraska – Online") exists at https://birds.outdoornebraska.gov/. I have tried to obtain and summarize biological and historical information of interest to birders, ornithologists, botanists, ecologists, naturalists, and others on the great majority of the state's federal, state, and privately owned natural areas as well as at a few of the state's natural history museums.

Over the last 60 years I have visited many if not most of the locations here described. The site descriptions in this book in part were derived from those experiences and from external data I gathered for several of my earlier books (including Johnsgard, 1979, 2007a, 2007b, 2009a, 2015b, and 2018a). The birding site descriptions in my 1979 book were later used by me to a large degree as the basis for writing digitized site descriptions used on the Nebraska Birding Trails website.

Chimney Rock

A Sampling of Nebraska's Greatest Natural and Historic Treasures

One of Nebraska's greatest, if often neglected, natural treasures is the **Platte River.** Although the Platte River's headwaters consist of two mountain-fed courses in Colorado and Wyoming, these streams merge in western Nebraska near North Platte, and the resulting river soon settles into a placid 70- to 80-mile stretch that extends from about Lexington to Grand Island in central Nebraska. There the river meanders slowly from west to east over the lower half of the state like a slightly sagging blue belt supporting a well-fed Cornhusker fan. The sand-bottom stream flows comfortably within a barely discernable 13-mile-wide and highly fertile valley, methodically if randomly and simultaneously depositing and eroding away countless sandy bars and islands during its seasonal flow fluctuations.

This otherwise inconspicuous stretch of the Platte River annually hosts one of the world's greatest bird spectacles during the month of March because the river here intercepts the middle of a north-south, roughly hourglass-shaped Central Flyway migration route that is used by nearly 30 species of waterfowl, 2 species of American cranes, and up to about 2 dozen species of shorebirds (Johnsgard, 1979, 1983, 2003b, 2011, 2012a). At least 373 bird species have been reported from the 10,000-square-mile central Platte Valley region (Brown and Johnsgard, 2013), representing more than 80 percent of the state's total recorded species list (463), the largest regional checklist for any Nebraska location, and one of the largest for any place in the entire Great Plains north of Texas. In early spring up to about 9 million waterfowl and almost a million sandhill cranes descend into the Platte valley and the adjoining Rainwater Basin south of the valley (Johnsgard, 2012a; Brown and Johnsgard, 2013). Estimates of waterfowl vary greatly. Actual numbers depend on water conditions, but it is commonly estimated that 7 million to 8 million snow geese may be here in mid-March, along with hundreds of thousands each of Canada geese and greater white-fronted geese. Probably at least 100,000 cackling geese are also present and perhaps as many as 40,000 Ross's geese; in 2016 more than 21,000 were calculated to be present within a mostly snow goose flock that was estimated at 1,074,000 birds.

The numbers of ducks are equally impressive, with mallards and northern pintails usually the most common and numbering in the tens or hundreds of thousands, and usually (along with common mergansers and common goldeneyes) the earliest ducks to arrive, some competing with the cranes and geese for unharvested corn. By the end of March, 20 or more duck species will have arrived in the Platte valley, while the geese and sandhill cranes will have begun to leave.

By early April, the central Platte's sandhill cranes (mostly Arctic tundra–breeding lesser sandhills headed for Alaska and Siberia) will have been replaced by the earliest of the shorebird migrants and family-sized groups of whooping cranes. The approximately two dozen species of shorebirds usually peak by the end of April or early May, their totals being estimated at 200,000 to 300,000 birds. There are no federal refuges on this important section of the Platte River, but much of it is now protected as a result of efforts by the Nature Conservancy, Platte River Recovery Implementation Program (PRRIP), National Audubon Society, the Crane Trust, and other conservation organizations.

The **Crane Trust** (originally known as the Platte River Whooping Crane Critical Habitat Maintenance Trust) was formed in the early 1970s as a result of a legal settlement over the environmental costs of building an upstream dam in Wyoming and now manages several thousand acres of riparian wetlands along the Platte River of importance to cranes and other wildlife. The trust's biologists perform annual surveys of sandhill crane usage, habitat surveys, and other avian and ecological research. See the Crane Trust website at https://cranetrust.org.

The **Lillian Annette Rowe Sanctuary and Iain Nicolson Audubon Center** is located about four miles southwest of Gibbon on Elm Island Road (drive south from I-80 at Exit 285 for 2.1 miles and then west on Elm Island Road for 2.1 miles). The sanctuary protects nearly five miles of prime crane habitat. As many as 70,000 roosting cranes can often be seen from its blinds. Least terns and piping plovers often nest on the barren sandbars that are also used by roosting cranes. Summer breeding birds include the

Cranes on the Platte River

Others might use a free elevated public viewing platform at the Platte River bridge on Gibbon Road (2 miles south of Exit 285 on I-80, just north of the turn onto Elm Island Road), the Richard Plautz Crane Viewing Site, which provides excellent free sunset and sunrise crane viewing. A similar viewing platform, the Alda Crane Viewing Site, is available south of I-80 at exit 305 (see the Crane Trust section). A hike-bike trail bridge across the Platte near the Fort Kearny SRA, about ten miles west of Rowe Sanctuary, off Nebraska Hwy. L-50A (the Platte River Road), also offers an alternate viewing choice, although a daily entrance fee to the park might be collected, especially late in the crane migration season. An Audubon-sponsored celebration of the cranes and Platte River valley natural history has been held annually for more than 40 years around the first day of spring in March. The Rowe Sanctuary address is 44450 Elm Island Road, Gibbon, NE 68440; phone 308-468-5282; website https://rowe.audubon.org/.

Other Major Natural and Historic Sites in Nebraska

Agate Fossil Beds National Monument. 3,055 acres. Agate Fossil Beds is located in Sioux County, 22 miles south of Harrison and 34 miles north of Mitchell on Nebraska Hwy. 29. This world-famous fossil site has been the source of vast numbers of early Miocene mammals, from sediments dating about 20 million to 22 million years ago (Maher, Engelmann, and Shuster, 2003; Johnsgard, 2015a). The fossil beds were discovered in 1904 by Capt. James Cook, a local rancher, one-time Indian Wars scout, and a friend of the Lakota Sioux. Since then the site has produced almost countless numbers of mammalian fossils that are represented in museums around the world, among them the Carnegie Museum of Natural History and the University of Nebraska State Museum (see section farther along). The fossils include such early mammals as *Miohippus* (horse), *Monceras* (rhino), *Amphycion* (bear-dog), *Daeodon* (antelodont), *Stenomylus* (camel), *Moropus* (chalcothere), and *Paleocaster* (land beaver). The recently remodeled visitor center has several reconstructed skeletons of *Moropus* and other fossils, and it also houses Captain Cook's personal collection of Lakota Sioux artifacts. Prairie rattlesnakes commonly sun themselves on the nearly mile-long trail to the old dig sites during summer, so caution is advised in selecting one's path. Carrying a canteen of drinking water on

dickcissel, upland sandpiper, and bobolink as well as riparian wooded-habitat species such as the rose-breasted grosbeak and willow flycatcher. Rowe Sanctuary is also immediately north of the western Rainwater Basin (see that section farther along), a region of seasonal wetlands of great importance to shorebirds and waterfowl. Rowe Sanctuary is located along the Platte River in the heart of the sandhill crane's spring staging area. The Iain Nicolson Audubon Center is open year-round and provides guided sunrise and sunset crane-viewing blind tours from early March until early April (although the visitor center was closed and blind trips were canceled in 2020 and 2021 because of the COVID-19 pandemic). Audubon's crane webcam provides year-round live-streaming video of crane roosting areas and river views via the internet. The largest blind accommodates up to 40 people and overlooks a roost that attracts thousands of cranes during peak migration in late March. Single or two-person blinds can also be rented for overnight use by photographers able to tolerate the cold.

hot days is important too. The Agate Fossil Beds address is 301 River Road, Harrison, NE 69346; phone 308-668-2211; website https://www.nps.gov/agfo/index.htm.

Ashfall Fossil Beds State Historical Park. 260 acres. Ashfall Fossil Beds is located in Antelope County, two miles west and six miles north of Royal on 517th Ave. This world-famous fossil site includes the exposed, in situ, fossil remains from dozens of mid-Miocene mammals, mostly rhinos, which died after a fallout of volcanic ash that originated from eruptions in the Yellowstone region about 12 million years ago (Voorhies, 1981; Maher, Engelmann, and Shuster, 2003; Johnsgard, 2015a). There are also one- and three-toed horses (five genera), camels (three genera), canids (three genera), saber-toothed deer (one genus), and a few birds—including a crane very similar to the modern African crowned cranes but distantly related to the two North American cranes. The park is operated by the University of Nebraska and the Nebraska Game and Parks Commission and open from May until mid-October, but check the days and hours before going. The Ashfall Fossil Beds address is 86930 517th Ave., Royal, NE 68773; phone 402-893-2000; website https://ashfall.unl.edu/.

Chimney Rock National Historic Site. 83 acres. The famous spire of Chimney Rock stands about 300 feet above the surrounding grasslands in western Nebraska and was one of the most mentioned landmarks on the Oregon Trail. A small visitor center has historic exhibits, a video presentation, and a variety of books for sale that focus on western and Oregon Trail history. Golden eagles once nested on bluffs to the south, prairie dogs are often also present near these bluffs, and burrowing owls might still sometimes be seen among the prairie dogs. A small alkaline marsh, Facus Springs, along the south side of Nebraska Hwy. 28/92 is about five miles east of Chimney Rock and often has migrant or nesting shorebirds, such as the Wilson's snipe, American avocet, and Wilson's phalarope. The Chimney Rock address is PO Box F, Bayard, NE 69334; phone 308-586-2581; website https://www.nps.gov/nr/travel/scotts_bluff/chimney_rock.html.

Crescent Lake NWR. 45,818 acres. Located 28 miles north of Oshkosh in Garden County (or 20 miles south of Lakeside), the enormous Crescent Lake refuge can be reached only by sand, gravel, and deteriorated hardtop roads. About 20 wetland complexes are contained in this sandhills refuge; these total 8,251 acres and compose almost 20 percent of the refuge. Crescent Lake NWR is in the central Nebraska Sandhills region, which extends over about 19,000 square miles and is the largest region of mostly stabilized dunes in North America (Johnsgard, 1995). At least 32 species of waterfowl have been reported at the refuge, and 14 are known or suspected breeders. Three grebes (western, eared, and pied-billed) are also breeders. Other fairly common wetland breeders include the double-crested cormorant, great blue heron, black-crowned night-heron, American bittern, sora, and Virginia rail (Johnsgard and Kren, 2020). The common yellowthroat, sedge wren, and marsh wren are abundant breeders, and the American avocet, white-faced ibis, and black-necked stilt breed locally but regularly. The marshes and shallow lakes in this large and remote Sandhills refuge vary greatly as to their relative alkalinity.

At the western edge of the refuge, Border Lake marks the eastern boundary of a multicounty (Garden, Morrill, and Sheridan) regional area of hypersaline water conditions; the Wilson's phalarope and American avocet are common breeders here, and cinnamon teal perhaps also breed occasionally. At least 66 bird species are common to abundant during spring versus 56 species during fall and 6 during winter (Jones, 1990). There are at least 83 nesting birds among the 233 listed in 1990 for the refuge by Jones. A total of 40 bird species were reported present year-round by Jones, so an estimated minimum of 83 percent of the refuge's total bird diversity is migratory. The refuge and its birds have been described by Farrar (2004) and Johnsgard (1995, 2001a). Bull snakes and ornate box turtles may often be seen along roadsides or crossing roads. The refuge headquarters has the only source of drinking water and public facilities on the refuge. A recent refuge bird list includes 273 species, with many wetland species, and is available from the refuge manager at 10630 Road 181, Ellsworth, NE 69340 (phone 308-762-4893). A bird checklist is also available online at https://www.fws.gov/refuge/Crescent_Lake/wildlife_and_habitat/index.html (scroll to Birds and "bird list").

Fort Atkinson State Historical Park. 186 acres. Fort Atkinson is a historically important site located one mile north of Fort Calhoun on County Road 34. The fort was founded in 1820 but abandoned in 1827 when western overland routes farther south made the Missouri River corridor less vital to national interests. Fort restoration began in the 1960s and now includes several restored buildings along with a visitor center. Fort Atkinson was situated on the summit of Council Bluff, the place where Lewis and Clark met with the Otoe-Missourias on August

3, 1804. It was Lewis and Clark's first formal meeting with any tribe of Native Americans. The site is now on the Nebraska side of the river as a result of channel shifting; the river has shifted some three miles east of the bluff summit, and because of timber growth the river is no longer visible from the bluff.

The nearby **Lewis and Clark National Historic Trail Headquarters Visitor Center** is located at 601 Riverfront Drive in Omaha (phone 402-661-1804). During resettlement in 1854, the Otoe-Missourias ceded their land to the US government and were initially confined to a reservation area of 160,000 acres along the present-day Nebraska-Kansas border. By 1880 most of the tribe had left the reservation to join the Sac and Fox Nation in Indian Territory. In 1881 those who remained also relocated to Indian Territory (now parts of Noble and Pawnee Counties, Oklahoma). It was the Otoe (historically also spelled Oto) who were responsible for giving Nebraska its name, from an Otoe word meaning "flat water," referring to the Platte River.

Much farther upstream on the Missouri River is a treeless, sedimentary cone made up of grayish yellow clays about 70 feet high that was discovered on September 7, 1804, and named **"The Cupola"** by Lewis and Clark expedition members. Locally known now as "Old Baldy," it is seven miles north of Lynch on privately owned land. The nearest public road (unnumbered but easily found) passes within about a half mile of the promontory and offers an excellent view of it and several miles of the nearby river valley, which is still fairly pristine. A colony of black-tailed prairie dogs was discovered here by Lewis and Clark. The colony is long gone, but others in the general vicinity have survived. Several prairie dogs and four black-billed magpies that Lewis and Clark had captured alive were sent back to Washington, DC, in April 1805 from Fort Mandan, along with many other acquisitions, before the group departed upstream. One of the prairie dogs and a magpie survived the thousand-plus-mile trip, and the prairie dog was Jefferson's guest for a time at the White House. Both animals were later preserved and displayed at Charles W. Peal's Philadelphia Museum, which eventually received nearly all of the Lewis and Clark specimens. The museum was housed in Independence Hall until 1838, after which it was moved the first of two times. Finally, in 1850 its contents were sold, some to P. T. Barnum and the rest to the Boston Museum. Some of the materials from the museum eventually were passed on to Harvard University, but most have since disappeared, including the prairie dog. However, the plant materials largely survived, and the more than 200 herbarium specimens brought back to Philadelphia were the basis for the naming of more than 100 new plant species.

The **Lewis and Clark Visitor Center** is located on Calumet Bluff, off Nebraska Hwy. 121 about four miles west of Yankton, South Dakota. It focuses on the ecology and history of the Missouri River, including the Lewis and Clark expedition. A regional bird checklist of about 240 species covers several counties and should be available at the visitor center (phone 402-667-2546).

Yet another center, in the southeast corner of the state, the **Missouri River Basin Lewis and Clark Visitor Center** and its interpretive trail, is located off Hwy. 2 at the eastern edge of Nebraska City on a wooded bluff overlooking the Missouri River. This center has exhibits on the Lewis and Clark expedition, especially its natural history aspects. It also has modern replicas of a 55-foot keelboat and a Plains Indian earth lodge. The Missouri River Basin address is 100 Valmont Dr., Nebraska City, NE 68410; phone 402-874-9900; website https://lewisandclarkvisitorcenter.org/.

Fort Niobrara National Wildlife Refuge. 19,122 acres. This refuge, located about five miles east of Valentine along Nebraska Hwy. 12, includes approximately 4,350 acres of mostly riparian woods and 375 acres of wetlands. Riparian hardwood forest occurs along the Niobrara River, and the uplands are sandhills prairie, with some spring-fed ponds. Notable wetland breeding species include the wood duck, upland sandpiper, and long-billed curlew. The most abundant Neotropical migrants nesting in the refuge area are the common yellowthroat, ovenbird, black-and-white warbler, and red-eyed vireo. At least 71 species are common to abundant during spring versus 67 species during fall and 14 during winter (Jones, 1990). There are at least 76 nesting birds among the 201 species listed for the refuge. A total of 25 bird species were reported present year-round by Jones, so an estimated minimum of 88 percent of the refuge's total bird diversity is migratory. The most recent refuge bird list includes 230 species, many of which are riparian woodland species with primarily eastern zoogeographic affinities, but some western species also occur, along with some hybrids between eastern and western counterpart species (Johnsgard, 2007c). A bird list is available from the refuge manager at 39983 Refuge Road, Valentine, NE 69201, phone 402-376-3789.

Fort Robinson State Park. 22,673 acres. Located three miles west of Crawford, at 3200 US Hwy. 20, this largest of Nebraska's state parks is one of special historic interest and also of great biological importance because of its Pine Ridge location. Established in 1874 to protect the Red Cloud Indian Agency, Fort Robinson is where the famous Lakota chief Thasunke Witco ("Crazy Horse") surrendered on September 5, 1877. "Crazy" is a racist translation of the original Lakota. "Fey" fits better than "Crazy" and means mysterious, or able to foretell the future or one's death. He was murdered that day by a bayonet stab from a military guard at Fort Robinson immediately after he had surrendered. His body was taken away and buried by his parents at a secret and still unknown location, but an unimpressive stacked stone memorial is present on the fort grounds. Another Lakota chief, Sitting Bull, also eventually surrendered in July 1881 and later died on December 15, 1890, at Standing Rock Reservation, South Dakota, by a gunshot wound from Indian Police. In 1891 the last remaining free-living Oglalas surrendered at South Dakota's Pine Ridge Agency, marking the end of the Indian Wars on the northern plains (Johnsgard, 2008a).

Besides a general history museum and a modest stone memorial to Crazy Horse on the grounds, there is also the **University of Nebraska State Museum Trailside** that describes the geology and rich fossil history of the region. The park is situated on the Arikaree geologic group of the late Oligocene and early Miocene epochs, below which are earlier sediments dating from the Oligocene's White River group (Maher, Engelmann, and Shuster, 2003). One of the more interesting museum displays is the skeletal heads of two Pleistocene-age Columbian mammoths that had died with their tusks intertwined in combat. The Trailside address is 3200 Hwy. 20, Crawford, NE 69339-0392; phone 308-665-2900; website http://outdoornebraska.gov/fortrobinson/.

Homestead National Historical Park. 195 acres. Located four miles west of Beatrice on Nebraska Hwy. 4, this park is the site of the first homestead acreage awarded through the Homestead Act of 1862. The property includes a restored log cabin of the 1860s and a modern heritage and education center, where visitors can research family histories online by using microfilms of early US census information and immigration data from Ellis Island. About 100 acres of tallgrass prairie, largely restored from original local prairie remnants, are near an approximate quarter-mile stretch of the Blue River's riparian woodland. A local bird list is available. The Homestead address is 8523 W. State Hwy. 4, Beatrice, NE 68310; phone 402-223-3514; website https://www.nps.gov/home/index.htm.

Indian Cave State Park. 2,831 acres. This site is a mature riverine hardwood forest park about ten miles east of Shubert on Nebraska Hwy. 64E and near the Lewis and Clark campsite of July 14, 1804. The park's centerpiece is a shallow, water-scourged, Cretaceous era limestone cave of upper Permian (Pennsylvanian) age, deposited during the major coal-forming period of early Paleozoic geologic history (Maher, Engelmann, and Shuster, 2003). The exposed rock surfaces also contain a few Native American animal petroglyphs, made during an unknown period of Native American or Paleo-Indian habitation, that are now mostly overwhelmed by recent visitors' scribbles. There are 20 miles of hiking trails, and camping is permitted. The Indian Cave address is 65296 720 Rd., Shubert, NE 68437; phone 402-883-2575; website http://outdoor-nebraska.gov/indiancave/.

Joslyn Art Museum. In addition to housing a world-class collection of fine art, Omaha's spectacular Joslyn Art Museum has the entire collection of the 359 magnificent watercolors made by Karl Bodmer during his trip up the Missouri River in 1832. The expedition was led by Alexander Philipp Maximilian, Prince of Wied-Neuwied, just three decades after the Lewis and Clark expedition. Many of these original paintings were later converted into hand-colored aquatint engravings and published in Europe. The Joslyn address is 2200 Dodge St., Omaha NE 68102; phone 402-342-3300; website https://www.joslyn.org/.

Lake McConaughy SRA. 41,192 acres. This largest of Nebraska's reservoirs (more than 30,000 acres when full) was developed for flood control, irrigation, and recreational use. It is about 22 miles long, 3 miles wide, up to 140 feet deep, and has 105 miles of shoreline when full. Including the adjacent Lake Ogallala SRA, the site totals about 5,500 land acres. Mostly bare sandy shorelines are on the northern side, but extensive wetlands exist at **Clear Creek WMA**, at the lake's western end. The lake is an important nesting area for both piping plovers and least terns and also hosts many nonbreeding double-crested cormorants and American white pelicans throughout summer. Western and Clark's grebes summer and breed here, and about 20,000 to 35,000 western grebes stage here during fall migration. Large numbers of waterfowl, gulls, other water birds, and eagles winter here. A recent bird checklist for the Lake McConaughy region has 362 species (Brown, Dinsmore, and Brown, 2012), a high percentage of which are wetland-dependent species. Lake McConaughy is located nine miles north of Ogallala on Nebraska Hwy. 61. A daily or seasonal state park entry

Incubating upland sandpiper

permit is required to enter the area. The SRA phone number is 308-284-8800; website http://outdoornebraska.gov/lakemcconaughy/ (and https://ilovelakemac.com/).

Missouri National Recreational River. This nationally so-designated part of the Missouri River is the northern boundary of Knox, Cedar, and Dixon Counties as well as a portion of Boyd County. Its history is briefly given in the *Wikipedia* article on this designation. It was first applied in 1978 to the 59-mile section of river between Gavins Point Dam and Ponca State Park. In 1991, the river between Fort Randall Dam and the town of Niobrara was added, another 39 miles. In the same year, the last 20 miles of the Niobrara River and 6 miles of Verdigre Creek were also added. These portions remain undammed and unchannelized and perhaps somewhat resemble the river conditions seen by Lewis and Clark and the native peoples they met. The original lower section of the national recreational river encompasses the locations of the Lewis and Clark campsites of August 22–25, 1804. The Yankton Sioux Indian Reservation (about 36,000 acres) is located directly north of the river in the upper portion. The reservation has been home to the Nakota-dialect (Yankton) Sioux, who first formally met Lewis and Clark in the vicinity of the present-day city of Yankton. The reservation-based population in 2000 was about 3,000 people, with another 3,000 living off the reservation. At the time of Lewis and Clark, the Sioux—including its Dakota (N), Lakota (SW), and Nakota (SE) divisions—was the most numerous of the Plains tribes, at one time numbering perhaps as many as 27,000 people.

Niobrara State Park. 1,632 acres. This state park is located one mile north of the town of Niobrara and mostly consists of mature riverine hardwood forest, not greatly altered from the area's natural state. It is situated at the now-impounded mouth of the Niobrara River, 20 miles of which is part of the Missouri National Recreational River system (see the previous paragraph). A two-mile trail traverses the entire northern boundary of the park, and an interpretive center has Lewis and Clark exhibits. Camping is permitted and a hiking trail is available. East of Niobrara State Park is the Santee Sioux Indian Reservation, whose members' ancestors were brought there in 1869 from the Crow Creek Reservation in western South Dakota. Still earlier, they had been removed from Minnesota. There they had engaged in a bloody uprising against the white settlers in 1862, after which 1,800 Santees were imprisoned and 33 were executed. The Santee Sioux Reservation in Nebraska originally consisted of 117,000 acres but was later substantially reduced. The current reservation population numbers about 600 residents.

Niobrara Valley Preserve. 56,000 acres. This Nature Conservancy preserve southwest of Springview in Brown and Keya Paha Counties is in the transition zone between western ponderosa pine forest and eastern deciduous forest. It includes 23 miles of shoreline along the Niobrara River and the northern edge of the Nebraska Sandhills (Johnsgard, 1995). The preserve is largely managed for bison, and research on bison foraging ecology and fire ecology is conducted here. A fire in 2012 burned 76,000 acres of this general region, including 29,000 acres of the preserve. Almost no tree regeneration has developed since that time. A list of 105 summering bird species has been published, and several of the breeding birds have east-west counterpart species or races (buntings, orioles, grosbeaks, flickers) that hybridize in this important continental ecological transition zone (Johnsgard, 2007c). A largely pristine 76-mile section of the Niobrara River that passes through the preserve has been designated as the Niobrara National Scenic River and is one of Nebraska's most popular rivers for canoeing and floating. The preserve address is 42269 Morel Road, Johnstown, NE 69214; phone 402-722-4440. The address of the scenic river park is 214 W. US Hwy. 20, Valentine, NE 69201; phone 402-376-1901.

North Platte NWR. 5,047 acres. Once part of the Crescent Lake NWR (see section), although distant from it, the North Platte NWR now includes Lake Alice (1,500 acres when full, but it's usually dry), Lake Minatare (737 acres), and Winter's Creek Lake (536 acres). The best wetland bird habitat is at Winter's Creek, which seasonally supports many waterfowl and sandhill cranes. The location is four miles north and eight miles east of Scottsbluff. The refuge bird list totals 228 species, including 85 wetland species (13 breeders), and is available from the refuge manager at 10630 Road 181, Ellsworth, NE 69340, phone 308-762-4893, or online at https://www.fws.gov/refuge/north_platte/wildlife_and_habitat/birds.html.

Oglala National Grassland. 94,344 acres. This enormous grassland in Sioux and Dawes Counties is seven miles north of Crawford on Nebraska Hwy. 104. It consists of shortgrass prairie over badlands of eroded clay and Cretaceous-age Pierre shale. Toadstool Geological Park (see section), also administered by the US Forest Service, is within the grassland, north of Fort Robinson State Park (see section). The Hudson-Meng Bison Kill Research and Visitor Center (20 acres) is also in the area (four miles north of Crawford on Nebraska Hwy. 2 and west on Toadstool Road, or about two miles southwest of Toadstool Park by trail). Here about 600 bison skeletal remains dating back 8,000 to 10,000 years (Alberta Culture period) have been excavated. About 50 mammal species have been reported from the Oglala National Grassland (Moul, 2006). A bird list of 302 species (covering the nearby Nebraska National Forest and entire associated Pine Ridge region of northwestern Nebraska) is available from the USFS at 270 Pine St., Chadron, NE 69337, phone 308-432-3367 or 308-432-4475.

Omaha Indian Reservation and **Winnebago Indian Reservation.** The Omaha and Winnebago reservations, located between Decatur and Homer, were established in 1856 and 1866, respectively. The Winnebagos had been moved here from South Dakota and, still earlier, from Minnesota. Blackbird Hill, on the Omaha Indian Reservation (12,421 acres), is the gravesite of Omaha chief Blackbird, which was visited by Lewis and Clark on August 11, 1804. Chief Blackbird died of smallpox in 1800 and was buried sitting erect on a horse. A wooden pole decorated with all the scalps he had taken was planted in the soil above. His gravesite is situated on the highest of the river bluffs between Decatur and Macy and is easily visible from nearby roads. The 300-foot-high and now mostly tree-covered promontory can best be observed about one mile east of Blackbird Scenic Overview at a site three miles north of Decatur (milepost 152 on US Hwy. 75).

The Omahas had moved into the region from the Ohio River valley by the 1700s, and by 1775 the tribe had a large village in this immediate area. During the smallpox epidemic of 1800, caused by contacts with Europeans, the Omahas' population was reduced from about 700 to 300, and its previous reputation as a powerful warrior society disappeared. During the later period of displacement of Native Americans to reservations in the mid-1800s, the Omahas were allowed to remain on part of their original homeland (originally 300,000 acres). The northern part of their ceded land was later given to the Winnebagos, and some of the remainder was later sold to white settlers. In spite of their peaceful nature, the Omahas were not accepted as US citizens until 1887, and their full rights of citizenship were not attained until 1924.

Similarly, the Pawnees of eastern Nebraska (the "Pani" or "Pania" of Lewis and Clark) were sent in the 1850s to a relatively tiny preserve (now part of Nance County) of about 300 square miles along the Loup River, an area representing less than 1 percent of their original vast homeland that centered on the Platte River valley. After their land was sold to settlers in 1872, the Pawnees were relocated in 1874 to a part of Indian Territory (now part of Oklahoma), in a region between the Arkansas and Cimarron Rivers. At the time of Lewis and Clark, the Pawnees were probably second only to the Lakotas in population size among Plains tribes, numbering perhaps 10,000 people. By comparison, the Omahas may have historically numbered about 2,800 at maximum. the Otoes about 1,800, and the Missourias about 500. By the year 2000, nearly 8,000 Native Americans were still living on reservations in Nebraska, including about 5,100 Omahas, 2,600 Winnebagos, and about 400 Santees.

Ponca State Park and **Ponca Indian Reservation.** The 2,400 acres of Ponca State Park are situated four miles north of Ponca on Nebraska Hwy. 12. The park consists of mature and old-growth riverine hardwood forest at the downstream end of the federally designated Missouri National Recreational River (see section), with 17 miles of hiking trails and a recently added adjoining Elk Point Bend WMA to the north. The park was named for the Ponca tribe, which had settled on the west bank of the Missouri River in present-day South Dakota during the early 1700s. At the time of Lewis and Clark, the Poncas numbered perhaps 800 people. Their initial reservation was established in 1858 and enlarged to 96,000 acres in 1865. However, it was taken over abruptly in 1868 by the federal government and made part of the Great Sioux Reservation.

The resulting conflicts with the Lakota Sioux, together with a government eviction order in 1876, forced the Poncas to resettle about 600 miles south in Indian Territory (now part of Oklahoma). Hundreds of adults and, later in spring, children were all forced to walk the entire distance with their few possessions. The Poncas were first assigned to the then-existing Quapaw Agency. During that winter of 1877–78, nearly one in five tribal members died of starvation or illnesses, including the daughter, Prairie Flower, of Chief Standing Bear, and then his eldest son, Bear Shield. However, Chief Standing Bear and 26 members of his tribe secretly returned to Nebraska the following spring to bury his son in an ancestral Ponca graveyard. Their trip took ten weeks, pulling three wagons.

Their arrival in Nebraska was soon discovered and led to the entire group's arrest and detention in Omaha. At that time, Native Americans were not legally regarded as US citizens and had no right of habeas corpus that might have achieved their release from prison. The resulting quandary over Standing Bear's captive status produced one of the most famous courtroom scenes in American history. It was centered on the critical legal question as to whether a Native American was a "person" under the interpretation of constitutional law and thus entitled to basic constitutional rights.

During the trial, Standing Bear argued emotionally that indeed, like white men, he too was a person. The case against him was eventually dismissed by the US Supreme Court and, after a presidential commission reviewed the tribe's sad history, a restoration of 26,236 acres of Ponca tribal land in the Niobrara valley was also granted in 1881.

In 1884 the Indian Territory population was moved to a new reservation in the Salt Fork River region, and later was moved again into what is now Oklahoma's Kay and Noble Counties. Adding to the tribe's endless difficulties, the Ponca Indian Reservation in Nebraska was dissolved in 1954, and for nearly 50 years the tribe was not recognized by the federal government, until it was officially restored in 1990.

The Missouri National Recreational River Resource and Education Center is located in Ponca State Park at the end of Hwy. Spur 26 E; it describes the ecology and history of the Missouri River. The Ponca State Park address is 88090 Spur 26 E, Ponca, NE 68770; phone 402-755-2284; website http://outdoornebraska.gov/ponca/.

Rainwater Basin. The Rainwater Basin is a large, diffuse region of seasonal playa wetlands spread widely across central and eastern Nebraska. It occurs south of the Platte River from Gosper and Dawson Counties in the west to Seward County in the east, and south from Franklin to Jefferson Counties. This region of clay soils and poor drainage once held an estimated 4,000 wetlands, of which more than 90 percent have been ditched and drained. However, some 22,000 acres are still protected as waterfowl production areas, and 12,000 acres are state-owned wildlife management areas (Johnsgard, 2012a). The Rainwater Basin Wetland Management District is a multicounty region south of the central Platte River that contains hundreds of temporary to seasonal playa wetlands. The Rainwater Basin Joint Venture coordinates the Rainwater Basin's wetland management, which involves the approximately 50 federally owned waterfowl production areas and about 30 state-owned wildlife management areas. They extend from Phelps County east to Butler and Saline Counties and are geographically divided into eastern and western components.

The Rainwater Basin's importance to Great Plains migrating shorebirds during April and early May is probably second only to Cheyenne Bottoms in Kansas (Jorgensen, 2012; Brown and Johnsgard, 2013). During wet springs, it also often holds millions of migrating geese (mostly snow and Ross's geese, plus some greater white-fronted, Canada, and cackling geese) in March. At least 29 species are common to abundant in the basin during spring versus 122 species during fall and 28 during winter. There are at least 102 nesting birds among the 256 species listed for the region by Jones (1990). A total of 49 bird species were reported present year-round by Jones, so an estimated minimum of 81 percent of the district's total bird diversity is migratory.

A collective bird list for the Rainwater Basin and adjacent central Platte River valley has more than 300 species, including 120 wetland species, and is available from the US Fish and Wildlife Service, 2610 Ave. QW, Kearney, NE 68847, phone 308-236-5015. Nebraska's playa wetlands are included within the multistate Playa Lakes Joint Venture program, which extends geographically from Nebraska to western Texas. The Playa Lakes Joint Venture address is 103 E. Simpson St., LaFayette, CO 80026, phone 303-926-0777. The address for the Rainwater Basin Wetland Management District is 73746 V Road, PO Box 8, Funk, NE 68940; phone 308-263-3000. The Rainwater Basin Joint Venture's address is 2550 N. Diers Ave., Suite L, Grand Island, NE 68803; phone 308-395-8586.

Rulo Bluffs Preserve. 444 acres. Rulo Bluffs is a Missouri valley forest, about six miles southeast of Rulo, that contains mature hardwood forests and some prairie vegetation on high, steep loess bluffs overlooking the Missouri River. It is important for its very high and southern-oriented botanical diversity, but because the area is undeveloped with no amenities or marked trails, access is restricted. It is now owned and managed by the Iowa Tribe of Kansas and Nebraska, and permission to enter must be obtained from the Tribal Administrative Office in White Cloud, Kansas, phone 785-595-3258.

Scotts Bluff National Monument. 4.7 square miles. This famous landmark on the Oregon Trail and at the southern edge of Nebraska's biologically unique Pine Ridge region is located just west of the city of Scottsbluff and refers to a promontory that rises 750 feet above the surrounding land. The face of the bluff exposes geological strata from the Tertiary period dated from 33 million to 22 million years ago. The top of the bluff is well vegetated with ponderosa pines and can be reached by a scenic summit road. From the bottom of the bluff, travelers pass sequentially through pink and tan siltstone of the early Oligocene's upper Brule formation of the White River group, two white volcanic ash layers also of the White River group, and lastly the even-bedded sandstones of the late Oligocene to early Miocene-age Gering and Monroe Creek formations of the Arikaree group (Maher, Engelmann, and Shuster, 2003).

From the bluff's summit, it is often possible to see flying raptors such as prairie falcons, red-tailed hawks, and ferruginous hawks as well as white-throated swifts and violet-green swallows that nest on the sheer sides of the monument. The visitor center is notable for holding the world's largest collection of drawings, photographs, and watercolor paintings of western scenes done by famed geologist and explorer William Henry Jackson in the late 1800s. The address is PO Box 27, Gering, NE 69341; phone 308-436-9970.

Spring Creek Prairie Audubon Center. About 850 acres. Located approximately 20 miles south of Lincoln and 3 miles south of Denton, this mostly virgin tallgrass prairie is on rolling glacial moraine (including a hilltop that is the highest elevation in Lancaster County) and is one of the largest such preserved tallgrass prairies in Nebraska. There are also wetlands, riparian edges, and deciduous woods. The property is owned by the Nebraska office of the National Audubon Society. It has a modern visitor/interpretive center (of hay-bale construction), many miles of trails, and nearly 400 documented species of plants, along with more than 200 birds, 30 mammals, and about 50 butterflies. Of the 200 or so prairie-adapted (non-tree and nonaquatic) plant species, native grasses compose about 20 percent of the flora, broad-leaved forbs about 70 percent, and shrubs and vines about 8 percent. Open daily year-round, except for major holidays. The Spring Creek address is 11700 SW 100th St., PO Box 117, Denton, NE 68339; phone 402-797-2301; website https://springcreek.audubon.org/.

Toadstool Geological Park. Toadstool is part of the Oglala National Grassland and is located 15 miles north of Crawford. From Crawford, go 4 miles north on Nebraska Hwy. 2 and 71. Turn northwest on Toadstool Road and go about 10 miles. Turn left at the sign to Toadstool Park and proceed another 1.5 miles.

The badland topography here consists of eroded sandstones and siltstones formed from streambed sediments deposited about 45 million to 25 million years ago, as well as more recent volcanic ash deposits, with most of the park's area exposing highly eroded sediments from the Orella member of the Oligocene's Brule formation from 35 million to 25 million years ago (Maher, Engelmann, and Shuster, 2003).

Fossil remains of several now long-extinct mammalian groups, such as oreodonts, brontotheres, entelodonts, and hyaenodons, have been found. Some fossils of still-surviving or post-Oligocene extinct groups, such as three-toed horses, saber-toothed cats, early rhinos, and other animals, have also been discovered. A one-mile loop trail circles through the formations, and the three-mile Bison Trail leads hikers to the Hudson-Meng Bison Kill bone bed (see Oglala National Grassland). Small groups of pronghorn are often seen in the vicinity, and prairie rattlesnakes and bull snakes are common. When hiking in hot weather, carry water because none might available at this remote site. The Toadstool address is US Forest Service, Nebraska National Forest, 125 N. Main St., Chadron, NE 69337; phone 308-432-0300.

University of Nebraska State Museum. Public exhibits of the museum's collections are located in Morrill Hall on the University of Nebraska–Lincoln main campus (on the southwest corner of 14th and Vine Streets). This museum has the world's most complete collection of fossil mammoths and mastodons, including the largest known complete fossil reconstruction of *Archidiskodon imperator*, a 14-foot-tall Columbian mammoth (Maher, Engelmann, and Shuster, 2003). A full-sized bronze version of this mammoth as it might have appeared in life stands near the museum's entrance.

There are also a series of mounted animals in dioramas representing many examples of Nebraska wildlife and habitats, an exhibition of Native American plains culture, exhibits of Paleozoic and Mesozoic life, and a planetarium. The museum address is 645 N. 14th St., University of Nebraska–Lincoln, Lincoln, NE 68588-0338; phone 402-472-2642; website https://museum.unl.edu/.

Valentine National Wildlife Refuge. 71,516 acres. About 22 miles south of Valentine, this location is Nebraska's largest national wildlife refuge. It consists mostly of sandhills prairie with sand dunes and intervening depressions that contain many shallow, sometimes lake-sized, marshes. The native plants are a mixture of local sand-adapted species (including a state-endemic penstemon species, *Penstemon haydenii*) and others from the more general mixed-grass and tallgrass Nebraska floras.

The refuge includes more than 30 shallow and mostly small lakes, plus numerous marshes, surrounded by sand dunes up to 200 feet high. Many typical grassland birds, such as the long-billed curlew and upland sandpiper, are abundant on this enormous refuge. Four grebes (eared, western, Clark's, and pied-billed) have regularly nested here, as have the white-faced ibis, long-billed curlew, upland sandpiper, Wilson's phalarope, and American avocet.

Up to 150,000 migrant ducks can be found on the refuge, with peak numbers occurring in May and October. At least 67 species are common to abundant during spring versus 66 species during fall and 8 during winter (Jones, 1990). There are at least 95 nesting birds among the 233 species listed for the refuge in 1990 by Jones. A total of 35 bird species were reported present year-round by Jones, so an estimated minimum of 85 percent of the refuge's total bird diversity is migratory. A more recent refuge checklist of 272 species includes 100 wetland species: 31 shorebirds, 24 waterfowl, 10 gulls and terns, 5 grebes, and 4 rails. The list is available from the refuge manager at 39679 Pony Lake Road, Valentine, NE 69201; phone 402-376-1889. The refuge website can be explored at https://www.fws.gov/refuge/valentine/.

Wildcat Hills and Wildcat Hills SRA and Nature Center. 1,094 acres. This modern center is managed by the Nebraska Game and Parks Commission and is ten miles south of Gering off Nebraska Hwy. 71, in the middle of the Nebraska panhandle's Wildcat Hills. Although mostly privately owned, some 30,000 acres of land are open for public use in the Wildcat Hills. This east-west ridge of sandstone, siltstone, volcanic ash, and limestone in western Nebraska has many of the same geological and biological features as Scotts Bluff and the Pine Ridge escarpment of northwestern Nebraska (see Scotts Bluff National Monument section).

When driving south on Hwy. 71 to the ridge summit, visitors pass through the Brule formation of the Oligocene epoch (34 million to 30 million years ago) on the lower slopes, followed by Miocene (Arikaree) deposits at the crest, where the nature center is located (Maher, Engelmann, and Shuster, 2003). The center exhibits samples of fossil mammals from the Oligocene epoch from about 30 million years ago that have been found locally during highway excavations. These include a four-horned deer (*Syndyoceras*), a hippo-like anthracothere, a tapir, a weasel, a camel, and a bear.

Hiking trails at the nature center and a half-mile boardwalk extend out from the center, where pygmy nuthatches, red crossbills, common poorwills, and other western species might be encountered. The northern saw-whet owl has nested in the Wildcat Hills recently. Large mammals of the area include introduced bighorn sheep and elk, plus pronghorns, mule and white-tailed deer, bobcats, and mountain lions. The Wildcat address is 210615 Hwy. 71, Gering, NE 69341; phone 308-436-3777.

Agate Fossil Beds National Monument

I. The Far Western Region

This beautiful part of Nebraska, its geographic "panhandle," is largely a ridge-and-canyon region, interspersed with High Plains topography and steppe vegetation. It is the land that Crazy Horse died trying to protect for his people, the Oglala Sioux (Lakota), and one laced with the bitter history of these brave people, as they vainly fought to retain their sacred lands from their loss to invading Europeans. Ultimately they were consigned to one of the most neglected and poorest Indian reservations in America, where alcoholism, suicide rates, life expectancies, and other shocking demographic statistics resemble those of the poorest countries.

The region's pine-covered hills and escarpments are like South Dakota's Black Hills to the north, and about 3.5 percent of the region's land is covered by wooded coniferous habitats. Several pine-adapted bird species that are common in the Black Hills breed only in this northwestern corner of Nebraska, such as Lewis's woodpecker, pinyon jay, dark-eyed junco (local white-winged race) western tanager, yellow-rumped warbler, Swainson's thrush, red-breasted nuthatch, and red crossbill. Some of these same species as well as the violet-green swallow, white-throated swift, and pygmy nuthatch also occur in the pine forests of the Scottsbluff area and the Wildcat Hills. The canyon-adapted cordilleran flycatcher is mostly limited to Sowbelly Canyon in Sioux County and to a few additional canyon sites, such as Monroe Canyon and East Ash Canyon in Dawes County (Johnsgard, 2018a).

The panhandle region also has more than 5.6 million acres of grassland, which support a few quite localized short-grass or arid plains species, such as the thick-billed and chestnut-collared longspurs and the mountain plover. A few sage-adapted species, including the sage thrasher and the Brewer's sparrow, are also local nesters. It is also a land rich in the fossil remains of early Cenozoic mammals, including an 8-million-year-old fossil bird bone that appears to be identical to one from a modern sandhill crane.

This still-unconvincing evidence would possibly make the sandhill crane the most archaic of all known extant birds, but at least it provides another reason for considering it a very special bird species. Sandhill cranes by the tens of thousands still pass through this region each spring and fall, but their major migratory pathway lies to the east, in the central Platte Valley.

Typical open-country panhandle birds include the prairie falcon, ferruginous hawk, golden eagle, merlin, Say's phoebe, western wood-pewee, Cassin's kingbird, pinyon jay, and rock wren, while the mountain bluebird, yellow-rumped warbler, western tanager, and pygmy nuthatch are more woods adapted.

The entire biologically diverse and scenic Pine Ridge is certainly one of the major birding attractions in the panhandle. However, the local area farther south around Lake McConaughy in Keith County has one of the very few local bird lists exceeding 325 reported species for any site north of Mexico (Brown, Dinsmore, and Brown, 2012).

About 75 miles northwest of Lake McConaughy is Crescent Lake NWR, a wilderness refuge in the western Sandhills that has the second-largest local bird list for the state, with 273 species. To the north of Crescent Lake, in northern Garden County and southern Sheridan County, are hundreds of highly saline Sandhills marshes that often abound with waterfowl, shorebirds, and marshland birds. The entire Sandhills region covers more than 22 counties, and 400 of the state's 463 reported bird species have been reported from the region (Johnsgard and Kren, 2020c).

Descriptions of Sites by Counties

1. Sioux County (Map 1)

Sioux County is in the heart of the Pine Ridge region, an area of ridge-and-canyon topography that is a southern outlier of the Black Hills region of South Dakota. The Pine Ridge is a north-facing escarpment largely covered by ponderosa pine forest and streamside deciduous forests, totaling some 68,000 acres. As such, it has several species that occur rarely, if at all, elsewhere in Nebraska, such as the cordilleran flycatcher and plumbeous vireo. There are also more than a million acres of short-grass plains, much of which is included in the Oglala National Grassland, which support a typical high plains avifauna. Tourist accommodations are available in Harrison.

A. Federal Areas

1. **Oglala National Grassland** (map locations 1 and 3). Area 93,344 acres. The area around Toadstool Geological Park offers Brewer's sparrows, sage thrashers, Swainson's and ferruginous hawks, and chestnut-collared longspurs. Horned larks, western meadowlarks, and lark buntings are common breeders in this vast region, which extends east into Dawes County. Large prairie dog towns occur north of Montrose. Rodent-eating predators such as ferruginous hawks and golden eagles are regularly present. For information contact the US Forest Service office at HC 75, Box 13A9, Chadron, NE 69337, phone 308-432-4475.

2. **Soldier Creek Wilderness** (map location 7). Area 9,600 acres. This is a large roadless ridge-and-canyon area that has an extensive hiking trail network as well as bridle trails. Water must be carried in, and facilities are lacking. Much of the area was burned in a 1989 fire. An eight-mile loop trail over ridges and canyons has its trailhead at the picnic area. For information contact the US Forest Service office mentioned in number 1.

3. **Agate Fossil Beds National Monument** (not shown on map; see a state highway map for the exact location). Includes nearly 2,000 acres of shortgrass plains, and two eroded promontories that house some of the richest sources of Miocene mammals in the world. At least 156 bird species have been reported for the site, including ferruginous hawk, mountain plover, burrowing owl, northern saw-whet owl, white-throated swift, Cassin's kingbird, pinyon jay, Townsend's warbler, western tanager, black-headed grosbeak, lazuli bunting, and three species of longspurs, including both thick-billed and chestnut-collared. A trail leads to the fossil quarries; a supply of water should be carried during summer. For information call the National Park Service office at 308-665-4113.

4. **Toadstool Geological Park** (map location 2). This area of badlands (about 300 acres) within the Oglala National Grassland supports rock wrens, Say's phoebes, golden eagles and prairie falcons, and sometimes also gray-crowned rosy finches during winter. A one-mile loop trail through part of the park that begins at the picnic area should turn up rock wrens and other topography-dependent birds. As at Agate Fossil Beds, water is at a premium here, and a canteen should be carried during hot weather. A small campground is available. For more information, call the Pine Ridge Ranger District at 308-432-0300.

5. **Nebraska National Forest, Pine Ridge Ranger District** (map location 10). This area comprises about 51,000 acres, with most of the holdings in Dawes County (see Dawes County).

B. State Areas

1. **Fort Robinson State Park** (map location 9). Area 22,000 acres. Although still a good pine habitat, a forest fire in 1989 destroyed much of the best sections of this beautiful park, which has numerous hiking trails. A nesting area of white-throated swifts is six miles west of the headquarters. For information, call 308-665-2900.

2. **Gilbert-Baker WMA** (map location 4). Area 2,457 acres. Located three miles north of Harrison via an oil-surfaced road, this WMA is an area of ridges covered with ponderosa pines, with scattered areas of grassland at the forest fringes. Monroe Creek traverses the area and is a clear trout stream. A gravel road that travels south along the Wyoming border (turn eight miles west of Harrison) crosses the Niobrara River and passes into ridge-and-valley topography that supports Say's phoebes and rock wrens as well as Brewer's sparrows, ferruginous hawks, long-billed curlews, and thick-billed longspurs, plus chestnut-collared longspurs farther south. At about eight miles south of the turn, a road goes east and connects back to state highway 29 (Rosche, 1990). Hiking trails penetrate the area. For information, call 308-665-2924.

3. **Peterson WMA** (map location 6). Area 2,460 acres. This area consists of habitats alternating between mature ponderosa pine forests and grasslands in typical ridge-and-canyon topography. Two streams bisect the area. No camping facilities are available.

4. **James Ranch** (map location 8). 10,000 acres. This large area of typical Pine Ridge habitat, the former James Arthur Ranch, became part of Fort Robinson State Park in 1972.

C. Other Areas

1. **Sowbelly Canyon** (map location 5). Although the land in this area is all privately owned, Sowbelly Canyon is worth visiting. It can be reached via a county road northeast of Harrison—drive one mile north and then turn east and proceed northeast for several miles along Sowbelly Creek. This road enters a narrow canyon and passes through a creek-bottom area (Coffee Park) where on-foot

birding can be done, about five miles from town. Many distinctly western species previously bred here, but forest fires in 2006 engulfed the entire canyon, and many other parts of the Pine Ridge, covering 65,000 acres and destroying a large portion of the region's ponderosa pine forests.

2. **Monroe Canyon.** This canyon lies directly north of Harrison; the lower portion of it is in the Gilbert-Baker WMA (see number 2 in the state areas section). That portion is mostly deciduous forest, whereas the upper part is ponderosa pine forest. Drive down the canyon road and stop every few hundred yards to watch and listen. About 200 yards north of campground entrance 22, a gravel track leads east to an impoundment that usually has violet-green swallows. The small side canyons are used by cordilleran flycatchers. The campground is at the bottom of the canyon along Monroe Creek.

3. **Smiley Canyon.** This canyon is reached from Fort Robinson State Park. About a mile west of the fort, take a paved road north that leads through short grasslands (look for bison) and into an area of ponderosa pine that was burned. Look for rare Lewis's, black-backed, and possibly even three-toed woodpeckers.

2. Dawes County (Map 2)

Dawes County is one of Nebraska's most scenic regions, with nearly 100,000 acres of wooded habitats and almost 600,000 acres of grasslands within its boundaries. Tourist accommodations are at Chadron and Crawford.

A. Federal Areas

1. **Pine Ridge National Recreation Area** (6,600 acres) and **Nebraska National Forest, Pine Ridge Ranger District** (52,000 acres) (map location 2). These areas are mostly ponderosa pine forest and intervening grasslands or farmlands. The topography of this area is often rugged, and the roads may not be in good condition, so it is good to check with the ranger office before venturing far from the main road. Cattle grazing is permitted here, so attention to gates is necessary. A fairly difficult four-mile trail starts at the Iron Horse Road meadow, and a less difficult three-mile hiking trail has a trailhead on East Ash Road. A fairly difficult eight-mile trail leads to Chadron State Park. For more information, contact the forest supervisor at 125 N. Main St. in Chadron, phone 308-432-0300.

Pronghorn male, Oglala National Grassland

2. **Oglala National Grassland** (map location 1). 94,394 acres. Note on the map that fine lines enclose actual holdings and broad lines show the maximum limits of the grassland district. See the Sioux County account for more information.

B. State Areas

1. **Fort Robinson State Park** (map locations 5 and 8). 20,000 acres. A state park entry permit is required; call 308-665-2900 for information and reservations. (See also the Sioux County account.)

2. **Chadron State Park** (map location 7). 801 acres. Chadron State Park is the best place in the region to see Lewis's woodpecker, and it also supports pygmy nuthatches, western tanagers, and common poorwills. On the way to the Black Hills lookout, watch for Lewis's woodpeckers perched on the tops of snags. At the lookout, it's possible to also see pinyon jays, yellow-rumped warblers, western tana-

gers, and mountain bluebirds as well as raptors (Boyle and Bauer, 1994). The Spotted Tail hiking trail extends for eight miles from the park boundary through the Nebraska National Forest, and the Black Hills Overlook trail extends for four miles from the park campground. A state park entry permit is required; call 308-432-6167 for information.

3. **Ponderosa WMA** (map location 6). 3,659 acres. Located southeast of Crawford, this area is largely covered by ponderosa pine forests, with grasslands on level areas and also some deciduous trees lining Squaw Creek. A hiking trail starts at Parking Area 5 that provides an excellent panorama and may offer views of such raptors as prairie falcons. National forest land adjoins the area to the south and southwest. About ten miles south of Crawford along state Hwy. 2 are ridgetop pine-wooded habitats where Cassin's kingbirds are rather easily seen, especially during September (Rosche, 1990).

4. **Box Butte SRA** (map location 3). Land area 612 acres. This SRA includes a 1,600-acre reservoir and is an outstanding birding area in the panhandle. Rock wrens, Say's phoebes, and ferruginous hawks are among the more interesting western species, and probable eastern breeders include the eastern bluebird, eastern wood-pewee, and wood thrush. Small passerines such as warblers and vireos are abundant during migration.

5. **Whitney Lake WMA** (map location 4). 900 acres (reservoir). Located two miles northwest of Whitney.

3. Box Butte County

Box Butte County is only slightly forested (about 5,000 wooded acres) but has more than 300,000 acres of remaining grasslands or farmlands. Tourist accommodations are available in Alliance.

A. Federal Areas — None

B. State Areas — None

C. Other Areas

1. **Kilpatrick Lake.** Located about 20 miles west of Alliance (go west on 10th St. for 11 miles and then south one mile and again west for five more miles). A trail goes left at a sign indicating the Snake Creek Ranch and leads to the dam. This privately owned reservoir is a major stopover point for snow geese and a few Ross's geese in spring. The meadows to the south of the dam around Snake Creek support willets, long-billed curlews, Wilson's snipes, eastern meadowlarks, and Savannah sparrows. Scan the drier areas for Cassin's sparrows (rare in Nebraska); these birds inhabit sand-sage grassland, and their distinctive vocalizations help locate them.

4. Sheridan County (Map 3)

Sheridan County has about 50,000 acres of wooded habitats and nearly 1.2 million acres of grasslands. It also has more than 20,000 acres of surface wetlands, much of which consist of Sandhills marshes. Tourist accommodations are available in Gordon and Rushville.

A. Federal Areas — None

B. State Areas

1. **Metcalf WMA.** 3,317 acres. Metcalf is located about ten miles north of Hay Springs. It has typical Pine Ridge habitat, which is mostly pine but with some open grasslands present. No camping facilities are available.

2. **Smith Lake WMA.** 640 acres. Located 20 miles south of Rushville. The area has a 222-acre lake, surrounding marsh and grasslands, and some wooded habitats. Primitive camping facilities and toilets are available. Fishing is permitted. Between Lakeside and Rushville, 50 miles apart, excellent birding opportunities exist, and nesting records for the long-eared owl, black-necked stilt, piping plover, and even the northern parula have been obtained (Rosche, 1990). The area and its ecology were lovingly described by Stephen Jones (2000).

3. **Walgren Lake WMA.** 130 acres. Located near Hay Springs; see a state highway map for the exact location. Primitive camping facilities are available. A great variety of migrant species are attracted to this lake, including such rarities as Sabine's and black-headed gulls and Townsend's warbler. Just a mile south of Walgren Lake is a prairie dog town with nesting burrowing owls and occasional chestnut-collared longspurs. The latter are more common along the first road going east to the north of the colony.

C. Other Areas

1. **Sandhills marshes near Lakeside** (map location 2). This

Bull elk, Pine Ridge area

area, extending both west and east from Lakeside on US Hwy. 2 and north on state Hwy. 250, provides views of many highly alkaline marshes that attract waterfowl, such as trumpeter swans, and many shorebirds, such as breeding black-necked stilts, American avocets, willets, and Wilson's phalaropes. The gravel road south from Lakeside travels 28 miles through Sandhills country (no gas or facilities) to Crescent Lake NWR (see Map 3 and the Garden County account) and past many wet meadows and very saline marshes. Those wetlands (north of the dashed line on Map 3) are highly attractive to shorebirds and waterfowl. Sandhills roads are narrow, hilly, and slippery when wet; careful driving is mandatory. State route 250 north from Lakeside is just as attractive; after about 20 miles an unimproved road that goes east connects with state route 27, which returns to US Hwy. 2 at Ellsworth. However, it might be better to backtrack from Smith Lake to Lakeside and make a similar two-way run north from Ellsworth for about 15 miles, beyond which the marshy wetlands peter out.

5. Scotts Bluff County (Map 4)

Scotts Bluff County has more than 25,000 acres of wooded habitats and over 180,000 acres of grasslands within its boundaries. Tourist accommodations are available at Gering and Scottsbluff.

A. Federal Areas

1. **North Platte NWR and Lake Minatare SRA** (map locations 2). 5,047 acres. The best part of the North Platte refuge is the 500-acre Winters Creek Lake unit northwest of Lake Minatare, where a marshy lake attracts a large number of migratory and breeding water birds, including western grebes. A bird list for the entire refuge includes 181 species, with 32 known nesters and 20 additional possible breeders. For information, contact the local US Fish and Wildlife Service office at 308-635-7851. See also https://www.fws.gov/refuge/north_platte/.

2. **Scotts Bluff National Monument** (map location 1). 3,000 acres. This famous bluff along the Oregon Trail is capped by ponderosa pine habitats and has steep sides that are used as nesting sites by white-throated swifts. At least 100 species have been reported for the area, including prairie falcon, burrowing owl, common poorwill, pinyon jay, both cuckoos, rock wren, yellow-rumped warbler, Baltimore and Bullock's orioles, blue and black-headed grosbeaks, green-tailed and spotted towhees, three races of dark-eyed juncos, and lazuli bunting. A three-mile nature trail leads from the summit parking lot to the visitor center. Three prairie dog towns totaling about 63 acres are present. For information, contact the superintendent at PO Box 27, Gering NE 69341, phone 308-436-9700. See also https://www.nps.gov/scbl/index.htm.

B. State Areas

1. **Nine Mile Creek WMA** (map location 3). 178 acres. Located north and east of Minatare, the area consists of grasslands, plus a trout stream.

2. **Wildcat Hills SRA** and **Buffalo Creek WMA** (map location 4). 3,935 acres. Buffalo Creek WMA consists of typical Wildcat Hills ridge-and-canyon habitats, covered by pines and junipers. It is nearly all wooded but has a seven-acre pond. Primitive camping facilities and a long trail are available. Pygmy nuthatches nest here, and violet-green swallows are fairly common. Several raptors, such as golden eagles, prairie falcons, and several buteos are good sighting possibilities. Some rarities that should potentially be seen here include common poorwill and white-throated swift. The Wildcat Hills Nature Center is part of the Wildcat Hills SRA and has a two-mile nature trail. Red crossbills and red-breasted nuthatches are regular at the bird feeders. For information, call 308-436-3777.

3. **Kiowa WMA** (not shown on map, located 2.5 miles south of Morrill). 540 acres (of which 326 are closed during goose-hunting season as a refuge). A large pool is situated at the east end of Kiowa WMA and seasonal wetlands toward the west. A small prairie dog colony is present, where burrowing owls are regular. About 20 waterfowl species have been reported, including large wintering populations. Nesting birds include American avocet and black-necked stilt. Listed as a Nebraska Important Bird Area.

6. Banner County

Banner County is a high plains county that is slightly wooded (under 25,000 acres of wooded habitats) but has about 235,000 acres of grassland habitats. Very little surface water is present. No tourist accommodations are available in the county.

A. Federal Areas — None

Scotts Bluff National Monument

B. State Areas

1. **Buffalo Creek WMA.** See Scotts Bluff County.

2. **Wildcat Hills SRA.** See Scotts Bluff County.

7. Kimball County (Map 5)

Kimball County is a high plains county with only about 500 acres of wooded habitats, a similar acreage of surface water, and about 180,000 acres of grasslands or farmlands. There are tourist accommodations at Kimball.

A. Federal Areas — None

B. State Areas

1. **Oliver Reservoir SRA** (map location 1). 1,187 acres. This reservoir of Lodgepole Creek (often dry) is an excellent birding location, attracting many migrants during spring and fall, especially warblers. Wilson's snipe have been reported to nest here (at the west-end marshes), and a population of song sparrows is the only one known in western Nebraska. This is the largest reservoir in southwestern Nebraska, and attracts many migrants in spring (late March to early June) and fall (late August to early November). Western rarities include dusky flycatcher (May and August–September), Cassin's vireo (August–September), and Townsend's warbler (August–October). More than 210 species have been seen here.

C. Other Areas

1. **Tri-state corner** (map location 2, highest point in Nebraska). This remote area can be reached by driving south from Bushnell—south 12.5 miles, west 4.2 miles, south 1 mile, west 2 miles, and south 2 miles, to nearly the Colorado line. Just past the H. Constable home is a right turn with a cattle guard and a sign reading "Panorama Point, Highest Point in Nebraska." After a mile, there is another cattle guard and another right turn, to the north. It is then 0.3 mile to the high point. There is a charge for driving to the high point, which is only very slightly higher than the surrounding area. Look for lark buntings, horned larks, thick-billed longspurs, and mountain plovers in the vicinity.

2. **Lodgepole Creek** (map location 3). This nearly dry creek should attract warblers and other passerines.

8. Morrill County (Map 6)

Morrill County has nearly 30,000 acres of wooded habitats, some 660,000 acres of grasslands, and almost 5,000 acres of surface water. Tourist accommodations are available in Bayard and Bridgeport.

A. Federal Areas

1. **Chimney Rock National Historic Site** (map location 1). 83 acres. Chimney Rock is located near Bayard, and the rimrock to the south is worth investigating for nesting golden eagles. An old cemetery lies to the northwest of Chimney Rock (see map), and burrowing owls are often found in a nearby prairie dog colony. Lazuli buntings are common in brushy areas. Websites: https://www.nps.gov/places/000/chimney-rock-national-historic-site.htm and https://history.nebraska.gov/rock.

B. State Areas

1. **Bridgeport SRA** (map location 4). 326 acres. This SRA is just west of Bridgeport and has five sandpit lakes. See http://outdoornebraska.gov/bridgeport/.

2. **Chet and Jane Fleisbach WMA** (map location 2). This WMA, also known as Facus Springs, preserves one of the best saline marshes in the North Platte River valley. It is a major stopover point for migrant shorebirds and also attracts ducks during migration. Some shorebirds, such as American avocets and Wilson's phalaropes, also nest, as does the cinnamon teal.

C. Other Areas

1. **Saline marsh near Bridgeport** (map location 3). Like the Chet and Jane Fleisbach WMA, this saline marsh between two railroad tracks northwest of Bridgeport attracts great numbers of shorebirds during migration. In wet years, other marshes may occur here too.

2. **Courthouse Rock** and **Jail Rock** (map location 6). These famous Oregon Trail landmarks once had nesting golden eagles (on Jail Rock, until one of the pair was shot by rifle-toting bikers). Breeding rock wrens are common. For a continuing tour, drive west on state route 88 to Redington and either take the Redington Gap road north to Facus Springs and back to Bridgeport or go south from Redington (see next).

I. THE FAR WESTERN REGION

Western grebes, Crescent Lake NWR

3. **Redington Gap road** (map location 5). This is a gravel road that also proceeds south of Redington (map location 7). One route is to drive south from US routes 26/92 past Facus Springs and pass over a long, eroded line of hills (Redington Gap), where many western species typical of the high plains may be seen. Within a mile, the road passes a meadow that supports a small population of savannah sparrows (rare in Nebraska). Continue to Redington and go south from there for 4.5 miles and then take a left fork and go 3 more miles until pines appear on a north-facing slope. This area (the eastern end of the Wildcat Hills) supports a good population of Cassin's kingbirds, plus the easternmost known pinyon jay population and such western birds as western wood-pewees and common poorwills.

9. Cheyenne County

Cheyenne County has almost no surface water, about 7,000 acres of wooded habitats, and more than 210,000 acres of grasslands or farmlands. Tourist accommodations are available at Lodgepole and Sidney.

A. Federal Areas — None

B. State Areas — None

10. Garden County (Maps 3 and 7)

Garden County has more than 22,000 acres of surface water, about 500 acres of wooded habitats, and nearly 900,000 acres of grasslands or farmlands. Tourist accommodations are available at Oshkosh.

A. Federal Areas

1. **Crescent Lake NWR** (map 3, location 1). 40,900 acres. Crescent Lake NWR is one of the great semi-wilderness refuges in the United States, and it supports a greater bird diversity than any other Nebraska site except the Lake McConaughy area. However, it is about 30 miles from the nearest source of gas, food, or lodging, and travelers must plan accordingly, taking a tow rope, if possible, and never parking on bare sand. Park or turn around on level, grassy spots, if possible. Water and a toilet are available at the refuge headquarters.

Goose Lake near the headquarters is excellent for eared grebes, and both Crescent Lake and Smith Lake have good populations of western grebes (and some Clark's grebes). Rush Lake (just outside the refuge boundary) has breeding ruddy ducks, canvasbacks, redheads, and black-crowned night herons. The western area near Border Lake is best for avocets, black-necked stilts, cinnamon teal, Wilson's phalaropes, and other shorebirds attracted to saline water conditions; Border Lake marks the boundary of such hypersaline conditions.

During most visits, no other people will be seen, but the birding will be spectacular and well worth the long ride over often bare sand roads. A free sharp-tailed grouse blind holds about three people; reservations for its use are required. The refuge is classified as a Nebraska Important Bird Area. For maps, a bird checklist, or other information, call the refuge office at 308-762-4893 or 308-783-2477. Website: https://www.fws.gov/refuge/crescent_lake/

B. State Areas

1. **Ash Hollow State Historical Park** (map 7, locations 1 and 3). This historically interesting park has a wide variety of habitats, from exposed rocky bluffs that are used by great horned owls, American kestrels, and sometimes

I. THE FAR WESTERN REGION

Burrowing owls, young and adult

prairie falcons; to grassy wet meadows where bobolinks and eastern meadowlarks are present; to riparian wooded habitats used by warbling vireos and other woods-type songbirds. There are also upland grassland areas with blue grosbeaks, shrubby areas with spotted towhees, and scattered yuccas where field and grasshopper sparrows sometimes perch. An air-conditioned interpretive center provides welcome relief from oppressive summer temperatures. The nearby US Hwy. 26 bridge across the North Platte River provides views of many marshland species, including least bitterns on rare occasions. A one-mile trail leads from the parking lot off Hwy. 26 to Windlass Hill, where old pioneer wagon ruts are still easily visible. Website: http://outdoornebraska.gov/ashhollow/

2. **Clear Creek WMA** (map 7, location 2). See the Keith County section.

C. Other Areas

1. **Oshkosh sewage lagoons** (map 7, location 7). These lagoons are reached by driving south on Route 27 for 0.5 mile from Oshkosh, turning east, and driving until the lagoons appear on the south side of the road. Three lagoons are accessible by walking. They attract a surprising array of waterfowl, including breeding wood ducks and even nesting ruddy ducks.

11. Deuel County (Map 7)

Deuel County has more than 1,000 acres each of wooded habitats and surface water, and nearly 64,000 acres of grasslands or farmlands. Tourist accommodations are available at Big Springs and Chappell.

A. Federal Areas — None

B. State Areas

1. **Bittersweet WMA** (map location 6). 76 acres. This WMA has South Platte River frontage.

2. **Goldeneye WMA** (map location 5). 25 acres. Goldeneye includes 11 acres of wetland with a large prairie dog town beside it and its associated shortgrass prairie birds, including horned larks, longspurs, and ferruginous hawks. Access is from the Big Springs I-80 exit—go one mile south, three miles west, and then back over I-80.

3. **Goldenrod WMA** (map location 4). 97 acres. Goldenrod is all mixed-grass prairie and woods habitat.

Burrowing owl family

II. The West-Central Region

The west-central portion of the state includes two of the very best bird-finding localities, namely the Valentine and Fort Niobrara NWRs, both with bird lists that are among the largest in Nebraska. Additionally, it includes those parts of the Niobrara and Platte Rivers that lie in the middle of the transition zone between the Rocky Mountain coniferous forest and eastern deciduous forest biogeographic regions. These transition zones, or "suture zones," include localities of hybridization between several species or nascent species pairs of birds that are now in secondary contact after having been isolated geographically for much or all of the Pleistocene geologic period. This transition zone is very wide in the Platte River valley but compressed to a distance of less than 100 miles in the Niobrara valley, most of which is not included within the boundaries of the Fort Niobrara NWR and the Nature Conservancy's Niobrara Valley Preserve.

The Niobrara valley also supports breeding populations of several eastern wooded habitats species that are otherwise mostly limited to Nebraska's Missouri River valley, including the wood thrush, black-and-white warbler, American redstart, ovenbird, and scarlet tanager. Along the upper Niobrara valley, several western or northern bird species likewise extend eastwardly, including the common poorwill, red-breasted nuthatch, chestnut-collared longspur, red crossbill, western wood-pewee, spotted towhee, black-headed grosbeak, lazuli bunting, and Bullock's oriole. All but the first four of these might hybridize with eastern relatives along this valley corridor. Beyond these regions, and lying directly between them, the region mostly consists of the Nebraska Sandhills.

The Sandhills region represents the largest natural ecosystem in the state, covering nearly 19,000 square miles, or almost a quarter of the state. It is also the largest remaining grassland ecosystem in the country that is still virtually intact, both faunistically and floristically. It is a land with far fewer people than cattle, where the roads are few and tourist facilities and accommodations are almost nonexistent. Those roads that do exist are little traveled and often consist of only slightly improved sandy trails leading to ranches.

However, the region is filled with breathtaking vistas, spectacular bird populations in the hundreds of lakes and marshes, and a pioneer spirit that requires everyone to help their neighbors—or any stranger who happens to fall afoul of trouble while on the road. It is a land designed for naturalists who would like to study virtually unaltered prairie ecosystems and who are prepared to deal with nature on its own terms. Many water birds and shorebirds nest almost only here in Nebraska, such as the American wigeon, canvasback, redhead, ruddy duck, Wilson's snipe, Forster's tern, marsh wren, and swamp sparrow . A summary of the natural history of the Nebraska Sandhills, along with an annotated bird checklist (400 species) may be in found in Johnsgard and Kren (2020).

1. Cherry County (Map 8)

Cherry County is by far the largest county in the state, and mostly consists of Sandhills habitat, with 3.7 million acres of grasslands, about 17,000 acres of wooded habitats, and 41,000 acres of surface wetlands. Tourist accommodations are available at Merriman and Valentine.

A. Federal Areas

1. **Fort Niobrara NWR** (map location 1). 19,122 acres. This refuge, originally established to protect bison and other large game animals, lies on the western edge of the east-west ecological transition zone between forest types, and thus has a fine mixture of eastern and western avifauna. Western-eastern species pairs that occur and may hybridize include such forms as western and eastern wood-pewees, black-headed and rose-breasted grosbeaks, eastern and spotted towhees, and Bullock's and Baltimore orioles. A total of 201 species (76 breeders) have been reported here. About two-thirds of the refuge consists of Sandhills prairie, and the rest is mostly of mixed riparian hardwoods. There is a good population of sharp-tailed grouse along with breeding burrowing owls, yellow-breasted chats, American redstarts, grasshopper and Savannah sparrows, and both meadowlarks. Wild turkey viewing blinds are available. Address 39983 Refuge Road, Valentine, NE 69201, phone 402-376-3789. *Note:* The John W. and Louise Seier National Wildlife Refuge in

Rock County is 25 miles south of Bassett and managed through the Fort Niobrara/Valentine NWRs. It is under development and not yet open to the public.

2. **Valentine NWR** (map location 7). 71,516 acres. This national wildlife refuge is Nebraska's largest and one that rivals Crescent Lake in its bird diversity, with 221 species (93 breeders) reported. Most of the refuge consists of Sandhills prairie, with dunes 40 to 200 feet high and interdune depressions that often contain shallow marshy lakes. Some of the lakes are open for canoeing or boating, offering great birding opportunities. Driving on the sandy trails requires care; a supply of water and an emergency tow rope are recommended. Several prairie-chicken and sharp-tailed grouse leks are present in the refuge, and two public-use blinds are located at prairie-chicken and sharp-tailed grouse leks.

Refuge wetlands offer breeding habitat for eared, western, and pied-billed grebes; a dozen species of waterfowl; and shorebirds such as soras, Wilson's snipes, and American avocets. The higher grasslands offer views of long-billed curlews, upland sandpipers, and Swainson's hawks. This refuge is classified as a Nebraska Important Bird Area. The contact information is for the refuge is the same as that for Fort Niobrara NWR. Website: https://www.fws.gov/refuge/valentine/

3. **Samuel R. McKelvie National Forest** (map location 2). 115,703 acres. This section of forest is similar to that of the Nebraska National Forest in the Bessey Ranger District (see Thomas County) but is not so rich in migrants. The adjoining Merritt Reservoir usually has many water birds, especially during migration. Sharp-tailed grouse leks are present in the area, but birders must provide their own blind. Phone 308-533-2257.

B. State Areas

1. **Schlagel Creek WMA** (map location 3). 600 acres. This area consists of Sandhills grassland including two miles of Schlagel Creek. No facilities for camping are present.

2. **Big Alkali WMA** (map location 5). 890 acres. Just north of the Valentine refuge, this WMA consists of 48 lakeside acres plus an 842-acre Sandhills lake. A campground is available.

3. **Ballards Marsh WMA** (map location 6). 1,561 acres. Also just north of the Valentine refuge and right on US Hwy. 83, this area includes a large marsh and adjoining

Bison and calf, Fort Niobrara NWR

Sandhills grasslands and farmlands. A campground is available.

4. **Smith Falls State Park.** 244 acres. This state park is located three miles west and four miles south of Sparks. The Niobrara River can be crossed by a walking bridge for a close view of Smith Falls, the highest waterfall in the state. A hiking trail and campground are available. For more information, see http://outdoornebraska.gov/smithfalls/.

5. **Merritt Reservoir WMA** (map location 4). 2,906-acre reservoir and 350 acres of upland Sandhills. Merritt Reservoir on the Snake River is located 26 miles southwest of Valentine. This area abuts the Samuel R. McKelvie National Forest land to the west and north. The lake attracts migrant waterfowl, pelicans, western grebes, and other species.

6. **Cottonwood–Steverson Lake WMA.** 2,919 acres. This WMA encompasses three lakes: Cottonwood, Steverson, and Home Valley. The western end of Steverson Lake has a fen and associated cold-climate plants that are relicts of the Pleistocene period. Other fens also occur in this headwaters area of the North Loup River. This area is

located about 30 miles south from Cottonwood Lake SRA on Nebraska Hwy. 61.

7. **Cottonwood Lake SRA.** 60-acre lake and 180 land acres. Located one mile southeast of Merriman. Camping facilities are available. Canada geese breed here. Five miles east of Merriman, off the north side of US Hwy. 20, is a marsh where trumpeter swans have nested. Website: http://outdoornebraska.gov/cottonwood/

8. **Bowring Ranch State Historical Park.** Bowring Ranch is located one mile north of Merriman. Trumpeter swans often forage on a marsh just north of this park, a working cattle ranch. A state park entry permit is required. For more information, see http://outdoornebraska.gov/bowringranch/.

9. **Chat Canyon WMA** (map location 8). 438 acres. Located about ten miles south of Nenzel or six miles west of Anderson Bridge along a Niobrara River road. This is a well-wooded habitat along the Niobrara River, across from the Samuel R. McKelvie National Forest. It has high bird diversity, with more than 90 species recorded on one weekend in May by the author and friends. An elk herd winters here, with limited fall hunting allowed.

2. Keya Paha County (Map 9)

Keya Paha County has more than 37,000 acres of wooded habitats, over 400,000 acres of grasslands, and about 1,300 acres of surface water. The only tourist accommodations are in Springview.

A. Federal Areas — None

B. State Areas

1. **Cub Creek Recreation Area** (map location 2). 300 acres. Cub Creek is managed by the Middle Niobrara Natural Resources District. The lake is about 31 acres, set in prairie and some pines. Migrating waterfowl and, now and then, trumpeter swans use the lake. Hiking trails and camping are available. (Note that a different Cub Creek Recreation Area is located in southern Nebraska.)

2. **Thomas Creek WMA** (map location 3). 692 acres. This area has steep topography around Thomas Creek, with grassland on the hills and woods along the creek bottoms.

C. Other Areas

1. **Niobrara Valley Preserve** (map location 1). See Brown County.

3. Brown County (Map 10)

Brown County has more than 21,000 acres of wooded habitats, nearly 700,000 acres of grasslands, and about 8,000 acres of surface water. Tourist accommodations are available in Ainsworth.

A. Federal Areas — None

B. State Areas

1. **Bobcat WMA** (map location 3). 893 acres. Nearly 90 percent of this area consists of steep pine- and cedar-covered canyons. Plum Creek passes through. The remainder is Sandhills grassland.

2. **Keller School Land WMA** and **Keller Park SRA** (map location 4). 836 acres (WMA 640 acres, SRA 196 acres). These areas consist of native prairie, wooded canyons, Bone Creek, and five small fishing ponds stocked with trout and other game fish. The ponds attract ducks, eagles, and other water birds; the prairies support grassland sparrows; and the mixed wooded habitats have a variety of both coniferous and deciduous forest birds, including wild turkeys, scarlet tanagers, and American redstarts.

3. **Pine Glen WMA** (map location 5). 960 acres. Located 7 miles west and 6.5 miles north of Bassett, this wildlife management area consists of canyons, a trout stream, and mixed grasslands and wooded habitats. No facilities are available.

4. **Long Pine WMA** (map location 6). 160 acres. Located just off US Hwy. 20 near the town of Long Pine. The area is about 85 percent pine and red cedar wooded habitats; the rest is native Sandhills grassland bisected by Long Pine Creek. The terrain is steep, and camping facilities are primitive.

5. **South Twin Lake WMA** (map location 7). 160 acres. South Twin Lake is a 60-acre lake surrounded by Sandhills grassland. This area and the following three nearby WMAs are similar and should offer birders some excellent views of Sandhills wildlife.

Niobrara River valley, Cherry County

6. **American Game Marsh WMA** (map location 8). 160 acres. True to its name, this management area consists of a large Sandhills marsh and surrounding grassland. No facilities are available.

7. **Long Lake SRA** (map location 9). 80 acres. Long Lake has 30 acres of upland grassland and 50 acres in a Sandhills lake. Facilities for primitive camping are provided. An entry permit is required.

8. **Willow Lake WMA** (map location 10). 511 acres. This area too has a Sandhills lake and surrounding grassland.

C. Other Areas

1. **Niobrara Valley Preserve** (map location 1; headquarters at map location 2). About 56,000 acres. including about 25 mi. of the Niobrara River, in the heart of the transition zone between western coniferous and eastern deciduous forest types. There is a bird checklist of 186 species, including a list of 75 definite and 30 more possibly breeding species (Brogie and Mossman, 1983). The preserve has been identified as a Globally Important Bird Area by the American Bird Conservancy. Among the breeding birds of special interest are the eastern and western forms that hybridize here, such as the Baltimore and Bullock's orioles, the lazuli and indigo buntings, and the rose-breasted and black-headed grosbeaks. The eastern and western wood-pewees both also occur here and potentially hybridize.

Two trails radiate out from the preserve headquarters and pass through several forest types and Sandhills prairie vegetation on the uplands. Each trail has a short loop and a long loop; the northern one is somewhat longer (three miles) and steeper. For information, phone 402-722-4440. The preserve lies within the Niobrara National Scenic River District, which is a popular canoeing destination (call 402-376-3241 for more information).

4. Rock County

Rock County Is, despite its name, mostly composed of Sandhills habitat, with about 11,000 acres of wooded habitats, more than 600,000 acres of grasslands, and about 11,000 acres of surface water. The only tourist accommodations are in Bassett.

A. Federal Areas

1. **John W. and Louise Seier NWR.** 2,400 acres. Located in southwestern Brown County 25 miles south of Bassett (via US Hwy. 183) and several miles west (via county road). Sandhills grasslands and marshes, including Hornburger Lake and the headwaters of Skull and Bloody Creeks. This refuge is still under development and is not yet (in 2021) open to the public. It is administered by the Fort Niobrara and Valentine NWRs, which can be contacted for more information.

B. State Areas

1. **Twin Lakes WMA.** 113 acres in two lakes; 30 acres of grassland. Rock County's Twin Lakes is located 18 miles south and 2 miles east of Bassett.

C. Other Areas

1. **Hutton Niobrara Ranch Wildlife Sanctuary.** 4,919 acres. Located 15 miles north of Bassett via Nebraska Hwy. 7 on bottomlands and uplands south of the Niobrara River. This former ranch was given to the Audubon Society of Kansas by its prior owner, Harold Hutton. It is managed for both for cattle and wildlife. An adjacent 160-acre farm with a four-bedroom home is used by students, volunteers, and other visitors. Red cedars that have invaded the grasslands are being removed to restore native prairie, and a cultivated field has been re-seeded to native grasses. Wet meadows along the river attract bobolinks and other meadow-nesting birds. There is a small educational exhibit of prairie dogs, otherwise absent from Rock County, and a sharp-tailed grouse lek near the main house. Sandhill cranes have nested here, and river otters often use the river area. Call 785-537-4385 or email aok@audubonofkansas.org for information about renting overnight accommodations. Website: https://www.niobrarasanctuary.org/

5. Grant County

Grant County is a sparsely populated Sandhills county with only about 400 acres of wooded habitats, about 3,500 acres of surface water, and more than 460,000 acres of grassland. No tourist accommodations are available in the county.

A. Federal Areas — None

B. State Areas — None

Cherry County sandhills

6. Hooker County

Hooker County is another sparsely populated Sandhills county, with 1,800 acres of wooded habitats, about 400 acres of surface water, and more than 450,000 acres of grasslands or farmlands. Tourist accommodations are available in Mullen. The Sandhills Motel and Glidden Canoe Rental on the west edge of town offers spring sunrise trips to prairie-chicken and sharp-tailed grouse leks, where birders can view displays of both species from the comfort of a school bus. For more information, call 308-546-2206 or see https://www.sandhillsmotel.com/.

A. Federal Areas — None

B. State Areas — None

7. Thomas County (Map 11)

Thomas County is in the heart of the Sandhills but has more than 16,000 acres of wooded habitats, most of which are in the planted pine "forest" near Halsey. There are also about 1,500 acres of surface water (mostly the Middle Loup and Dismal Rivers) and almost 380,000 acres of grassland. Tourist accommodations are available at Halsey and Thedford.

A. Federal Areas

1. **Nebraska National Forest, Bessey Ranger District** (map location 1; map locations 2 and 3 indicate traditional lek locations with public-use blinds). 90,445 acres. Grasslands around and in this entirely planted "forest" support greater prairie-chickens, sharp-tailed grouse, upland sandpipers, horned larks, and western meadowlarks. The conifers provide habitat for great horned owls, black-capped chickadees, and red crossbills. Brushy and riparian thicket areas attract several woodpeckers, brown thrashers, towhees, chipping sparrows, and Baltimore orioles. At least six warbler species nest here, including the yellow warbler, black-and-white warbler, American redstart, ovenbird, common yellowthroat, and yellow-breasted chat. Three vireos (Bell's, warbling, and red-eyed) also nest here, as does the northern saw-whet owl. Townsend's solitaires and red-breasted nuthatches are common in winter.

There is a bird checklist available at the headquarters, where information on the grouse blinds is also available (Boyle and Bauer, 1994). One small prairie dog town may still be present, but regrettably one other has been destroyed by hunters. A fire in the 1960s burned much of the forest, as did another in 2006, but most of the original 25,000 acres of woods still survive. Three grouse-viewing blinds have long been present, each holding about four adults. There is a six-mile hiking trail that begins at the parking lot off Nebraska Hwy. 2. For more information, contact the US Forest Service office at PO Box 39, Halsey, NE 69142 or phone 308-533-2257.

B. State Areas — None

8. Blaine County (Map 11)

Blaine County is a Sandhills county with 1,600 acres of wooded habitats, about 1,000 acres of surface water, and nearly 440,000 acres of grassland. No tourist accommodations are available in the county.

A. Federal Areas — None

B. State Areas

1. **Nebraska National Forest, Bessey Ranger District** (map location 1). See Thomas County.

2. **Milburn Dam WMA.** 672 acres. Located 14 miles southeast of Brewster in the Middle Loup River valley, with extensive mud flats present around the reservoir.

9. Loup County

Loup County is a Sandhills County with about 7,000 acres of surface water, nearly 1,000 acres of wooded habitats, and more than 325,000 acres of grasslands or farmlands. The only tourist accommodations are at Taylor.

A. Federal Areas — None

B. State Areas

1. **Calamus Reservoir SRA/WMA.** 10,312 acres total with a 5,124-acre reservoir. Calamus Reservoir is a major stopover point for migrating American white pelicans, with up to about 700 often present in May. Calamus crosses the Garfield County–Loup County boundary. See also Garfield County.

10. Arthur County (Map 12)

Arthur County is another sparsely populated Sandhills county with almost 3,000 acres of surface water, about 200 acres of wooded habitats, and 427,000 acres of grasslands or farmlands. There are no tourist accommodations in the county.

A. *Federal Areas* — None

B. *State Areas* — None

C. *Other Areas*

1. **Marshes near the McPherson County border** (map locations shown by several arrowheads are the better birding marshes). These Sandhills marshes and creeks are often used by trumpeter swans.

11. McPherson County

McPherson County is a very sparsely populated Sandhills county, with about 600 acres of surface water, 1,000 acres of wooded habitats, and more than 520,000 acres of grasslands or farmlands. No tourist accommodations are available in the county.

A. *Federal Areas* — None

B. *State Areas* — None

C. *Other Areas*

1. **Marshes near the Arthur County border.** Several large marshes occur near the Arthur County border, such as Diamond Bar Lake, which is about 3.5 miles south of Nebraska Hwy. 92 (the turn is about five miles east of the Arthur County line) on a secondary road, with only a bare sandy trail for close access. Trumpeter swans are regular here. Whitewater Lake, Dry Lake, and Brown Lake are located north of Hwy. 92 and are also on unmarked secondary roads; they are poorly documented biologically. See also Arthur County.

12. Logan County

Logan County is a Sandhills county with only 250 acres of surface water, about 300 acres of wooded habitats, and more than 520,000 acres of grasslands or farmlands. No tourist accommodations are present in the county.

A. *Federal Areas* — None

B. *State Areas* — None

13. Custer County

Custer County is a mostly Sandhills county with about 2,500 acres of surface water, more than 10,000 acres of wooded habitats, and about 1.1 million acres of grasslands or farmlands. Tourist accommodations are available at Arnold, Broken Bow, Callaway, and Sargent.

A. *Federal Areas* — None

B. *State Areas*

1. **Victoria Springs SRA.** 60 acres. Here, a small campground and lake are surrounded by deciduous forest with cottonwoods. Wood ducks often nest here. A state park entry permit is required. Website: http://outdoornebraska.gov/victoriasprings/

2. **Pressey WMA.** 1,640 acres. This wildlife management area is located five miles north of Oconto. It has South Loup River valley grasslands, hills, and steep canyons as well as agricultural areas. Toilets and a campground are available, and there are are hiking trails. Sharp-tailed grouse are in the area, and great blue herons have a rookery.

3. **Arcadia Diversion Dam SRA.** 925 acres. Located 8.5 miles northwest of Arcadia, this recreation area in the Middle Loup River valley has mostly of grasslands and planted trees but also deciduous wooded habitats lining the river. Campgrounds are available on both sides of the river. A state park entry permit is required.

14. Keith County (Map 13)

Keith County is notable in having more than 37,000 acres of surface water, nearly 6,000 acres of wooded habitats, and over 420,000 acres of mainly Sandhills grasslands or farmlands. Tourist accommodations are available at Keystone, Lemoyne, Ogallala, and Paxton.

A. *Federal Areas* — None

Loup River valley sandhills

II. THE WEST-CENTRAL REGION

B. State Areas

1. **Clear Creek WMA** (map location 1). 5,709 acres. This wildlife area was partly developed as Clear Creek Refuge (2,500 acres, the west half) and partly as a controlled hunting area. The latter part includes the west end of Lake McConaughy and the Platte River inflow area. The low meadows support nesting bobolinks and probably breeding Wilson's snipes, and the groves of tall trees hold many breeding passerines. White pelicans are common, and least bitterns have been sighted.

   This is one of the state's best birding areas, but mosquitoes can be a problem during summer. Barn owl nest cavities usually can be seen in the cutbanks at the turnoff from Hwy. 26; nests in this part of the state are usually in such excavated sites rather than in old buildings. Rosche (1994) has described this area and its birds very well. It's also one of the state's few known nesting areas for Clark's grebe.

2. **Lake McConaughy SRA** (map location 2). 6,492 acres. The SRA occupies much of the north side of the Lake McConaughy reservoir, the largest body of water in Nebraska. A small area on the south side is also included (map location 6). This area has produced the longest bird list of any location in the state, including about 340 species, with 104 known breeders, 17 additional possible breeders, and about 200 transients (Brown et al., 1996; Brown and Brown, 2001). The large water area attracts great numbers of migrant waterfowl, grebes (especially western grebes), gulls (including many rarities), and shorebirds.

   A good spotting scope is needed to cover the huge expanse of this reservoir, but many of the waterfowl congregate near the dam spillway during winter and toward the western end of the lake during summer (see Clear Creek WMA). Bald eagles build up in number during the winter, attracted by dead fish and the wintering duck and goose populations. The reservoir has well over 100 miles of shoreline, with the southern shoreline rocky and steep and the northern shore sandy, which supports nesting piping plovers and least terns. Lake McConaughy is classified as a Nebraska Important Bird Area.

   Some of the rarer birds found here are trumpeter swan, cinnamon teal, Clark's grebe, all three jaegers, Sabine's gull, and common tern. Snowy plovers have nested in recent years, as have piping plovers and least terns. Both eastern and western wood-pewees occur, as do east-west species pairs of orioles, grosbeaks, and buntings. For more information, call 308-284-8800 or see http://outdoornebraska.gov/lakemcconaughy/.

Coyote eating a cottontail rabbit

3. **Kingsley Dam and Lake Ogallala SRA** (map location 3). 339 acres. Kingsley Dam offers a good vantage point for birds both on the deeper end of Lake McConaughy and on the shallower and much smaller Lake Ogallala located at the base of the opposite side of the dam. Lake Ogallala (and its eastern end, often called Lake Keystone) receives the spillway water from Lake McConaughy, and its level fluctuates greatly. However, it is very attractive to migrant gulls, ducks, ospreys, Caspian terns, cliff swallows, American white pelicans, double-crested cormorants, and other summering species. It is used by Canada geese and numerous bald eagles in winter. An eagle-watching blind is available below Kingsley Dam during peak periods, when 200 to 300 eagles are sometimes present, generally late December through early Match. Then, the blind is open on Thursdays and Fridays, 8 a.m. to noon, and Saturdays and Sundays, 8 a.m. to 4 p.m. The northern shoreline of Lake Ogallala has deciduous wooded habitats with a rich array of nesting passerines, but lake fluctuations limit nesting for aquatic species. Lake Ogallala SRA is classified as a Nebraska Important Bird Area. Some of the rare gulls seen here include mew, Iceland, glaucous, and lesser black-backed. Rare waterfowl include trumpeter swan, greater scaup, all three scoters, long-tailed duck,

and Barrow's goldeneye. For eagle-viewing information, phone the Central Nebraska Public Power and Irrigation District at 308-284-2332.

4. Cedar Point Biological Station (map location 4). Although an extension of the University of Nebraska and a summer field station and thus not usually open to the public, ornithological research at the Cedar Point Biological Station has made its avifauna the best known of any area in the state (Brown and Brown, 2001). Ornithology courses have been taught here on a regular basis since 1977, and studies on species such as the cliff swallow and orchard oriole have been of national significance. The area is classified as a Nebraska Important Bird Area.

5. Ogallala Strip WMA (map location 5). 453 acres (includes 2.5 miles of South Platte River frontage). This stretch of riparian wooded habitats supports many of the same species found around Lake Ogallala, such as house wren, yellow warbler, common yellowthroat, eastern and western kingbirds, killdeer, and others. Mississippi kites breed in nearby Ogallala.

6. Lake View Campground (map location 6). The road leading down the canyon to Lake View Campground, and a similar road that travels through Eagle Canyon six miles farther west, may offer views of rock wrens, turkey vultures, rough-winged swallows, and with luck, occasional prairie falcons or ferruginous hawks. Turkey vultures nest along the south side of Lake McConaughy, usually in eroded crevices or recesses well out of view. These canyon roads are often in poor condition, so caution must be exercised when driving over them.

15. Perkins County

Perkins County is a high plains county with only about 200 acres of surface water, about 1,000 acres of wooded habitats, and 125,000 acres of grasslands or farmlands. However, in wet springs hundreds of shallow playa lakes develop in northern Perkins County and southern Keith County, attracting large numbers of waterfowl and shorebirds. The state's largest remaining area of sand sage is southeast of Grant near the Chase County line. No tourist accommodations are available.

A. Federal Areas — None

B. State Areas — None

16. Lincoln County (Map 14)

Lincoln County straddles the Platte River valley, with nearly 10,000 acres of surface water, about 36,000 acres of wooded habitats, and about 1.2 million acres of grasslands or farmlands. Tourist accommodations are available in North Platte and Sutherland.

A. Federal Areas — None

B. State Areas

1. Sutherland Reservoir SRA (map location 1). 37 acres upland grassland with a 3,020-acre reservoir. At least ten gull species have been observed at Sutherland Reservoir. These include such rarities as Iceland, glaucous, great and lesser black-backed, and even Ross's gulls. There are often large flocks of wintering grebes, diving ducks, double-crested cormorants, and American white pelicans during mild winters. During spring, large flocks of snow, greater white-fronted, and occasional Ross's geese stop here.

2. Lake Maloney SRA (map location 2). 1,732 acres with a 1,600-acre reservoir. Lake Maloney is used during spring by American white pelicans and double-crested cormorants and by many shorebirds when the water levels subside.

3. Jeffrey Canyon WMA and Jeffrey Reservoir (map location 3). 35 acres with a 900-acre reservoir. This area consists of canyon-and-upland topography, with grasses and scattered deciduous trees and cedars. Public access is very limited at the dam and boat ramp.

4. North River WMA (map location 4). 681 acres (with 2 miles of North Platte River frontage). There are woods along the river, and grassland beyond that is used by sandhill cranes. This is one of the westernmost crane roosting sites; the birds use the southeastern part of the area, in less-than-ideal roosting habitat.

5. Muskrat Run WMA (map location 5). 224 acres. Mostly riparian wooded habitats and marshy areas.

6. East Sutherland WMA (map location 6). 27 acres with an 8-acre lake.

7. Hershey WMA (map location 7). 53 acres with an 80-acre lake.

8. **East Hershey WMA** (map location 8). 20 acres with a 20-acre lake.

9. **Birdwood Lake WMA** (map location 9). 20 acres with a 13-acre lake.

10. **Fremont Slough WMA** (map location 10). 30 acres with an 11-acre lake.

11. **Platte WMA** (map location 11). 242 acres (with 0.5 mile of Platte River frontage). This wildlife management area is mostly riparian wooded habitats.

12. **Fort McPherson National Cemetery** (map location 12). 30 acres with a pond.

13. **West Brady WMA** (map location 13). 10 acres with a 6-acre lake.

14. **Chester Island WMA** (map location 14). 69 acres with ponds (includes 0.3 mile of Platte River frontage).

15. **Box Elder Canyon WMA.** 20 acres. This area is located three miles south and 2.5 miles west of Maxwell, and it consists of native grasslands and deciduous wooded habitats along the Tri-County Supply Canal. The nearby Cottonwood and Snell Canyons, both on private land, along with Box Elder Canyon, support black-headed grosbeaks, Say's phoebes, and rock wrens in summer and mountain bluebirds, eastern bluebirds, Townsend's solitaires, and cedar waxwings during winter.

16. **Wellfleet WMA.** 65 acres. This area is just west of the village of Wellfleet, or 20 miles south of North Platte. It lies along Medicine Creek and provides a diversity of habitats that usually attract a wide variety of small passerines and water birds. In the summer, yellow-breasted chats, Bell's vireos, and other bush-loving species are common.

17. **Wapiti WMA.** 1,920 acres. The Wapiti WMA is made up of loess hills, mixed-grass prairie, trees and shrubs, and cedar woodlands (40–50 percent). Birds to see include rock wrens, Say's phoebes, black-headed grosbeaks, and some eastern species such as great crested flycatchers. To get there, from the I-80 interchange at Maxwell drive south about two miles, turn south again at the Y junction onto Cottonwood Road, go seven miles, stay to the right at the next Y junction to reach South Effenbeck Road, and then after 1.5 miles, turn right onto a minimum maintenance road for about one more mile. The loess road is hazardous when wet.

Long-billed curlew, female incubating

C. Other Areas

1. **North Platte sewage lagoons** (map location 15). North Platte's sewage lagoons are reached by leaving I-80 at exit 179 and going north on spur road L56G. Cross the South Platte River and turn east on a dead-end gravel road that will take you to the lagoons. These lagoons attract many water birds during migration. Also, several wetlands north of North Platte (Whitehorse Marsh, Jackson Lake, and Ambler Lake) support typical Sandhills marsh birds and waterfowl.

2. **Birdwood Creek.** Go north out of Sutherland (from US Hwy. 30 on the east side of town), cross the North Platte River, and turn right on a gravel road. Follow this road until you cross Birdwood Creek and then turn north and follow the creek for six to seven miles. Look for trumpeter swans and other waterfowl.

17. Dawson County (Map 15)

Dawson County is another Platte River valley county with about 8,000 acres of surface water, more than 17,000 acres of wooded habitats, and over 250,000 acres of grasslands.

A. Federal Areas — None

B. State Areas

1. **Willow Island WMA** (map location 1). 45 acres with a 35-acre lake. This wildlife management area has riparian wooded habitats.

2. **East Willow Island WMA** (map location 2). 16 acres with a 21-acre wetland. The East Willow Island area includes 0.3 mile of Platte River frontage, with mostly riparian wooded habitats.

3. **West Cozad WMA** (map location 3). 19 acres with a 29-acre lake.

4. **Cozad WMA** (map location 4). 182 acres with a 16-acre wetland. This wildlife area has 0.5 mile of river frontage.

5. **East Cozad WMA** (map location 5). 18 acres, all upland.

6. **Darr Strip WMA** (map location 6). 976 acres (767 land acres and 2.5 miles of river frontage).

7. **Dogwood WMA** (map location 7). 402 acres with a 10-acre lake (and 1.5 miles of river frontage). Good shorebird viewing, especially in April, May, July, and August. The county roads nearest the Platte River are worth driving any time of the year.

8. **Midway Lake WMA** (map location 8). Midway Lake is a reservoir near the Tri-County Supply Canal. At its upper (southern) end is Midway Canyon, an eroded area of loess hills.

9. **Gallagher Canyon SRA** (map location 9). 24 acres with a 400-acre reservoir. This recreation area is situated in a deep canyon in the loess hills with an associated irrigation reservoir.

10. **Plum Creek WMA** (map location 10). 152 acres with a 320-acre reservoir.

11. **Johnson Lake SRA** (map location 11). 81 acres with a 2,061-acre reservoir. Johnson Lake is in both Dawson and Gosper Counties, and the recreation area is in Gosper County, seven miles south of Lexington on US Hwy. 283. Habitat includes the reservoir and 68 acres of upland. The best birding is in late fall, winter, and early spring, when few people are around. It is a good area for gulls, waterfowl, cormorants, eagles, loons, and grebes. Excellent camping and water sports are hallmarks of this popular area in the summer. Though relatively small, the SRA provides three access points to the lake, and it's at the heart of a complex of lakes on the Tri-County Supply Canal. Elwood Reservoir (1,330 acres) and its recreation area are nearby.

12. **Bitterns Call WMA**. 80 acres. This area of mixed upland and wetland habitat is located about fives miles west of Lexington on Nebraska Hwy. 21 and then three miles north.

18. Chase County (Map 16)

Chase County is a high plains county with about 2,200 acres of surface water (nearly all reservoirs), about 1,400 acres of wooded habitats, and 290,000 acres of grasslands or farmlands. The only tourist accommodations are at Imperial. Some sand sage still exists in western Chase County, especially from Lamar south to the Dundy County border and in northern Chase County.

A. Federal Areas — None

B. State Areas

1. **Enders Reservoir SRA** (map location 1). 3,643 acres with a 2,146-acre reservoir. This SRA is nearly all open grassland, with rolling to rugged topography. The reservoir attracts large numbers of mallards and Canada geese; most of its western half and the surrounding area are in a wildlife refuge. The north side of the reservoir is sand-sage prairie, which possibly supports the rare Cassin's sparrow. Two prairie dog towns encompass about 35 acres. Campgrounds are available.

2. **Enders Reservoir WMA** (map location 2). This area to the west of the reservoir is managed for big game and upland game hunting.

3. **Wannamaker WMA** (map location 3). 160 acres. This wildlife management area is located about one mile west of Imperial and consists mostly of planted grasslands and shelterbelts.

4. **Champion Lake SRA** (map location 4). 13 acres. A park entry permit is required.

Other Areas

1. **Imperial Reservoir** (not shown on map). 640 acres. Located four miles south and then two miles west and northwest from Imperial, this municipal dam and reservoir are surrounded by sand-sage and shortgrass prairie with a cattail marsh and riparian cottonwoods.

19. Hayes County

Hayes County is a high plains county with less than 800 acres of surface water, about 2,000 acres of wooded habitats, and 255,000 acres of grasslands or farmlands. The only tourist accommodations are at Benkelman.

A. Federal Areas — None

B. State Areas

1. **Hayes Center WMA.** 78 acres. Located 12 miles northeast of Hayes Center, this wildlife management area consists of native high plains grasslands, scattered wooded habitats, and a 40-acre reservoir. The shrubby riparian vegetation attracts many passerines, and some eastern species such as eastern phoebes, red-bellied woodpeckers, and northern bobwhites breed here. To the north, along Nebraska Hwy. 25, western birds such as Say's phoebe, rock wren, and ferruginous hawk may at times be seen. A cattail marsh at the upper end of the reservoir supports green herons, Virginia rails, and marsh wrens.

20. Frontier County (Map 17)

Frontier County is a high plains county with about 3,500 acres of surface water (nearly all reservoirs), 1,300 acres of wooded habitats, and almost 330,000 acres of grasslands or farmlands. No tourist accommodations are available.

A. Federal Areas — None

B. State Areas

1. **Red Willow Reservoir SRA/WMA** (map location 1). 4,320 acres with a 1,628-acre reservoir. This reservoir in a water-poor region attracts good numbers of migratory water birds, including many geese and ducks. Burrowing owls should be searched for in the prairie dog town north of the county road near the Spring Creek arm and at Prairie Dog Point on the Red Willow arm. A park entry permit is required for the SRA. Modern camping facilities are available. See also Red Willow County.

2. **Medicine Creek Reservoir and Medicine Creek SRA/WMA** (map location 2). WMA 6,726 acres, SRA 1,200 acres with 1,768-acre reservoir. Seventeen hiking trails are available along with both primitive and modern camping facilities. A park entry permit is required for the SRA.

21. Gosper County (Map 18)

Gosper County is a mostly high plains county with less than 4,000 acres of surface water, nearly 1,700 acres of wooded habitats, and nearly 140,000 acres of grassland. The only tourist accommodations are at Elwood.

A. Federal Areas

1. **Victor Lakes WPA** (map location 2). 168 acres wetland, 70 acres upland.

2. **Elley WPA** (map location 6). 33 acres wetland, 29 acres upland.

3. **Peterson WPA** (map location 7). 527 acres wetland, 627 acres upland.

B. State Areas

1. **Johnson Lake SRA.** 81 acres with 2,061-acre reservoir. Developed facilities. See Dawson County.

2. **Elwood Reservoir WMA.** 900 acres with 1,330-acre reservoir. This wildlife management area is located two miles north of Elwood and is mostly grassland with some wooded sites and the reservoir. No camping facilities.

3. **J-2 Hydro Power Plant** (map location 1). This powerplant, operated by the Central Nebraska Public Power and Irrigation District, is located on a canal six miles south and

Sharp-tailed grouse, male on lek

0.5 mile east of Lexington. The plant is open seasonally for eagle viewing. During winter months, up to 100 bald eagles may gather along the powerplant spillway, feeding on dead and stunned fish. Viewing is from windows in the plant. Access is free, but public viewing hours and days are limited. For information, call 308-324-2811 or see https://www.cnppid.com/eagles/.

22. Phelps County (Map 18)

Phelps County is a Platte River valley county at the western edge of the Rainwater Basin, with fewer than 200 acres of permanent surface water (plus temporary wetlands), 3,800 acres of wooded habitats, and more than 72,000 acres of grasslands or farmlands. The only tourist accommodations are at Holdrege.

A. Federal Areas

1. **Cottonwood WPA** (map location 3). 560 acres. Cottonwood is located one mile north and two miles east of Bertrand. The waterfowl production area habitat includes 201 acres of wetland and 359 acres of upland. A pipeline delivers water directly to the wetland.

2. **Linder WPA** (map location 4). 160 acres. Linder is located just a couple miles east of Cottonwood WPA. Whooping cranes often stop here.

3. **Johnson WPA** (map location 5). 252 acres wetland, 326 acres upland. The view is best from the east side looking west. The mudflats on the west side are excellent for shorebirds.

4. **Funk WPA** (map location 8). 1,163 acres wetland, 826 acres upland. Located one mile east and three miles north of the town of Funk. This is the largest Rainwater Basin marsh at 1,989 total acres and perhaps the best. It is one of the few basins with permanent water and has some of the best marsh vegetation. During spring it hosts hundreds of thousands of geese (especially greater white-fronted) and some 20 species of ducks. Thousands of shorebirds use this site from March through May and again in the early fall. In April and October, whooping cranes have used this area. From May through September, birders might see cattle egrets, black-crowned night herons, great blue herons, and great egrets. White-faced ibis and cinnamon teal are regularly seen here. White pelicans, double-crested cormorants, and eared grebes are common in the deeper water areas.

Birds that nest here include great-tailed grackles, yellow-headed blackbirds, eared and pied-billed grebes, least bitterns, Virginia rails, northern harriers, and common yellowthroats. The amount of surface water present each spring greatly affects waterfowl usage, and natural runoff might be supplemented by groundwater pumping when needed. Funk lagoon sometimes seasonally impounds large areas of open water, moist soil wetlands, and restored native grasslands.

Hiking trails along dikes offer excellent opportunities to view wildlife any time of the year. A three-mile loop begins and ends at the main parking lot, which has an information kiosk with maps. A nearby handicap-accessible observation blind looks out over the marsh. The wetland is the collecting area for runoff from a large watershed. It can quickly go from nearly dry to flooded after a heavy summer rain.

5. **Atlanta WPA** (map location 9). 453 acres wetland, 659 acres upland. Located six miles west and three miles south of Holdrege, this waterfowl production area is seasonally open to public hunting for pheasant, waterfowl,

Great horned owl, on nest in Cherry County

and doves. It contains a large wetland basin that requires a significant runoff event to provide adequate water for migratory waterfowl; the basin is often dry in low snowfall years.

6. **Jones WPA** (map location 10). 90 acres wetland, 76 acres upland. Located three miles west and three miles south of Holdrege.

B. State Areas

1. **West Sacramento WMA** (map location 11). 200 acres wetland, 188 acres upland. A prairie dog town of four to five acres is present here.

2. **Sacramento-Wilcox WMA** (map location 12). 1,050 acres wetland, 1,263 acres upland. Located about 2.5 miles west of Wilcox. "Sac" offers a nice variety of habitat types, including freshwater marsh, prairie, creek, and woodland. Several controlled water impoundments ensure that some water is always available. A wide variety of birds can be seen here. This area serves both as a waterfowl refuge and as a public hunting area. Approximately 500 of its 2,313 acres are designated as refuge, and a

viewing blind overlooks a good waterfowl and shorebird area when water is present. Many ducks visit the area each fall, and duck hunting is available from established blinds. Intensive habitat development—including the planting and managing of trees, shrubs, and grasses—has provided a wealth of cover diversity. Camping is available in a designated area. The headquarters is located on the east end of the property. Long-eared owls roost here in winter.

23. Dundy County

Dundy County is a high plains county with less than 500 acres of surface water, about 5,200 acres of wooded habitats, and 384,000 acres of grasslands or farmlands. No tourist accommodations are available in the county. Scattered areas of sand sage still exit in western areas.

A. Federal Areas — None

B. State Areas

1. **Rock Creek Lake SRA.** 165 acres. Located ten miles west and four miles north of Benkelman (and one mile south of the fish hatchery). This may be the best birding area in southwestern Nebraska. The surrounding vegetation is one of the few protected areas of sand sage prairie in Nebraska, with its associated birds such as Cassin's sparrow. The 54-acre reservoir is one of the few locations in the region where migrating water birds can settle; thus, it attracts ducks, shorebirds, and other water birds during both spring and fall. It also attracts many passerine migrants, especially in autumn, and migrating ospreys. A park entry permit is required.

24. Hitchcock County (Map 19)

Hitchcock County is a Republican River valley county with more than 5,600 acres of surface water (mostly reservoir), about 2,000 acres of wooded habitats, and over 200,000 acres of grasslands or farmlands. Tourist accommodations are available in Trenton and Culbertson.

A. Federal Areas — None

B. State Areas

1. **Swanson Reservoir and WMA** (map location 1). 1,157 acres upland with a 4,973-acre reservoir. Primitive and

modern camping facilities are available, along with 13 hiking trails. Swanson Reservoir attracts many migrant water birds, some of which might overwinter. The wet meadows south of Stratton also attract many water birds during migration, including sandhill cranes and white-faced ibis. About 3,000 acres are open to hunting and other public use; this is the largest of the area's reservoirs and has a large fish population, which should attract eagles and other fish-eating birds. A prairie dog town occupies about six acres.

25. Red Willow County

Red Willow County is also a Republican River valley county with about 2,700 acres of surface water, 7,000 acres of wooded habitats, and nearly 180,000 acres of grasslands or farmlands. Tourist accommodations are available at Indianola and McCook.

A. Federal Areas — None

B. State Areas

1. **Red Willow Reservoir SRA/WMA.** 5,948 acres with a 1,628-acre reservoir. Located 12 miles north of McCook on US Hwy. 83 and then two miles west, Red Willow consists mostly of high plains grasslands or farmlands. Camping facilities are available. The associated reservoir (Hugh Butler Lake) extends into Frontier County (see additional information there). A park entry permit is required.

2. **Bartley Diversion Dam WMA.** This wildlife area is located one mile south and 1.5 miles east of Indianola. It is a small area of grasslands, rolling hills, and scattered trees around a campground.

C. Other Areas

1. **Barnett Park.** Located in McCook on the north side of the Republican River, Barnett Park has a small lake and a nature trail along the river.

26. Furnas County

Furnas County is a Republican River valley county with nearly 5,600 acres of surface water, 8,300 acres of wooded habitats, and more than 175,000 acres of grasslands or farmlands. Tourist accommodations are available in Arapahoe, Beaver City, Cambridge, and Oxford.

A. Federal Areas — None

B. State Areas

1. **Cambridge Diversion Dam.** Located two miles east of Cambridge, this area includes 21 acres of grassland bordering the Republican River as well as brushy bottomland.

27. Harlan County (Map 20)

Harlan County is a Republican River valley county with nearly 15,000 acres of surface water (mostly reservoir), nearly 9,000 acres of wooded habitats, and almost 120,000 acres of grasslands or farmlands. Tourist accommodations are available at Alma, Orleans, and Republican City.

A. Federal Areas

1. **Harlan County Lake** (map location 1). 17,278 acres with a 13,338-acre reservoir. This largest reservoir in south-central Nebraska attracts bald eagles, geese (especially Canada geese), and some sandhill cranes during spring and fall. The area has a population of greater prairie-chickens (on the south side of the reservoir) as well. Near the south end of the dam is an eagle roost. Look for burrowing owls in the prairie dog colony between Republican City and the dam administration area that is located between the town and the dam. During spring and fall good numbers of double-crested cormorants and American white pelicans are present (some perhaps staying through summer). Gulls also accumulate in good numbers here, and migrating raptors are often seen.

B. State Areas

1. **South Sacramento WMA** (map location 2). 90 upland acres, 77 wetland acres.

2. **Southeast Sacramento WMA** (map location 3). 45 upland acres, 140 acres wetland. A prairie dog town occupies about four acres.

III. The East-Central Region

The central Platte River valley and nearby Rainwater Basin provide some of the best spring birding opportunities in all of North America. For most of March, about 7 million waterfowl and about half a million sandhill cranes pour into the region, remaining until late March for the waterfowl and about the first week of April for the sandhill cranes. As the last sandhill cranes are leaving, whooping cranes begin to arrive, as do the early shorebirds, continuing the amazing spring spectacle until about the end of April.

Birding in the central Platte valley during March is a chancy affair in terms of weather. Late winter snowstorms may blanket the entire area in a foot of snow, which when it melts leaves country roads slippery at best, and thus driving requires a good deal of care. This is especially true in the Rainwater Basin, an area of clay soils that prevent water from percolating down and thus is rich in temporary wetlands (locally called "lagoons") just at the peak of spring waterfowl populations. The wetlands occur only during years when winter snowfalls or spring rains allow the basins to fill; in drier years only the deepest lagoons or those that are kept wet by pumping (Harvard, Massie, Smith, etc.) can accommodate the hordes of ducks and geese passing through. During dry years, the stresses caused by bad weather and overcrowding can set off outbreaks of fowl cholera and kill tens of thousands of birds in just a short time. Some of these birds are consumed by wintering bald eagles, hundreds of which occur along ice-free areas of the Platte from late fall until early spring. A good viewing area for eagles is at the J-2 Hydro Power Plant near Lexington (see the Gosper County section for more information).

The best way to watch cranes during the day is observing them from a parked car, with observers remaining quiet and inside the car, while the cranes are feeding in the fields. Opening a door and leaving the car will guarantee a rapid departure of the birds. Gravel roads on the south side of the Platte River are usually better for crane viewing than those on the north side of Interstate 80. However, the most rewarding way to watch cranes is from a riverside blind near their roosting locations (see accompanying maps). Such blinds are maintained by the Crane Trust on Mormon Island (reservations required) and Audubon's Lillian Annette Rowe Sanctuary near Gibbon (reservations required).

If it is not possible to arrange a blind for viewing, several bridges such as the hike-bike trail bridge near Fort Kearny or the bridge over the middle Platte River channel two miles south of Alda (see maps 26 and 27) provide a less thrilling but still exciting view, both at sunset and sunrise. Information on crane viewing and accommodations can be obtained from the Kearney Visitors Bureau (phone 308-237-3178), Grand Island Tourism (phone 308-382-4400), or Visit Hastings Nebraska (phone 800-967-2189). The Hastings Museum (at 1330 N. Burlington Ave., phone 402-461-2399) and the Stuhr Museum (at the southern edge of Grand Island on US Hwy. 34, phone 308-385-5316) both provide tourist information and sell informative books or pamphlets on local tourist attractions.

The Nebraska Game and Parks Commission (phone 308-865-5310 in Kearney or 402-471-0641 in Lincoln) can provide free informative materials, including an excellent eight-page "Spring Migration Guide" that centers on Platte valley birding. Some its maps showing wildlife viewing areas are reproduced here by permission. The commission also published (1997) a 96-page booklet by Joseph Knue that includes descriptions of 68 viewing sites in the state. It may sometimes be obtained from used bookstores. (See also https://platteriverprogram.org/visitors.)

A collection of county road maps is also available from the Nebraska Department of Transportation in Lincoln (phone 402-471-4567). Bound sets of maps covering the entire state can be found in the DeLorme *Nebraska Atlas and Gazetteer*. Both describe and list local tourist attractions, offer camping information, and provide other similar information. The latter book is based on contour maps and the former emphasizes hunting and fishing sites.

The Rainwater Basin area is just as attractive as the Platte River valley during early spring, when snowmelt accumulates in the clay-rich lowlands and an estimated 7 million to 9 million ducks and 2 million to 3 million geese pass through. These flocks include 90 percent of

Sandhill crane roost, Lillian Annette Rowe Sanctuary

the midcontinental greater white-fronted goose population, 50 percent of the mid-continental mallard population, and 30 percent of the entire continent's northern pintail population. Increasing numbers of snow geese also use the more easterly parts of the area each spring, their numbers recently exceeding a million birds. Some of the shallower wetlands are also of great importance to migrant shorebirds. Joel Jorgensen (2012) analyzed shorebird migration patterns in the eastern Rainwater Basin. He reported that, in decreasing order, the most numerous shorebirds (out of 38 total species) seen there over a several-year period in spring were white-rumped sandpiper, Wilson's phalarope, semipalmated sandpiper, long-billed dowitcher, lesser yellowlegs, least sandpiper, and Baird's sandpiper. Pectoral sandpiper, long-billed dowitcher, lesser yellowlegs, least sandpiper, and stilt sandpiper were progressively less numerous during fall.

The region may be of hemispheric migratory importance to the very localized buff-breasted sandpiper, which stages in various mixed-grass sites around the eastern Rainwater Basin. A suggested eastern loop tour starting from the I-80 exit at Aurora is mapped and available at https://www.fws.gov/refuge/Rainwater_Basin_WMD/map.html (scroll down and look for the "Driving Tour Map—Eastern" map). This route over generally improved roads includes the most important wetlands of the eastern Rainwater Basin. The Rainwater Basin Wetland Management District comprises about 84 wetlands occupying 28,600 acres (including 21,742 federally owned acres and about 6,900 state-owned acres).

Sites such as Harvard, Massie, and Smith lagoons and Mallard Haven are of special value to these birds, as they usually are kept well watered and are prime birding locations in the eastern basin, while Funk lagoon is a special attraction in the western basin. Sites of special shorebird significance include Harvard, Mallard Haven, Massie, and Sinninger. A bird checklist, with nearly 200 species, including more than 100 breeding species, is available from the US Fish and Wildlife Service Rainwater Basin headquarters in Funk (phone 308-263-3000). The Kearney office of the Nebraska Game and Parks Commission is located at 1617 First Ave., phone 308-865-5310.

1. Boyd County

Boyd County is a Niobrara River valley county with about 2,500 acres of surface water, 1,600 acres of wooded habitats, and 200,000 acres of grasslands or farmlands. The only tourist accommodations are at Spencer.

A. Federal Areas

1. **Missouri National Recreational River.** The northeastern boundary of Boyd County is the Missouri River, and along this length it is designated the Missouri National Recreational River and managed by the National Park Service. The nearest visitor center is located in Niobrara State Park.

B. State Areas

1. **Parshall Bridge WMA.** 230 acres. Located five miles south of Butte, this wildlife management area has riparian wooded habitats along the Niobrara River.

2. **Hull Lake WMA.** 36 acres. Located three miles south and one mile west of Butte. At this site, hilly uplands with oaks, conifers, and grasslands surround a three-acre lake.

2. Holt County

Holt County is a mostly Sandhills county with more than 12,000 acres of surface water, almost 69,000 acres of wooded habitats, and 1.2 million acres of grasslands or farmlands. The only tourist accommodations are at Atkinson and O'Neill.

A. Federal Areas — None

B. State Areas

1. **Atkinson Lake SRA.** 54 acres. Located at the northwest edge of Atkinson, this recreation area includes a 14-acre reservoir on the Elkhorn River. A state park entry permit is required.

2. **Goose Lake WMA.** 349 acres. Located four miles east of US Hwy. 281 and two miles north of the Wheeler County boundary (23 miles south of O'Neill and 4 miles east). The area is mostly lake but also includes grassy and wooded uplands.

3. **Redbird WMA.** 433 acres. Located a few miles south of Lynch on 503rd Ave., just south of the Redbird Bridge over the Niobrara River, this area is mostly bur oak and cedar, bisected by Louse Creek, with steep, wooded slopes and rolling grasslands.

4. Spencer Dam WMA. 9 acres. The acreage of this site is in the Niobrara River valley, providing river access. It is located 23 miles north of O'Neill on US Hwy 281.

3. Knox County (Map 21)

Knox County contains portions of the Niobrara and Missouri Rivers and thus has more than 41,000 acres of surface water as well as 38,000 acres of wooded habitats and almost 320,000 acres of grasslands or farmlands. Tourist accommodations are available in Bloomfield, Creighton, Crofton, Niobrara, and Wausa.

A. Federal Areas

1. **Missouri National Recreational River.** The northern boundary of Knox County is the Missouri River, and along this length it is designated the Missouri National Recreational River and managed by the National Park Service. A visitor center is located in Niobrara State Park.

B. State Areas

1. **Gavins Point Dam and Lewis and Clark Lake SRA** (map location 1). 1,227 acres with a 32,000-acre reservoir. See the Cedar County section.

2. **Bazile Creek WMA** (map location 2). 4,500 acres. Bordered for nine miles by the Missouri River and Lewis and Clark Lake, this wildlife management area has mixed woods, grasslands, and marshy areas. The area is extensively marshy, as it includes the upper end of Lewis and Clark Lake, formed by the impoundment of the Missouri River, so many wetland birds are present. A hiking trail is available. A state park entry permit is required.

3. **Niobrara State Park** (map location 3). 1,632 acres. This state park is located at the confluence of the Niobrara and Missouri Rivers. It is mostly grassland but also has riparian wooded habitats. More than 12 miles of hiking trails are available, and a 2-mile hike-bike trail extends along the park's northern boundary. Wooded-habitat birds include whip-poor-wills, and both bald eagles and ospreys are present seasonally. This place is classified as a Nebraska Important Bird Area. The park provides an interpretive center and both modern cabins and primitive camping facilities. A state park entry permit is required. Phone 402-857-3373 for more information.

4. **Bohemia Prairie WMA** (map location 4). 600 acres. This site is mainly grasslands with some woods and two ponds.

5. **Greenvale WMA.** 200 acres. Middle Verdigre Creek bisects this mostly wooded wildlife management area located ten miles west and three miles south of Verdigre.

4. Antelope County (Map 22)

Antelope County is an Elkhorn River valley county with less than 900 acres of surface water, more than 21,000 acres of wooded habitats, and nearly 200,000 acres of grasslands or farmlands. Tourist accommodations are available at Elgin, Neligh, and Orchard.

A. Federal Areas — None

B. State Areas

1. **Ashfall Fossil Beds State Historical Park** (map location 1). 360 acres. This extremely important paleontological site preserves the fossils of horses, rhinos, camels, and other animals (including crowned cranes) killed and interred under a thick layer of volcanic dust that settled here about 10 million years ago. The area is now mostly rugged range country, with grassland species most common. However, rock wrens can often be seen near the excavation site. The center is open from Memorial Day through Labor Day, Wednesday–Sunday, 9:30 a.m.–4:30 p.m. Hours vary during May and September. Both an admission fee and state park permit are required. For more information see https://ashfall.unl.edu/ or phone 402-893-2000.

2. **Grove Lake WMA** (map location 2). 1,746 acres with a 35-acre reservoir. This wildlife management area is rolling grassland with scattered mixed hardwood trees along the East Branch of Verdigre Creek. There is also a small reservoir and trout-rearing facility. Most of the birds are grassland species, but ospreys and belted kingfishers are also possible to see.

3. **Hackberry Creek WMA** (map location 3). 180 acres. This area includes a mile of Elkhorn River frontage, several marshy oxbows, mixed woods, and grassland.

4. **Redwing WMA** (map location 4). 320 acres. Like Hackberry Creek WMA, this area also includes Elkhorn River

frontage—about a mile and a half. The habitat is mostly riparian woods with some grassland and marshes.

5. Pierce County (Map 23)

Pierce County has less than 4,000 acres of surface water, about 5,000 acres of wooded habitats, and nearly 125,000 acres of grasslands or farmlands. Tourist accommodations are available in Osmond and Plainview.

A. Federal Areas — None

B. State Areas

1. **Willow Creek SRA** (map location 1). 1,600 acres with a 700-acre reservoir. Willow Creek is a fishing and camping area. A hiking trail is available. A state park entry permit is required.

6. Garfield County

Garfield County is a Sandhills county with about 6,000 acres of surface water (nearly all reservoir), 5,500 acres of wooded habitats, and more than 320,000 acres of grasslands or farmlands. Tourist accommodations are available in Burwell.

A. Federal Areas — None

B. State Areas

1. **Calamus Reservoir SRA/WMA.** 4,958 acres with a 5,123-acre reservoir. Located about five miles northwest of Burwell, this Sandhills recreation area provides several types of camping facilities, boating, fishing, swimming, and more. A fish hatchery is located below the Calamus Reservoir dam. The area is classified as a Nebraska Important Bird Area largely because of the huge migratory populations of white pelicans it attracts as well as good numbers of migrating shorebirds, waterfowl, and other water birds. In early spring when winter-killed fish appear, bald eagles are often abundant. A state park permit is required.

7. Wheeler County

Wheeler County is an eastern Sandhills county with 1,300 acres of surface water, almost 24,000 acres of wooded habitats, and nearly 330,000 acres of grasslands or farmlands. Tourist accommodations are available in Ericson.

A. Federal Areas — None

B. State Areas

1. **Pibel Lake Recreation Area.** 72 acres with a 24-acre lake. Located seven miles east and two miles south of Ericson, this area is owned and operated by Lower Loup Natural Resources District. Pibel Lake is a beautiful Sandhills lake with a variety of water birds present during spring and summer.

8. Valley County

Valley County is a Loup River valley county with nearly 3,000 acres of surface water, 2,300 acres of wooded habitats, and 200,000 acres of grasslands or farmlands. Tourist accommodations are available at Ord.

A. Federal Areas — None

B. State Areas

1. **Fort Hartsuff State Historical Park.** 18.4 acres. Located about three miles north and one mile west of Elyria. This restored 1870s fort was built to protect settlers from Native Americans and to help separate the Pawnees from the Sioux to the north. It is mainly of interest for historical reasons, but passerines should be present seasonally. The grounds are open daily year round, while facilities are open a variety of days and hours seasonally; check http://outdoornebraska.gov/forthartsuff/ or phone 308-346-4715. A state park permit is required, and the visitor interpreter center charges a small fee.

2. **Davis Creek Recreation Area.** About 2,000 acres with a 1,145-acre reservoir. Located about three miles south of the town of North Loup, this Lower Loup Natural Resources District area is mostly grassy, surrounding the irrigation reservoir. Hiking trails and camping are available.

3. **Scotia Canal WMA.** Located near the North Loup River, 4.5 miles north of the town of North Loup, this small wildlife management area is mostly covered by grassy uplands and mixed wooded habitats.

9. Greeley County

Greeley County is an eastern Sandhills and loess hills county with nearly 2,500 acres of surface water (mostly reservoir acreage), almost 3,000 acres of wooded habitats, and more than 200,000 acres of grasslands or farmlands. Tourist accommodations are available near Spalding.

A. Federal Areas — None

B. State Areas

1. **Davis Creek Recreation Area.** 2,000 acres with a 1,145-acre reservoir. See the Valley County description.

10. Boone County

Boone County is a mostly loess hills county with about 1,100 acres of surface water, 2,600 acres of wooded habitats, and more than 160,000 acres of grasslands or farmlands. Tourist accommodations are available at Albion.

A. Federal Areas — None

B. State Areas

1. **Beaver Bend WMA.** 27 acres. Located one mile northwest of St. Edward along Beaver Creek, this area has good riparian wooded habitats.

11. Madison County (Map 23)

Madison County is a loess hills and Elkhorn River valley county with less than 800 acres of surface water, about 10,000 acres of wooded habitats, and more than 80,000 acres of grasslands or farmlands. Tourist accommodations are available at Newman Grove, Norfolk, and Tilden.

A. Federal Areas — None

B. State Areas

1. **Yellowbanks WMA** (map location 2). 680 acres. Yellowbanks includes 1.5 miles of frontage along the Elkhorn River and has steep riverine bluffs that support mature hardwood forest and some grassy uplands.

2. **Oak Valley WMA** (map location 3). 640 acres. Oak Valley includes a hardwood bottomland forest, bisected by Battle Creek, and otherwise mostly grassy uplands.

12. Platte County (Map 24)

Platte County is a mostly loess hills county with almost 3,000 acres of surface water, 7,400 acres of wooded habitats, and nearly 90,000 acres of grasslands or farmlands. Tourist accommodations are available in Columbus and Humphrey.

A. Federal Areas — None

B. State Areas

1. **George Syas WMA** (map location 4). 917 acres. This area includes 1.5 miles of Loup River frontage and is about half wooded with the rest in grasses, crops, and planted shrubs.

2. **Wilkinson WMA.** 957 acres. Wilkinson WMA is mostly upland grassland and managed wetlands. It is located five miles west and one mile north of Columbus, just off US Hwy. 81. Large numbers of waterfowl and shorebirds are present in spring. (Not shown on map.)

3. **Lookingglass Creek WMA.** 87 acres. About half wooded with the rest in grassland and two small lakes, this area is located scarcely a mile south of Monroe. (Not shown on map.)

C. Other Areas

1. **Lake Babcock Waterfowl Refuge** (map location 6). 600 acres. Lake Babcock is a reservoir on the Loup River Canal, just outside of Columbus.

2. **Lake North** (map location 7). 200 acres. Lake North is a city lake developed for fishing and swimming and probably of limited nature potential.

3. **Pawnee Park.** Pawnee Park is a city park on the banks of the Loup River, which offers a good riparian zone for viewing spring warblers.

13. Sherman County (Map 25)

Sherman County is a Loup River valley county with more than 4,000 acres of surface water (mostly reservoir acreage), 3,000 acres of wooded habitats, and over 200,000 acres of grasslands or farmlands. Tourist accommodations are available in Loup City.

A. Federal Areas — None

B. State Areas

1. **Sherman Reservoir SRA/WMA** (map location 1). 4,721 acres with a 2,845-acre reservoir. These areas are mostly rolling prairie grasslands with woody growth along creeks. Ten hiking trails are maintained along with many spots for primitive camping. Two prairie dog towns totaling about 12 acres can be viewed. A state park entry permit is required.

2. **Bowman Lake SRA** (map location 2). 23 acres. Bowman is a small SRA with a lake just outside of Loup City. A state park entry permit is required.

14. Howard County

Howard County is a Loup River valley county with nearly 3,000 acres of surface water, more than 5,000 acres of wooded habitats, and about 190,000 acres of grasslands or farmlands. Tourist accommodations are available at Dannebrog and St. Paul.

A. Federal Areas — None

B. State Areas

1. **Harold W. Andersen WMA.** 272 acres. Located four miles south and two miles west of St. Paul, Andersen WMA consists of about 12 miles of Loup River frontage with bottomland timber and a marshy oxbow.

2. **Loup Junction WMA.** 328 acres. Loup Junction is located three miles north and two miles east of St. Paul. Bordered on the north by the North Loup River and on the south by the Middle Loup River, this confluence region is mostly riparian flooded habitats with marshes and grassy areas.

15. Nance County (Map 24)

Nance County is a Loup and Platte Valley county with almost 3,000 acres of surface water, over 5,000 acres of wooded habitats, and over 190,000 acres of grasslands or farmlands. Historically, part of it comprised the Pawnee Reservation, with Genoa the headquarters and site of an Indian School. There are tourist accommodations at Genoa and Fullerton.

A. Federal Areas — None

B. State Areas

1. **Loup Lands WMA** (map locations 1 and 2). 485 acres. Similar to Prairie Wolf WMA.

2. **Prairie Wolf WMA** (map location 3). 972 acres. This area is mainly bottomlands along the Loup River with restored grasslands, marshes, and some timber.

3. **Sunny Hollow WMA** (map location 5). 160 acres. This site is mostly grassy uplands with two marshes and an excavated wetland.

4. **Council Creek WMA.** 160 acres. Located 6.5 miles west and one mile south of Genoa, Council Creek has a mixture of alfalfa fields, restored grassland, and riparian woods. (Not shown on map.)

16. Polk County

Polk County is a Platte River valley county with less than 500 acres of surface water, nearly 5,000 acres of wooded habitats, and 54,000 acres of grasslands or farmlands. Tourist accommodations are available in Osceola.

A. Federal Areas — None

B. State Areas — None

17. Buffalo County (Map 26)

Buffalo County is a Platte River and Loup River valley county with 4,400 acres of surface water, 9,600 acres of wooded habitats, and nearly 225,000 acres of grasslands or farmlands. Tourist accommodations are available in Elm Creek, Gibbon, and Kearney.

III. THE EAST-CENTRAL REGION

Greater prairie-chicken males displaying to a female

A. Federal Areas — None

B. State Areas

1. **Ravenna Lake SRA** (map location 1). 53 acres. Situated along the South Loup River, this SRA also has a small reservoir. A state park entry permit is required.

2. **Blue Hole WMA** (map location 2). 530 acres. Blue Hole has a 30-acre pond and two miles of Platte River frontage with mostly riparian wooded habitats.

3. **Sandy Channel SRA** (map location 3). 133 acres. Sandy Channel has 11 small lakes and ponds that together total 47 acres. A state park entry permit is required.

4. **Union Pacific SRA** (map location 4). 26 acres with a 15-acre pond. A state park permit is required.

5. **East Odessa SRA** (map location 5). 71 acres with a seven-acre pond. A state park permit is required.

6. **Cottonmill Lake Public Use Area** (map location 6). A hike-bike trail extends six miles from this area to the outskirts of Kearney.

7. **Bassway Strip WMA** (map location 10). 636 acres. Bassway Strip has four ponds and seven miles of Platte River frontage. It includes 90 acres of lakes and sandpits, mostly wooded. In spite of the river frontage, this area is not used by sandhill cranes to any great extent.

8. **War Axe SRA** (map location 8). 9 acres with a 12-acre pond. War Axe was developed for fishing and tourists. A state park permit is required.

9. **Windmill SRA** (map location 9). 168 acres with five ponds. A state park entry permit is required.

C. Other Areas

1. **Lillian Annette Rowe Sanctuary and Iain Nicolson Audubon Center** (map location 7). About 2,900 acres (including recent acquisitions). This sanctuary, the largest Audubon refuge in the state, protects prime sandhill and whooping crane habitats near Kearney, and includes nearly five miles of river frontage, plus about 1,000 acres of native prairie. Several riverside blinds are located on the property, and spring sunrise or sunset excursions to the blinds can be arranged between early March and mid-April (reservations are needed). A self-guided hiking/birding trail is also available.

The Audubon Center headquarters provides information and sells books and other bird-related materials. Summer breeding birds include dickcissel, upland sandpiper, and bobolink as well as species such as the rose-breasted grosbeak and willow flycatcher that use riparian wooded habitats. Least terns and piping plovers often nest on barren sandbars that are also used by roosting cranes. The sanctuary is classified as a Globally Important Bird Area. The Iain Nicolson Center is of modern haybale construction; its north side is lined with windows for easy bird watching. A webcam provides 24-hour coverage of Platte River crane roosts.

The sanctuary's address is 44450 Elm Island Road, Gibbon, NE 68840, phone 308-468-5282, email rowe@nctic.net. Office hours are 9 a.m.–5 p.m. Monday through Friday, 1–5 p.m. Sunday; open seven days a week during crane season. No admission is charged to visit, but a donation is suggested.

2. **Prairie-chicken lek.** Prairie-chickens often have a lek visible from the road near Kearney. Drive west 6.5 miles from the town center, turn right (north) on Evergreen Road, and go to 56th Road and turn left (west). At 3.2 miles, you will be at the top of a hill with two windmills

visible. The lek is on the north side of the road, about 300 yards away, so a spotting scope is needed.

3. **Richard Plautz Crane Viewing Site** (map location 11). This bridge, 1.5 miles south of I-80 exit 285 in Buffalo County, provides a parking area and viewing platform for watching crane roosting flights. The Central Platte Natural Resources District has provided two crane viewing decks for use by visitors. The decks offer a safe, elevated area for viewing cranes and other wildlife on the Platte River. Best times are sunset and sunrise. Cranes, herons, egrets, pelicans, waterfowl, song sparrows, and a host of other birds can be seen comfortably from these wooden observation decks. Be careful to avoid standing on the bridge itself, where traffic can be quite fast.

18. Hall County (Map 27)

Hall County is a Platte River valley county with nearly 2,000 acres of surface water, 3,900 acres of wooded habitats, and almost 120,000 acres of grasslands or farmlands. Tourist accommodations are available at Alda, Grand Island, and Wood River.

A. Federal Areas

1. **Hannon WPA.** 659 acres. This waterfowl production area is located one mile east and two miles north of the I-80 Shelton exit (number 291). The habitat includes wet meadows and surrounding grassy uplands with 105 acres of water. Common summer residents include marsh and sedge wrens, upland sandpipers, bobolinks, dickcissels, and a variety of native sparrows. This site has had good use by waterfowl when water is present and excellent use by sandhill cranes after a prescribed burn. There are several small ponds and a slough that runs through the area in wet years, which is attractive to shorebirds such as snipe. Some years this area has seen heavy use by migrating sandhill cranes.

B. State Areas

1. **Cornhusker WMA** (map location 2). 840 acres. Cornhusker is all upland habitats with various planted cover types. The birds include such brush-loving winter species as Harris's sparrows and American tree sparrows.

2. **Mormon Island SRA** (map location 10). 152 acres with a 61-acre lake. Mormon Island SRA is located 0.25 mile north of I-80 at the Grand Island exit number 312. Habitats include three lakes and their surrounding riparian woodlands. Camping, restrooms, swimming, shelters, and an office are available at this site. It is a popular fishing, camping, and swimming spot just off I-80 that occasionally attracts large concentrations of waterfowl in the spring, despite the potential for disturbance. Historically, this location was used as a winter stopover by Mormon emigrants heading westward.

A good variety of waterfowl and shorebirds comes to this area before heading farther north. Ask park personnel for more information about the best times and locations to view these impressive wildlife displays. Because of its depth, the main lake sometimes hosts loons, pelicans, mergansers, and a variety of grebes. The slough running through the SRA is a good place to search for Wilson's snipe. Cedar waxwings, woodpeckers, and brown creepers are common, as are owls. At other times of the year, this area rarely attracts many waterfowl because of the high human disturbance level.

3. **Martin's Reach WMA** (map location 12). 89 acres. This site is located one mile south and three miles west of the Wood River I-80 interchange (exit 300). It includes about 0.7 mile of frontage on the middle channel of the Platte River. A slough running through the center of the area provides nesting habitat for shorebirds and ducks. As many as 88 species have been seen here in a single day.

4. **Loch Linda WMA.** 38 acres. Located three miles east of the Alda I-80 exit (number 305), then a mile south over the interstate, and another two miles east, this area is a 29-acre wet cattail marsh surrounded by nine acres of pastureland and mature riparian forest adjoining the Platte River. Ducks, wild turkeys, yellow-headed blackbirds, common yellowthroats, and herons are common in the marsh. Shorebirds should be visible along the Platte.

C. Other Areas

1. **Taylor Ranch road** (map location 1). Taylor Ranch is located four miles west and three miles north of Grand Island. It is a privately owned 7,000-acre ranch with extensive Sandhills prairie and numerous small wetlands that are attractive to migrating ducks and shorebirds during wet years. County roads along the perimeter of this ranch provide an opportunity to watch displaying greater prairie-chickens from a parked car. Active prairie-chicken leks can be located by driving to this area around sunrise and stopping every few hundred yards to listen for the

Sandhill cranes, landing on a Platte River roost

males' "booming" from mid-March into May. A few sharp-tailed grouse are also sometimes present, and a good variety of raptors can be found too.

About 90 species of birds have been observed in this area. Blue grosbeaks have nested in the plum thickets; burrowing owls have also nested here. The lower arrowhead on the map points toward one such location where a grouse lek usually is located. (Farther north in the Sandhills, sharp-tailed grouse outnumber the greater prairie-chickens.)

2. Crane Trust (map location 3). 6,500 acres. This preserve was the second Platte River valley crane sanctuary to be established and, along with the Rowe Sanctuary farther west, is the most important. More than 70,000 cranes have been seen on its pristine wet meadows, and up to 200,000 birds roost along its river shorelines. More than 280 bird species have been reported here. This facility is generally not open to the public.

For more information about the Crane Trust, call 308-382-1820. Crane observation blinds are located on Crane Trust land and operated from early March to early April (see the Crane Trust Nature and Visitor Center section next). A blind visit ($35 per person in 2020, reservations are usually needed) can be reserved by contacting the trust or the visitor center.

3. Crane Trust Nature and Visitor Center (map location 5). This large nature center is on the south side of the Alda I-80 interchange (exit 305) and is operated by the Crane Trust. Here, guided tours to crane-viewing blinds may be arranged during the crane migration season (early March to early April), and staff are available to help provide birding information. Hiking trails are open year-round Monday through Saturday, 9 a.m.–4:00 p.m., with some restrictions during crane season. The center's address is 9325 S. Alda Road, Wood River, NE 68883.

4. Shoemaker Island road (map location 4). One starting point of the road across the western portion of Shoemaker Island is located two miles south of the I-80 Alda exit (number 305). The road extends east to west about six miles to the next intersection, which is one mile south of the Wood River I-80 interchange (exit 300). This gravel road thus traverses most of the length of Shoemaker Island, where many wet meadows attract foraging flocks of sandhill cranes. There are also large stands of riparian forest where rose-breasted and black-headed grosbeaks can be observed, along with eastern wood-pewees, wild turkey, and red-headed woodpeckers. The area is partly privately owned, so birding away from the road may require landowner permission. Cattle egrets and eastern bluebirds are common here. Road ditches often contain some water, and wood ducks, sora rails, and American bitterns sometimes make use of them.

Greater prairie-chickens have been infrequently observed on this island. American woodcock perform their courtship sky dance along the wooded river drainage in April and May. This stretch of the Platte River is heavily used not just by migrating cranes but also waterfowl, eagles, shorebirds, and nesting piping plovers and least terns. At least 205 species of birds have been recorded in this area. The adjacent native prairie provides nesting sites for prairie species such as dickcissels, upland sandpipers, bobolinks, grasshopper sparrows, and Bell's vireos. Riparian areas provide habitat for a variety of passerines, including orchard orioles and willow flycatchers.

5. Alda Crane Viewing Site (map location 6). Near the Alda bridge over the middle Platte River channel (two miles south of I-80 exit 305) is the Central Platte Natural Resources District Alda Crane Viewing Site, a wooden platform where people can watch the sunrise and sunset roosting flights of cranes. The Central Platte NRD built two free crane-viewing decks (the other is the Richard Plautz Crane Viewing Site in Buffalo County) that provide a safe area to view cranes and other wildlife on the Platte River. This one is near a sandpit lake that may attract up to 40,000 geese, but the lake is on private property and can be viewed only from the highway vicinity. The handicap-accessible viewing platform provides an excellent view of cranes and waterfowl roosting on both sides of the Platte's Alda bridge at sunrise and sunset. Parking is available, and this site also has a hiking trail. Besides the cranes, it's possible to see herons, egrets, pelicans, song sparrows, and a host of other birds from this deck.

6. Platte River Road (map location 7). This paved road that travels west from Doniphan to Kearney is a good route for observing field-feeding cranes during the daytime. Although it extends west to the Kearney area, the density of crane use is greatest toward the eastern end. Generally the cranes are best seen from the road nearest the south bank of the Platte River, especially in early morning and late afternoon, among cornfields or the occasional wet meadows that still exist.

7. Amick Acres (map location 8). This small subdivision has several sandpit lakes that attract large flocks of

Sandhill crane roost, Crane Trust

Canada and cackling geese in early March. Do not stray from the road, as the area is entirely private property.

8. **Nine Bridges Bridge** (map location 9). This narrow bridge over one of the few remaining river channels north of Doniphan (nine river channels were once present within the approximately eight-mile Grand Island–to–Doniphan distance) provides views of a small crane flock often present on the downstream side. However, no parking is allowed near the bridge, so some walking is necessary.

9. **George Clayton Hall County Park** and **Stuhr Museum of the Prairie Pioneer** (map location 11). George Clayton Hall County Park is located one mile south of Grand Island on US Hwys. 34/281 (or about three miles north of the I-80 interchange) and 0.5 mile east on Schimmer Drive. This county park allows free entry and offers wooded trails for birding. Warblers, thrushes, woodpeckers, and kinglets are seen here. Occasionally a Carolina wren, American redstart, or long-eared owl can be found here too. This heavily wooded 38-acre park is the remnant of dried-up Schimmer Lake; Wood River forms its northern boundary. Tent and RV camping facilities are provided for a fee. This park is just south of the Stuhr Museum (https://stuhrmuseum.org/). The museum has an admission charge, but there is free access to the museum shop. For more information about the museum call 308-385-5316.

10. **Eagle Scout Park.** 90 acres. Located at the southwest corner of Broadwell Ave. and Airport Road north of Grand Island, Eagle Scout Park has an 80-acre lake surrounded by a 1.2-mile paved hiking trail. Trees, shrubs, and mowed grassy areas border the lake. Playground and restroom facilities are available along with parking lots on the south, east, and north sides. This park is a well-used haven for waterfowl, shorebirds, and waders, including egrets, avocets, mergansers, and pelicans. Look for sparrows and warblers in the surrounding trees and brush, including song sparrows, Nelson's (sharp-tailed) sparrow (on migration), and yellow warblers.

11. **Mormon Island Crane Meadows.** 2,500 acres. Located one mile south of I-80 exit 312 on US Hwy 281 and then west on Elm Island Road, this is the largest remaining wet meadow left along the Platte River. It is owned and managed by the Crane Trust. The preserve contains an extensive area of sedge meadows along with native tall grass prairie surrounded by channels of the Platte River. More than 70,000 cranes have been seen foraging together on its pristine wet meadows and more than 300 species of vascular plants have been documented from Mormon Island. As many as 200,000 sandhill cranes roost along its river shorelines during peak usage. Birds totaling more than 280 species have been reported here. Upland sandpipers, bobolinks, sedge wrens, dickcissels, and grasshopper sparrows nest from May to August. Prairie falcons, short-eared owls, and northern harriers are seasonally common here. Crane-observation blinds are operated here from the first week of March into early April with an admission fee. Access is by permission only. For more information call 308-382-1820.

19. Merrick County (Map 24)

Merrick County is a Platte River valley county with about 600 acres of surface water, more than 13,000 acres of wooded habitats, and over 113,000 acres of grasslands or farmlands. Tourist accommodations are available in Central City.

A. Federal Areas — None

B. State Areas

1. **Dr. Bruce Cowgill WMA** (map location 8). 150 acres. Located just 1.5 miles east of the town of Silver Creek and south of US Hwy. 30, this WMA has Platte River frontage with riparian timber, planted grasslands, and wet meadows.

C. Other Areas

1. **Bader Memorial Park Natural Area.** 80 acres. This park is located three miles south of Chapman and includes a stretch of Platte River wooded habitats and adjacent native prairie, with trails through all of the local habitat types. American woodcocks occur here, and sandhill cranes sometimes visit during spring. Ducks, geese, marsh birds, and shorebirds are abundant during migration. An entry fee is required. (Not shown on map.)

20. Hamilton County (Map 28)

Hamilton County is a Platte River valley and Rainwater Basin county with less than 1,000 acres of permanent surface water, 2,400 acres of wooded habitats, and almost 50,000 acres of grasslands or farmlands. Tourist accommodations are available in Aurora.

A. Federal Areas

1. **Springer WPA** (map location 3). 397 wetland acres, 243 upland acres. Located six miles west and one mile south of Aurora, this large, flat wetland provides excellent habitat for waterfowl and other water birds. A well is located on the property, which is routinely pumped to provide water during spring and fall migration.

2. **Troester WPA** (map location 4, right). 268 wetland acres, 49 upland acres.

3. **Nelson WPA** (map location 5). 145 wetland acres, 17 upland acres.

B. State Areas

1. **Pintail WMA** (map location 4, left). 118 upland acres, 360 wetland acres. This area is located 2.5 miles south and 2 miles east of the Aurora I-80 (exit 332) interchange. It has a large basin and includes a shallow seasonal pond and mixed upland and lowland habitats. In wet springs this marsh may attract up to 100,000 geese, primarily greater white-fronted, and it is a favorite stopover for pintails and white-fronted geese. In the morning, a parking lot on the east side provides the best viewing access to the marsh. During the afternoon, the west side offers better viewing, and the road is closer to the marsh. Look for pheasants, northern harriers, and migrating peregrines in the uplands. Shorebirds, waders, American white pelicans, black terns, and a variety of waterfowl rest here during spring migration.

2. **Gadwall WMA** (map location 1). 90 acres with 70 acres of wetlands. The wetland acreage includes two excavated areas and a narrow slough.

3. **Deep Well WMA** (map location 2). 78 acres. Known locally as the "Phillips Basin," and located three miles south of Phillips, the habitat includes 35 acres of semipermanent wetlands and 25 acres of permanent wetlands. Mudflats and emergent vegetation harbor semipalmated plover, marbled godwit, willet, black tern, and a host of other water birds in May. Waterfowl concentrations peak in mid-March. Yellow-headed blackbirds and pied-billed grebes occasionally nest here. A king rail was seen here in 1992. The best viewing is from the road on the south side of the wetland. Common yellowthroats, yellow warblers and yellow-rumped warblers can be seen as well. Extensive renovation was completed in the early 2000s, followed by heavy shorebird use in the spring and great waterfowl use in the fall.

21. York County (Map 29)

York County is a Rainwater Basin county with nearly 3,000 acres of permanent surface water, 2,400 acres of wooded habitats, and more than 50,000 acres of grasslands or farmlands. Tourist accommodations are available in Henderson and York.

A. Federal Areas

1. **County Line WPA** (map location 8). 176 acres upland, 232 acres wetland. The county road that leads to this marsh usually floods in spring. Large flocks of dabbling ducks often gather at County Line marsh in early March. (See also Fillmore County.)

2. **Waco Basin WPA** (map location 3). 159 acres. Located one mile west and 0.5 mile north of Waco, this WPA has 113 acres of mixed marsh habitat and 46 acres of upland habitat. The wetland basin is now deeper, making it very difficult for canary grass to reestablish. Waco Basin WPA adjoins Spikerush WMA.

3. **Sinninger Lagoon WPA** (map location 7). 115 upland acres, 42 wetland acres. Located 2.5 miles east and 2 miles south of McCool Junction, this cattle-yard basin is best viewed in the evening; it is tough viewing looking into the morning sun. Satellite basins such as South Sinninger (southeast edge of WPA) and Q2 Basin (at intersection of county roads Q and 2) can also be very productive of birds. Between 1997 and 2001, this marsh supported more than 6,000 spring shorebirds and may be the best all-around basin for ease of viewing and the number and variety of birds. Expect good numbers of Hudsonian godwit and ruddy turnstone. It is also very good in the fall with area high counts for willet, long-billed dowitcher, red knot, and Hudsonian godwit.

B. State Areas

1. **Spikerush WMA** (map location 4). 194 acres. Spikerush consists of mixed marsh and upland habitats.

2. **Kirkpatrick Basin North WMA and Kirkpatrick Basin South WMA** (map locations 5 and 6). 615 acres total. To reach the northern WMA, take I-80 exit 348 north a half mile and and then east one mile. Take the same exit for the southern WMA, but proceed south 1.5 miles and west 1.5 miles. The northern portion contains 70 acres of semipermanent wetlands, 175 acres of seasonal wetlands, and about 110 acres in upland grasses; the southern WMA has a shallow wetland of 305 acres. These are excellent areas in spring for seeing migrating ducks and geese, especially snow geese. Slightly later (April–June), they attract a host of shorebirds, including American avocets and long-billed dowitchers. The northern area is visible from I-80, a few miles west of the York interchange.

3. **Hidden Marsh WMA.** 120 acres. Hidden Marsh is located just two miles east of Spikerush WMA. (Not shown on map.)

4. **Renquist Basin WMA.** 107 acres. Renquist Basin, northwest of Benedict, has mixed upland and marshland.

C. Other Areas

1. **Bruce L. Anderson Recreation Area (Recharge Lake).** 120 acres with a 50-acre reservoir. Located 1.5 miles west of York, this area is operated by the Upper Big Blue Natural Resources District. Originally developed for a groundwater recharge study, it is now dedicated to recreation, including camping, fishing, hiking, and wildlife viewing. Yellow-crowned night heron, piping plover, black tern, western sandpiper, and dunlin are a few of the species that have been reported from this site.

22. Kearney County (Map 30)

Kearney County is a Platte River valley county with about 200 acres of permanent surface water, 300 acres of wooded habitats, and more than 70,000 acres of grasslands or farmlands. Tourist accommodations are available in Minden.

A. Federal Areas

Note: The following federal sites are temporary wetlands of fairly small size, but they might be attractive to migrant water birds during wet springs.

1. **Bluestem WPA** (map location 4). 32 acres upland, 44 acres wetland.

2. **Gleason WPA** (map location 5). 372 acres upland, 197 acres wetland. Gleason lagoon is located four miles south and four miles west of Minden. Good waterfowl and shorebird viewing during spring migration depends upon water conditions, but water is pumped during dry migratory seasons. The area offers a good variety of waterfowl, waders, and shorebirds. White-faced ibis, pectoral sandpipers, American bitterns, black-crowned night herons, and whooping cranes have been reported here in recent years. (Courtesy of Erick Volden.)

3. **Prairie Dog WPA** (map location 6). 421 acres upland, 471 acres wetland. Located 5.5 miles south of Axtel, Prairie Dog marsh has a small black-tailed prairie dog colony on the higher ground near the southeast end of the WPA that is consistently used by burrowing owls (which usually arrive in May). It is one of the very few active prairie dog colonies left in the central Platte River valley. Whooping cranes have been observed here in April, and it is a great place for waders and shorebirds in late spring and late summer. The best birding is from the south parking area and may require some walking to get a good view.

4. **Lindau WPA** (map location 7). 47 acres upland, 105 acres wetland.

5. **Clark WPA** (map location 12). 222 acres upland, 227 acres wetland.

6. **Youngson WPA** (map location 8). 70 acres upland, 113 acres wetland. Youngson lagoon is located six miles south and one mile east of Norman. This WPA is sometimes good to excellent for seeing shorebirds and waterfowl.

7. **Frerichs WPA** (map location 10). 10 acres upland, 33 acres wetland.

8. **Killdeer WPA** (map location 11). 2 acres upland, 36 acres wetland.

9. **Jensen Lagoon WPA** (map location 9). 278 acres upland, 187 acres wetland.

B. State Areas

1. **Fort Kearny Hike-Bike Trail** (map location 1). The Hike-Bike Trail is a mile east of Fort Kearny Historical Park and is a well-maintained, handicapped-accessible trail that crosses the Platte River on a former railroad bridge and continues on into the city of Kearney. The bridge provides

Whooping crane, adult foraging

an excellent view of the river and the woods along its banks and islands. Birds that can be seen along the trail near the river include bald eagles, geese, and ducks in January and February; sandhill cranes and American woodcock in March; and warblers and other passerines in April, May, and June. This is one of the few public state areas where hunting is not allowed, so birds are there in the fall as well. The bridge is a very good area for watching sandhill cranes at sunset and sunrise during migration. Sometimes American woodcock can be seen displaying near the north end of the bridge at sunset. Stop at Fort Kearny for information and a park permit. A four-mile trail leads northwest to Bassway Strip WMA along the two northernmost channels of the Platte (see Buffalo County). Park entry permit required. Phone 308-865-5305 for more information.

2. **Fort Kearny SRA** (map location 2). 163 acres. This area has primitive camping facilities and provides nearby parking for the hike-bike trail and bridge (see above).

3. **Fort Kearny State Historical Park** (map location 3). Located three miles south and four miles east of I-80 exit 272 at Kearney, this park has a restored version of nineteenth-century Fort Kearny, including a stockade, parade grounds, blacksmith shop, and pony express stage station. The fort was originally built to protect and supply overland travelers headed for California, Oregon, and other points west. The park has primitive camping, a concessions area, and an interpretive center, which blends the history of the Platte River valley with its ecology and natural history. Fort Kearny is also a place to watch field-feeding sandhill cranes in the spring. The visitor center opens in early March for the crane migration and provides information about crane and waterfowl viewing. It has a gift shop and a variety of displays.

4. **Northeast Sacramento WMA.** 10 acres upland, 30 acres wetland. (Not shown on map.)

23. Adams County (Map 31)

Adams County is a Rainwater Basin county with about 900 acres of permanent surface water, 1,200 acres of wooded habitats, and more than 83,000 acres of grasslands or farmlands. Tourist accommodations are available in Hastings.

Prairie falcon and chick with green-winged teal

A. Federal Areas

1. **Weseman WPA.** 81 acres upland, 82 acres wetland. This waterfowl production area is located nine miles west and four miles south of Hastings. A parking lot is available on the east side. The wetland generally has standing water only after heavy rains or snowmelt.

2. **Kenesaw WPA** (map location 1). 70 acres upland, 161 acres wetland. Located 0.5 mile southeast of Kenesaw, this WPA attracts a large variety of water birds during spring. Birds are best observed from county roads on the south or west side of the lagoon. The mudflat area on the southwest side attracts shorebirds, waterfowl, and waders in spring.

B. State Areas

1. **Prairie Lake Recreation Area** (map location 3). 125 acres with a 30-acre lake. Operated by the Little Blue Natural Resources District, Prairie Lake is mainly a fishing lake, with limited attractiveness to birds.

2. **Crystal Lake Recreation Area** (map location 4). 33 acres. Crystal Lake is located 1.5 miles north of Ayr, which owns the area and manages it with the Lower Blue Natural Resources District. Camping, electrical hookups, and picnic shelters are available. The surrounding mature

woodlands are good for warblers, thrushes, sparrows, and flycatchers. The lake is attractive to a variety of waders and waterfowl but is mostly developed for fishing.

3. **DLD State Wayside Recreation Area** (map location 6). 7 acres. DLD offers primitive camping and picnicking. (DLD stands for the historic Detroit–Lincoln–Denver rail and then highway route, popularly remembered as a "Damned Long Drive.")

C. Other Areas

1. **Little Blue River** (map location 2). The Little Blue River passes through the southern third of Adams County and is its dominant drainage feature. The wooded riparian zone of the Little Blue contains cottonwoods and hackberries with a thick understory that should be searched for passerines during spring and fall migration periods. Early May and September are the best times for viewing birds.

2. **Hastings Museum and Lake Hastings** (map location 7). The Hastings Museum has a notable exhibit area for a small-town museum, including a diorama with ten whooping cranes. It sells materials of interest to naturalists, has an I-MAX theater and planetarium, and provides advice on local attractions. Phone 402-461-2399 for more information. Lake Hastings is a city-owned lake that might seasonally attract some birds, and it is a short distance north of the museum on US Hwy. 281/34. The Adams County Convention and Visitors Bureau (800-967-2189) might also be of assistance to visitors.

3. **Ayr Lake** (map location 5). Ayr Lake is a privately owned seasonal wetland that sometimes attracts good numbers of migrating water birds. Access is limited to the peripheral road. The area is mostly noted for shorebirds and wading birds and to a lesser extent waterfowl. April and May are the best times to find American golden-plovers, American avocets, and many other species.

4. **Holstein Hills.** Located 2 miles west of Holstein, or 20 miles east of Minden, this hilly, mixed-grass prairie region known as Holstein Hills is home to several prairie-chicken leks. The prairie-chickens display from March into early May each spring. Also common are grasshopper sparrows, dickcissels, horned larks, and a variety of raptors. Drive the side roads, but be aware that many are minimum-maintenance dirt roads that are impassable when wet. All land in this area is privately owned, so stay in your car and on the road for viewing.

24. Clay County (Map 28)

Clay County is a Rainwater Basin county with more than 4,000 acres of permanent surface water, 900 acres of wooded habitats, and nearly 76,000 acres of grasslands or farmlands. Tourist accommodations are available in Clay Center and Sutton.

A. Federal Areas

Note: All of these waterfowl production areas vary greatly in size and in relative wetland permanence.

1. **Sandpiper (North Hultine) WPA** (map location 6). 214 acres upland, 226 acres wetland. This area is one of the best sites for seeing migrating shorebirds in the region, especially during late March and April.

2. **Hultine WPA** (map location 7). 74 acres upland, 164 acres wetland.

3. **Harvard WPA** (map location 8). 724 acres upland, 760 acres wetland. Harvard marsh is a deep permanent marsh that attracts tens of thousands of snow, Canada, and greater white-fronted geese each March. Access from the east is via a narrow, often slippery road and is better from the south, at least to the railroad tracks. Driving beyond is not recommended after rains. A parking area is located on the north side, but it is quite far from the nearest water or marshy areas. Later in spring, this area is used by many shorebirds, including several sandpipers and piping plovers. Breeders include northern harriers and short-eared owls as well as some ducks ad wading birds. Occasional flocks of sandhill cranes stop, and bald eagles are regular in early spring. Altogether it is one of the best birding wetlands in the entire region; up to 500,000 waterfowl have been seen here at the peak of spring migration. Later on as water levels drop, the main basin and several smaller wetlands to the south offer excellent shorebird watching, and breeding by a variety of generally uncommon wetland birds has occurred. It also is one of the better fall migration wetlands.

4. **Lange WPA** (map location 10). 101 acres upland, 59 acres wetland. Lange lagoon is located 0.25 mile east and 2 miles south of Sutton. It is a "migrant trap" worth checking during migrations. The grove of elm trees takes a few minutes to check and can be a good indicator of "fallout." An area of permanent water exists but often cannot be viewed because of the immense stand of cattails. View

the wetland from the east side and search the trees on the north side.

5. **Theesen WPA** (map location 11). 34 acres upland, 46 acres wetland. Theesen lagoon is located 1.5 miles northwest of Glenville. The private property across the road to the west usually has good mudflats for shorebirds in spring and late summer.

6. **Massie WPA** (map location 12). 359 acres upland, 494 acres wetland. Massie lagoon is located 2.5 miles south of Clay Center and is an excellent spot to see shoreline, edge, and grassland bird species. It is one of the best Rainwater Basin lagoons for seeing waterfowl and shorebirds. Water levels in spring are maintained by pumping. Waterfowl species include snow geese, greater white-fronted geese, Canada geese, pintails, and mallards. An observation blind is located close to the parking lot on the south side of the lagoon; this access point is recommended over the others.

7. **Glenvil WPA** (map location 13). 37 acres upland, 83 acres wetland. No detailed information for this basin.

8. **Kissinger Basin WPA** (map location 14). 342 acres. No detailed information for this basin.

9. **Meadowlark WPA** (map location 15). 35 acres upland, 45 acres wetland. No detailed information for this area.

10. **Harms WPA** (map location 16). 25 acres upland, 34 acres wetland. No detailed information.

11. **Moger WPA** (map location 17). 123 acres upland, 72 acres wetland. Moger WPA is located three miles east and two miles south of Clay Center.

12. **Shuck WPA** (map location 18). 24 acres upland, 56 acres wetland.

13. **Green Acres WPA** (map location 19). 15 acres upland, 48 acres wetland. Green Acres is located six miles east and four miles south of Clay Center.

14. **Eckhardt Lagoon WPA** (map location 20). 108 acres upland, 66 acres wetland. Eckhardt Lagoon is located eight miles east and four miles south of Clay Center, not far from Green Acres WPA.

15. **Smith WPA** (map location 21). 254 acres upland, 226 acres wetland. Smith lagoon is located six miles south and 3.5 miles east of Clay Center. The wetland habitat is maintained by seasonal water pumping. Snow geese use the wetland heavily toward the peak of their migration.

16. **Hansen WPA** (map location 23). 173 acres upland, 147 acres wetland. Hansen lagoon is located 0.25 mile west and 3.5 miles north of Ong. This is an excellent basin for bird-watching. The eastern portion has been better in recent years, but because of cattail overgrowth, it may be necessary to walk west from the parking area to a large lagoon for best viewing.

B. State Areas

1. **McMurtrey Marsh** (map location 9). 1,071 acres. No public access to this refuge, and it is closed to hunting.

2. **Bluewing WMA**. 160 acres. Located four miles west and 0.5 mile south of Edgar, Bluewing is all lowland and seasonal wetland habitat.

3. **Bulrush WMA**. 160 acres. Located 2.5 miles south and 1.5 miles east of Fairfield, Bulrush includes a mix of upland and marshes.

4. **Greenhead WMA** (map location 22). 60 acres. Greenhead includes a dug-out pond and mainly marshy habitats.

5. **Greenwing WMA** (map location 24). 80 acres. Greenwing is located 3 miles north and 0.5 mile east of Ong and includes marsh, uplands, and scattered thickets.

6. **Whitefront WMA**. 175 acres. Located 1.5 miles west and 1.5 miles north of Clay Center, Whitefront WMA includes 7 acres of permanent wetland, 158 acres of cropland, and 10 acres of pasture.

25. Fillmore County (Map 29)

Fillmore County is a Rainwater Basin county with 1,600 acres of permanent surface water, 2,100 acres of wooded habitats, and about 55,000 acres of grasslands or farmlands. Tourist accommodations are available in Geneva.

III. THE EAST-CENTRAL REGION

A. Federal Areas

1. **County Line WPA** (map location 8). 408 acres. County Line marsh is located three miles south and three miles east of McCool Junction. This site contains 232 acres of wetland and 176 acres of upland. The county road leading to this marsh sometimes floods in spring. Very large flocks of dabbling ducks gather here in early March. (See also York County.)

2. **Real WPA** (map location 9). 39 acres upland, 121 acres wetland.

3. **Wilkins WPA** (map location 11). 208 acres upland, 324 acres wetland. Wilkins lagoon is located a mile south and a mile east of Grafton. This large but seasonal "spring" basin should be checked during that season; however, wet periods can make access impossible because dirt roads approach the area from every direction.

4. **Morphy WPA** (map location 12). 9 acres upland, 81 acres wetland. No detailed information about this lagoon.

5. **Rolland WPA** (map location 13). 76 acres upland, 53 acres wetland. No detailed information about this lagoon.

6. **Griess WPA** (map location 14). 20 acres upland, 20 acres wetland. No detailed information about this area.

7. **Rauscher WPA** (map location 15). 119 acres upland, 132 acres wetland. No detailed information about this lagoon.

8. **Weis Lagoon.** 40 acres upland, 120 acres wetland. Weis Lagoon is located just north of Mallard Haven WPA.

9. **Krause WPA** (map location 17). 227 acres upland, 306 acres wetland. Krause lagoon is located 3 miles north and a mile or two west of Shickley. It has a heavy growth of cattails, and a very large area of native grasses surrounds the wetland, especially on the east.

10. **Mallard Haven WPA** (map location 18). 454 acres upland, 634 acres wetland. Located about one mile north of Shickley, Mallard Haven WPA is one of the largest and perhaps best marshes for waterfowl during spring. This basin provides habitat for thousands of white-fronted geese, snow geese, and ducks during late February and early March. Many wetland birds remain here to breed, including northern harriers, great-tailed grackles, and yellow-headed blackbirds. Several parking lots provide access points.

11. **Brauning WPA.** 241 acres. Located three miles south and 3.5 miles west of Grafton, Brauning WPA includes 75 acres of uplands and 166 acres of wetlands.

B. State Areas

1. **Marsh Hawk WMA** (map location 10, left) and **Bluebill Hawk WMA** (map location 10, right). Just north of Grafton, this pair of wildlife management areas comprise 173 and 60 acres, respectively. Marsh Hawk WMA is mostly seasonal wetlands with some trees and shrubs. Bluebill WMA includes two marshes separated by higher ground.

2. **Sandpiper WMA** (map location 16). 160 acres. Located 5 miles west and 1.5 miles south of Geneva, Sandpiper WMA includes 56 acres of marsh with plum, willow, cottonwood, and Osage orange on the uplands. This is one of the best sites in the region for seeing migrating shorebirds, especially during late March and April.

26. Franklin County (Map 30)

Franklin County is a Republican River valley county with about 1,500 acres of surface water, more than 5,000 acres of wooded habitats, and over 160,000 acres of grasslands or farmlands. No tourist accommodations are available in the county.

A. Federal Areas

1. **Quadhamer Marsh WPA** (map location 13). 287 acres upland, 311 acres wetland.

2. **Ritterbush Marsh WPA** (map location 14). 32 acres upland, 48 acres wetland.

3. **Macon Lakes WPA** (map location 15). 505 acres upland, 604 acres wetland.

B. State Areas

1. **Ash Grove WMA.** 74 acres. Includes rolling hills, grasses, rock outcrops, and a small stream.

2. **Limestone Bluffs WMA.** 479 acres. Includes rolling hills with grasses, rock outcrops, and wooded ravines with a spring-fed stream.

27. Webster County

Webster County is a Republican River valley county with more than 2,600 acres of surface water, nearly 4,000 acres of wooded habitats, and over 160,000 acres of grasslands or farmlands. Tourist accommodations are available in Red Cloud.

A. Federal Areas — None

B. State Areas

1. **Elm Creek WMA.** 120 acres. Located three miles south of Cowles, Elm Creek WMA is mostly wooded with a creek and slough at one end.

2. **Indian Creek WMA.** 114 acres. Indian Creek WMA is located one mile south of Red Cloud. Part of it is riparian woods along the Republican River, where wood ducks, ospreys, and eagles might be seen as well as woodpeckers and passerines.

C. Other Areas

1. **Willa Cather Memorial Prairie.** 612 acres. This loess hills prairie owned by the Willa Cather Foundation is located six miles south of Red Cloud. Its management includes grazing, but it is an unplowed, native, mixed-grass prairie. Plant species ranging in count from 164 to 219 have been found by Steve Rothenburger and others on various remnant loess hills prairies in this region.

American tree sparrow in winter

2. **Smartweed Marsh West WMA.** 38 acres. Located one mile south and three miles west of Edgar, this WMA is also mostly grassy lowlands but with some upland habitats.

28. Nuckolls County

Nuckolls County is a Republican River valley county with 1,200 acres of surface water, more than 10,000 acres of wooded habitats, and over 125,000 acres of grasslands or farmlands. Tourist accommodations are available in Nelson and Superior.

A. Federal Areas — None

B. State Areas

1. **Smartweed Marsh WMA.** 6 acres upland, 74 acres wetland. Located two miles south and two miles west of Edgar, Smartweed Marsh WMA is mostly grassy lowlands with some marshy areas.

29. Thayer County

Thayer County is a dissected plains county with about 1,800 acres of surface water, more than 5,000 acres of wooded habitats, and 113,000 acres of grasslands or farmlands. Tourist accommodations are available in Hebron.

A. Federal Areas — None

B. State Areas

1. **Little Blue WMA.** 303 acres. Located three miles east of Hebron, Little Blue WMA is mostly flat wooded bottomland of the Little Blue River, with some grasslands and croplands.

2. **Prairie Marsh WMA.** 160 acres. Located two miles west of Bruning, Prairie Marsh WMA consists of seasonal wetlands and adjoining uplands.

IV. The Eastern Region

The eastern region of Nebraska is a land that until about 20,000 years ago was ruthlessly scraped over by repeated glaciers and which later was mantled by tallgrass prairies and riparian deciduous forests with eastern biogeographic affinities. It is bounded to the east by the Missouri River, which is now mostly channeled, narrowed, and much degraded as far as wildlife habitat is concerned—in an extremely expensive but failed effort to control flooding and provide for barge traffic. However, some stretches, such as around Ponca State Park, provide a faint idea of what the river once was like.

The Missouri River valley is still a migratory pathway not only for Arctic-breeding waterfowl such as snow geese, which alone now number more than a million birds using this narrow flyway, but also myriads of forest-adapted Neotropic migrants, especially warblers and vireos. Remnant stands of mature deciduous forest still exist at Rulo Bluffs Preserve and Indian Cave State Park in Richardson County, Fontenelle Forest and Neale Woods in the Omaha area, DeSoto NWR near Blair, and Ponca State Park in Dixon County. These are among the best places that can be visited in early May to see such wonderful birds as they journey north to breeding grounds in the Upper Midwest and southern Canada.

This region is the most heavily populated part of the state and thus has the fewest areas of native prairie vegetation persisting, but in such extant areas, grassland species such as greater prairie-chickens still gather at sunrise every spring on traditional display grounds made sacred by decades, if not centuries, of use. Similarly, other prairie species such as long-billed curlews and upland sandpiper rarely occur here anymore, but grassland sparrows still announce their territories from fenceposts, and house wrens, gray catbirds, and brown thrashers sing every spring from plum thickets along roadside ditches.

Many other eastern or southeastern species occur and locally breed here, including Henslow's sparrow; Kentucky, northern parula, and prothonotary warblers; and possibly red-shouldered and broad-winged hawks. Furthermore, chuck-will's-widows certainly must nest in the wooded habitats bordering the southeastern corner of the state, and pileated woodpeckers sometimes also nest here, making it an area of special interest to birders.

Trumpeter swan family, Missouri River valley wetland

Nebraska breeders that are largely limited to the forested Missouri River valley are the American woodcock, barred owl, chuck-will's-widow, whip-poor-will, ruby-throated hummingbird, yellow-throated vireo, tufted titmouse, blue-gray gnatcatcher, Louisiana waterthrush, Kentucky warbler, summer tanager, and scarlet tanager. Cerulean warblers occur very rarely.

More than 100 bird species are believed to nest in Iowa's adjoining loess hills region on the east side of the Missouri River, including the state's densest breeding populations of the turkey vulture, American kestrel, Bell's vireo, orchard oriole, chuck-will's-widow, and summer tanager. The most common nesting species in the loess hills region include the brown-headed cowbird, northern cardinal, brown thrasher, house wren, mourning dove, American crow, blue jay, and red-headed woodpecker.

1. Cedar County

Cedar County is a Missouri River valley county with 3,900 acres of surface water, 10,700 acres of wooded habitats, and almost 134,000 acres of grasslands or farmlands. Tourist accommodations are available in Hartington, Laurel, and Randolph.

A. Federal Areas

1. **Missouri National Recreational River.** The northern boundary of Cedar County is the Missouri River, and along this length it is designated the Missouri National Recreational River and managed by the National Park Service. The nearest visitor center is the Lewis and Clark Visitor Center at Gavins Point Dam, located on Calumet Bluff off Nebraska Hwy. 121.

2. **Gavins Point Dam.** See a state highway map for the location. Birding from the dam should offer views of gulls, waterfowl, and other birds, including numerous bald eagles during migration periods. A nature trail is nearby, as is an aquarium in the associated US Fish and Wildlife Service Gavins Point National Fish Hatchery.

3. **Lake Yankton.** Located just below Gavins Point Dam and partly in South Dakota, Lake Yankton is a 250-acre reservoir that was once part of the main channel of the Missouri River. It offers good birding along its wooded shoreline.

B. State Areas

1. **Chalkrock WMA.** 130 acres. Chalkrock WMA is located four miles south of the Missouri River bridge on US Hwy. 81 and 1.5 miles east of the highway. It consists of 90 upland acres and a 45-acre reservoir.

2. **Wiseman WMA.** 365 acres. Located one mile north and five miles east of Wynot, just south of the Missouri River, this area includes steep wooded bluffs and grassy ridges. The woods are mostly bur oak, cedar, hackberry, and ash.

2. Dixon County (Map 32)

Dixon County is a Missouri River valley county with more than 5,000 acres of surface water, 10,000 acres of wooded habitats, and over 73,000 acres of grasslands or farmlands. Tourist accommodations are available in Ponca.

A. Federal Areas

1. **Missouri National Recreational River.** The northern boundary of Dixon County is the Missouri River, and along most of this length—to Ponca State Park—it is designated the Missouri National Recreational River and managed by the National Park Service. The Missouri National Recreational River Resource and Education Center is located in Ponca State Park.

B. State Areas

1. **Ponca State Park** (map location 1). 2,166 acres. Ponca State Park is mostly forested with stands of bur oak, walnut, hackberry, and elms; one of the oaks is more than 375 years old. A bird list of 297 species and 70 breeders covers the park plus adjoining parts of northern Nebraska, southeastern South Dakota, and northwestern Iowa. Twenty-two miles of hiking trails and modern cabins are available, as is a tent campground. Whip-poor-wills are common in summer, and bald eagles are present during much of the year. Snow geese migrate past the area in great numbers during spring and fall, and the nearby Missouri River is still unchanneled here and thus resembles its original state. The park is classified as a Nebraska Important Bird Area. A state park entry permit is required.

2. **Buckskin Hills WMA.** Located two miles west and two miles south of Newcastle, Buckskin Hills WMA consists of 340 acres of grasslands and woods around a 75-acre reservoir.

3. **Elk Point Bend WMA.** 624 acres. This area is located about two miles north of Ponca State Park and consists of oak savanna and riparian wetlands near the Missouri River. It is excellent for waterfowl watching during migrations. Not located on the map; for more information contact Ponca State Park at 402-755-2284.

3. Dakota County (Map 32)

Dakota County is a Missouri River valley county with 3,400 acres of surface water, 6,800 acres of wooded habitats, and more than 28,000 acres of grasslands or farmlands. Tourist accommodations are available in South Sioux City.

A. Federal Areas — None

Young raccoon, Missouri River valley woods

B. State Areas

1. **Basswood Ridge WMA** (map location 2). 360 acres. Basswood Ridge WMA consists of very rugged and heavily wooded uplands with some Native American petroglyphs near the north end.

2. **Omadi Bend WMA** (map location 3). 33 acres. This area is bottomland forest along an oxbow lake.

4. Wayne County

Wayne County consists of glaciated uplands with 180 acres of surface water, 2,100 acres of wooded habitats, and nearly 46,000 acres of grasslands or farmlands. Tourist accommodations are available in Wayne.

A. Federal Areas — None

B. State Areas

1. **Sioux Strip WMA.** 25 acres. Sioux Strip WMA is located at western edge of the village of Sholes and consists of upland grasses along an old railroad bed.

5. Thurston County

Thurston County is a Missouri River valley county with nearly 1,500 acres of surface water, more than 22,000 acres of wooded habitats, and nearly 34,000 acres of grasslands or farmlands. No tourist accommodations are available in the county.

A. Federal Areas

1. **Missouri River federal access areas.** The Missouri River has numerous small access points for boats, as posted. See the Nebraska Game and Parks Commission's access guide at https://maps.outdoornebraska.gov/MRRecreationGuide/.

B. State Areas — None

6. Stanton County

Stanton County is an Elkhorn River valley county with fewer than 800 acres of surface water, 5,200 acres of wooded habitats, and 75,000 acres of grasslands or farmlands. No tourist accommodations are available in the county.

A. Federal Areas — None

B. State Areas

1. **Red Fox WMA.** 537 acres. Located one mile south of Pilger, Red Fox WMA includes a flooded remnant oxbow, a 25-acre sandpit lake, 0.6 mile of Elkhorn River frontage, and 163 acres of grassland.

2. **Wood Duck WMA.** 1,528 acres. Wood Duck WMA is located about two miles south and four miles west of Stanton. It consists of riparian wooded habitats bordering the Elkhorn River with several oxbow lakes and a stream. Many eastern songbirds nest here, and the marshy lakes are used by large numbers of geese, ducks, pelicans, cormorants, and occasionally swans. The perimeter roads are often wet and sometimes even flooded during wet springs, so caution is needed when driving.

C. Other Areas

1. **Maskenthine Lake Recreation Area.** Maskenthine Lake is a Lower Elkhorn Natural Resources District flood-control reservoir (98 acres) located one mile north of Stanton. The area offers open water, wetland, riparian woodland, and a trail around the lake.

7. Cuming County

Cuming County is an Elkhorn River valley county, with about 800 acres of surface water, 3,000 acres of wooded habitats, and more than 75,000 acres of grasslands or farmlands. Tourist accommodations are available in Beemer, West Point, and Wisner.

A. Federal Areas — None

B. State Areas

1. **Black Island WMA.** 240 acres. Black Island WMA is located one mile north and four miles west of Wisner. To get there, from the intersection of US Hwy. 275 and state route 15, drive one mile east, 0.5 mile south, another 1.5 miles east, and then south again on the entrance road. This area is a mixture of woodlands (primarily cottonwoods), grassy and weedy vegetation, some wet grassy areas, and 0.75 mile of the Elkhorn River. There are possibilities for viewing migrating, breeding, and wintering passerines as well as waterfowl, shorebirds, and other water birds. The area is open to public hunting and fishing, so use caution during hunting seasons.

C. Other Areas

1. **Elkhorn River.** The Elkhorn River throughout Cuming County is bounded by deciduous riverine forest along most of its length and should provide for good birding opportunities.

2. **Wilderness Park and Neligh Park.** Wilderness Park is a 120-acre undeveloped municipal natural preserve located on the eastern edge of West Point. It is wooded with grassy open areas and hiking trails. Neligh Park, in West Point, has a fishing lake and large trees along with camping and many recreational options.

8. Burt County

Burt County is a Missouri River valley county with 3,200 acres of surface water, 5,500 acres of wooded habitats, and almost 39,000 acres of grasslands or farmlands. Tourist accommodations are available in Lyons, Oakland, and Tekamah.

A. Federal Areas — None

B. State Areas

1. **Middle Decatur Bend WMA.** 133 acres. This wildlife management area is located three miles east of Decatur along the Missouri River.

2. **Pelican Point SRA.** 36 acres. Pelican Point is located along the Missouri River about 4 miles east, 3.5 miles north, and another mile east from Tekamah. The area has riverine wooded habitats and includes a small primitive campground and access to the Missouri River. The campground and surrounding area is dominated by large cottonwoods with some shrubby understory. This is a good place to see migratory and breeding bird species such as warblers, vireos, thrushes, orioles, flycatchers, woodpeckers, and other passerines as well as larger birds that tend to follow the river during migration. A state park entry permit is required.

3. **Summit Reservoir SRA.** 535 acres. Summit Reservoir SRA is located about three miles west and south of Tekamah and provides for camping, picnicking, and hiking. The 190-acre lake has been developed for fishing. A state park entry permit is required.

9. Colfax County

Colfax County is a Platte River valley county with about 1,300 acres of surface water, 5,900 acres of wooded habitats, and 44,000 acres of grasslands or farmlands. Tourist accommodations are available at Schuyler.

A. Federal Areas — None

B. State Areas

1. **Whitetail WMA.** 216 acres. Located two miles south and one mile west of Schuyler, Whitetail WMA consists of 93 acres of Platte River bottomland forest and 123

White-tailed deer, doe

acres of islands and river. This WMA features a variety of wooded habitats ranging from cottonwood savannah to open woods with shrubs to dense cottonwood forest. There are some shallow oxbow wetlands and access to the Platte River. A sandpit lake northwest of the parking lot (on private property) occasionally has gulls, terns, and waterfowl on it. This is a good area for viewing migratory and breeding passerine species, shorebirds, and larger migratory species.

10. Dodge County (Map 33)

Dodge County is an Elkhorn River and Platte River valleys county with 1,800 acres of surface water, more than 3,000 acres of wooded habitats, and almost 40,000 acres of grasslands or farmlands. Tourist accommodations are available in Fremont.

A. Federal Areas — None

B. State Areas

1. **Dead Timber SRA** (map location 1, right). 150 acres with a 50-acre lake. Dead Timber is a recreational facility northwest of Scribner developed for fishing. It has an old oxbow lake beside the Elkhorn River. The wooded high bank along the northeastern part of the area has many seeps, which hold many birds in the area through the winter. A state park entry permit is required.

2. **Powder Horn WMA** (map location 1, left). 289 acres. Powder Horn consists of riparian wooded habitats that bound the Elkhorn River plus adjoining grasslands, marshes, and croplands.

3. **Fremont Lakes SRA** (map location 2). 670 acres. Fremont Lakes SRA, a few miles west of Fremont on the Platte River, includes 20 small sandpit lakes totaling 280 acres and many recreational facilities. A state park entry permit is required.

11. Washington County (Map 34)

Washington County is a Missouri River valley county with more than 3,000 acres of surface water, nearly 15,000 acres of wooded habitats, and nearly 33,000 acres of grasslands or farmlands. Tourist accommodations are available in Blair.

A. Federal Areas

1. **DeSoto NWR** (map location 1). 7,823 acres total. This important national wildlife refuge is located around an old oxbow of the Missouri River and consists mostly of riverine deciduous forest, an oxbow lake, and croplands. It supports an enormous fall population of snow geese (including up to 5 percent Ross's geese), which may reach a peak of about 800,000 birds in late October or early November. A superb interpretive center has large windows facing a 788-acre lake that allow wonderful views of the geese, other waterfowl, and numerous bald eagles in late fall and early spring. Outdoor viewing platforms are also available for close viewing. The refuge bird checklist contains 240 species, including 81 breeders. Peak populations of ducks, mostly mallards, may reach 125,000. A 12-mile drive loops through the refuge, and four trails are available for hiking. The address for the refuge is 1434 316th Lane, Missouri Valley, IA 51555, phone 712-388-4808. The interior refuge roads are closed during some

Migrating snow geese, Lancaster County

periods; inquire at the interpretive center for a schedule. A daily admission fee charged. See also https://www.fws.gov/refuge/Desoto/.

2. **Boyer Chute NWR** (map location 3). Located along the Missouri River, this fairly new refuge (1992) of about 2,000 acres is a cooperative project involving the US Army Corps of Engineers and several state agencies. It has several river access points, two miles of roads, and about five miles of trails, including a mile of paved trail. The area is managed from DeSoto NWR, which is the contact for more information. Boyer Chute is classified as a Nebraska Important Bird Area. See also https://www.fws.gov/refuge/boyer_chute/.

B. State Areas

1. **Fort Atkinson State Historical Park** (map location 2). Fort Atkinson was established in 1820 on a Missouri River bluff that Lewis and Clark had recommended for a military post. It operated until 1827 with more than 1,000 soliders at its peak and has been under reconstruction since the 1960s. Artifacts and historical displays can also be viewed in the Harold W. Andersen Visitor Center. Living history events take place periodically May through October. A hiking trail travels through trees and native prairie. A state park entry permit is required, and the visitor interpreter center has a small admission fee. See also http://outdoornebraska.gov/fortatkinson/ and https://www.fortatkinsononline.org/.

12. Butler County

Butler County is a Platte River valley county with about 700 acres of surface water, 6,000 acres of wooded habitats, and 84,000 acres of grasslands or farmlands. Tourist accommodations are available in David City.

A. Federal Areas — None

B. State Areas

1. **Redtail WMA.** 320 acres with a 17-acre reservoir. Located one mile east of Dwight, Redtail WMA includes grassland, wooded draws, and a pond.

2. **Timber Point.** 160 acres. Located one mile south and two miles east of Brainard, this Lower Platte South Natural Resources District area has a 29-acre lake. Tent camping, fishing, no-wake boating, and picnicking are permitted.

13. Saunders County (Map 35)

Saunders County is a Platte River valley county with more than 4,000 acres of surface water, over 9,000 acres of wooded habitats, and 103,000 acres of grasslands or farmlands. Tourist accommodations are available in Wahoo.

A. Federal Areas — None

B. State Areas

1. **Jack Sinn Memorial WMA** (map location 7). See Lancaster County.

2. **Red Cedar Lake** (map location 2). 175 acres with a 51-acre lake. Red Cedar is a Lower Platte South Natural Resources District property where no-wake boating, camping, hunting, and fishing are permitted. Adjacent **Madigan Prairie** (23 acres) is located one mile east of the Butler County line and two miles south of state Hwy. 92. This prairie was never grazed or plowed and is now mowed for hay. It is owned by the University of Nebraska Foundation and managed by the University of Nebraska School of Biological Sciences for research and education. Contact the Natural Areas Committee for permission to visit Madigan Prairie (see http://snr.unl.edu/aboutus/where/fieldsites/madiganprairie.aspx).

3. **Larkspur WMA** (map location 3). 160 acres. Larkspur WMA includes 37 acres of bur oak wooded habitats plus areas of native prairie and seeded grassland.

4. **Czechland Lake Recreation Area.** Czechland Lake is an 85-acre Lower Platte North Natural Resources District reservoir surrounded by grassland and riparian timber. It is located one mile north of Prague (not shown on map). Hiking trails are available, as are hunting, fishing, boating, picnicking, and camping.

14. Douglas County (Map 36)

Douglas County is a Platte River and Missouri River valleys county, with 12,800 acres of surface water, more than 3,000 acres of wooded habitats, and 20,000 acres of grasslands or farmlands. Tourist accommodations are available in Omaha.

A. Federal Areas — None

B. State Areas

1. **Two Rivers SRA/WMA** (map location 1). SRA 643 acres, WMA 312 acres. The Two Rivers SRA was developed for recreational purposes. Located just south of the SRA, the WMA consists of timbered Platte River–bottom forest, marshes, and croplands. Hiking trails are available. A state park entry permit is required for the SRA. See http://outdoornebraska.gov/tworivers/.

C. Other Areas

1. **Neale Woods Nature Center** (map location 7). 600 acres. Neale Woods is owned and operated by Fontenelle Forest. It includes nine miles of trails through hardwood forests, restored prairie uplands, and riverine wooded habitats. A checklist of 190 bird species either seen or expected in the area is available. Fifty-seven are likely breeders, including barred owl, whip-poor-will, ruby-throated hummingbird, eastern wood-pewee, American redstart, scarlet tanager, rose-breasted grosbeak, and indigo bunting. Neale Woods is classified as a Nebraska Important Bird Area. The address is 14323 Edith Marie Ave., Omaha. For more information, phone Fontenelle Forest at 402-731-3140. There is an admission fee. See also www.fontenelleforest.org.

2. **Standing Bear Lake** (map location 5). Standing Bear Lake is a flood-control reservoir of 135 acres. It attracts migrant waterfowl seasonally and has 3.3 miles of hiking trails. Free access.

3. **Glenn Cunningham Lake** (map location 6). 1,050 acres. Glenn Cunningham Lake is a US Army Corps of Engineers flood-control and recreation reservoir of 390 acres. It is the largest reservoir in the Omaha area and as such is important for migrating water birds. Free access.

4. **Papio D-4 Lake.** Located just east of Glenn Cunningham Lake, Papio D-4 Lake is a 30-acre reservoir that sometimes attracts migrant gulls and waterfowl. Free access.

5. **Zorinsky Lake Park** (map location 9). 770 acres. The park has Zorinsky Lake, a flood-control reservoir of 255 acres, and Bauermeister Prairie, a 40-acre native tall-

White-tailed deer, fawn in native prairie

grass prairie, as well as recreational facilities and hiking trails. Free access.

15. Sarpy County (Map 36)

Sarpy County is a Platte River and Missouri River valleys county with 2,500 acres of surface water, nearly 15,000 acres of wooded habitats, and 21,000 acres of grasslands or farmlands. Tourist accommodations are available in Bellevue, Gretna, and Papillion.

A. Federal Areas — None

B. State Areas

1. **Chalco Hills Recreation Area** (map location 2). 1,200 acres. At Chalco Hills, 245-acre Wehrspann Lake is the main feature. This developed area has boating and catch-and-release fishing as well as an arboretum, nature trail and natural resource center, wildlife observation blind, and more than seven miles of trails. It's managed by the Papio-Missouri River Natural Resources District.

2. **Schramm Park SRA** (map location 3). 340 acres. This Platte River valley area includes the Schramm Education Center (formerly known as the Aksarben Aquarium) and some excellent wooded habitats that teem with warblers during spring migration. Whip-poor-wills can be heard here, and Kentucky warblers probably breed. There are five miles of trails with 1.5-mile and 3-mile loops. A state park entry permit is required, and the education center has a fee. Phone 402-332-5022 for more information.

C. Other Areas

1. **Fontenelle Forest** (map location 4). 1,300 acres. This large area of mature riverine hardwood forest includes 17 miles of trails as well as a mile-long boardwalk and a combined nature center and museum. The preserve has a bird checklist of 246 species, and more than 100 of these are summering species that potentially breed. Summer species of special interest include American woodcock, broad-winged and red-shouldered hawks, whip-poor-will, Acadian flycatcher, Carolina wren, yellow-throated vireo, wood thrush, American redstart, prothonotary and Kentucky warblers, brown creeper, and scarlet and summer tanagers.

The yellow-throated warbler has also been found to nest here, a location well to the north of its known breeding range, and the pileated woodpecker has regularly bred here. An observation blind overlooks a marsh, and staff facilitate organized bird and nature hikes, plus many other programs. The center is open 8 a.m. to 5 p.m. daily; there is an admission fee. The address is 1111 Bellevue Blvd. N. in Bellevue. Phone 402-731-3140 for more information. See also https://fontenelleforest.org/.

2. **Gifford Point** (map location 8). **Gifford Point WMA** is a 1,300-acre area of Missouri River–bottom forest located just east of Fontenelle Forest. **Gifford Farm Education Center** is a 420-acre farm and woodlands, now owned and operated by Educational Service Unit #3 and dedicated to environmental and historical education. The address is 700 Camp Gifford Road in Bellevue. Phone 402-597-4920 for more information. See also http://www.esu3.org/GF/Home.

3. **Neale Woods Nature Center.** See Douglas County.

16. Seward County (Maps 29 and 37)

Seward County is a loess plains county with 1,500 acres of surface water, about 6,000 acres of wooded habitats, and more than 110,000 acres of grasslands or farmlands. Tourist accommodations are available in Seward.

A. Federal Areas

1. **Freeman Lakes WPA** (map 29, location 1). 188 acres. Located northwest of Utica, Freeman Lakes includes 42 upland acres and 146 acres of wetland.

2. **Tamora WPA.** 260 acres. Tamora basin is located six miles west and two miles south of Seward and includes 52 acres of upland habitat and 228 acres of wetlands. This is the farthest east Rainwater Basin waterfowl production area.

B. State Areas

1. **Meadowlark Recreation Area** (map 37, location 1). 320 acres. This recreation area managed by the Lower Platte South Natural Resources District includes 55-acre Meadowlark Lake, native prairie, and a walnut plantation. No-wake boating, fishing, hunting, and tent camping are permitted.

2. **Oak Glen WMA** (map 37, location 2). 632 acres. Oak Glen consists of 260 acres of mature oak wooded habitats with some grassland, including native prairie.

3. **Branched Oak SRA** (map 37, location 3). See Lancaster County.

4. **Bur Oak WMA** (map 37, location 4). 143 acres. Located along US Hwy. 34 east of Seward, Bur Oak WMA comprises mature bur oak wooded habitats with some green ash and native grassland.

5. **Twin Lakes WMA** (map 37, location 5). 1,300 acres. Twin Lakes includes 255- and 50-acre reservoirs plus marshes, wooded bottomlands, upland prairie, grasslands, and small ponds. Although part of the prairie has been reseeded, other portions are native. Dickcissels, eastern and western meadowlarks, sedge wrens, eastern bluebirds, and other prairie or forest-edge species occur here. Fishing from boats is allowed on the two lakes but only with electric motors (not gasoline), and no waterfowl hunting is permitted, so undisturbed birding is possible.

The area is closed to public access from October 15 to the end of the hunting season for Canada geese.

6. **North Lake Basin WMA** (map 29, location 2). Located one mile north of Utica, North Lake Basin has 364 acres of marsh and adjoining uplands. Usually this area attracts large numbers of waterfowl during spring migration.

17. Lancaster County (Maps 35 and 38)

Lancaster County is in an area of glacial till plains, with nearly 6,000 acres of surface water, more than 7,000 acres of wooded habitats, and 140,000 acres of grasslands or farmlands. Tourist accommodations are available in Lincoln.

A. Federal Areas — None

B. State Areas

Note: Most of the following sites are flood-control reservoirs built during the 1960s to control flooding in the Salt Creek watershed. Silting-in has affected all of these reservoirs, producing marshlike habitats at the places where creeks feed into the reservoirs; such areas usually provide the best birding sites. Flooded trees (now dead and falling down) are also usually present, providing perching sites for bald eagles and cormorants.

1. **Pawnee Lake SRA** (map 38, location 4). 1,906 acres with a 740-acre reservoir. This fairly large reservoir (second only to Branched Oak Lake in area) attracts many migrant waterfowl during spring; the surrounding acreage also has many prairie species. A hiking trail is available. A state park entry permit is required.

2. **Conestoga Lake SRA** (map 38, location 8). 486 acres with a 230-acre reservoir. Similar to Pawnee Lake in its bird life, this lake is also surrounded by grasslands and some wooded habitats. A state park entry permit is required.

3. **Yankee Hill Lake WMA** (map 38, location 9). 728 acres with a 210-acre reservoir. Yankee Hill Lake is surrounded by rolling grassland and wooded bottomland.

4. **Killdeer WMA** (map 38, location 10). 69 acres with a 20-acre reservoir. Killdeer WMA has a small lake with surrounding marsh, wooded draws, and uplands.

5. **Bluestem Lake SRA** (map 38, location 11). 483 acres with a 325-acre reservoir. The silted-in upper (northern) end of this reservoir is quite marshlike and good for finding marsh birds. A state park entry permit is required.

6. **Olive Creek SRA** (map 38, location 12). 438 acres with a 175-acre reservoir. This small lake seems to attract rare waterfowl, especially scoters. A state park entry permit is required.

7. **Teal WMA** (map 38, location 13). 66 acres with a 27-acre reservoir. Teal WMA has a small lake with surrounding wooded bottomland and rolling upland.

8. **Stagecoach Lake SRA** (map 38, location 15). 607 acres with a 195-acre reservoir. Stagecoach provides for hunting, boating, fishing, camping, and picnicking. A state park entry permit is required.

9. **Cottontail Lake** (map 38, location 14). 148 acres with a 29-acre reservoir. Cottontail Lake is owned and operated by the Lower Platte South Natural Resources District. The area provides for hunting, boating, fishing, and camping.

10. **Wagon Train Lake SRA** (map 38, location 17). 750 acres with a 315-acre reservoir. Much like the other lakes in the area, Wagon Train Lake has many flooded trees. Located three miles east of Hickman. A state park entry permit is required.

11. **Hedgefield Lake WMA** (map 38, location 18). 114 acres with a 44-acre reservoir. The surrounding area is rolling upland and some wooded vegetation.

12. **Branched Oak SRA** (map 35, location 5). 4,406 acres with an 1,800-acre reservoir. This lake is the biggest of the reservoirs in Lancaster County, and one that seems to attract many rare birds (gulls, waterfowl, loons) during fall, winter, and early spring. Vast flocks of snow geese visit it in early March, along with Canada and greater white-fronted geese. Eagles are common during the spring when the ice is breaking up, and ospreys may also be seen on migration. Many species of ducks and white pelicans are common during migration. The shorebirds are best during fall, and the flooded timber at the northern end of the lake attracts cormorants too. Snowy owls sometimes turn up here, and the brushy vegetation supports wintering American tree sparrows and Harris's sparrows, among many others. A hiking trail is available. A state park entry permit is needed for some parts of the area.

13. **Wildwood Lake WMA** (map 35, location 4). 491 acres with a 107-acre reservoir. Wildwood Lake is surrounded by native wooded habitats, hilly grassland, and crops.

14. **Jack Sinn Memorial WMA** (map 35, locations 6 and 7). 1,600 acres. This WMA consists of mostly seasonally wet lowlands that occur along a creek drainage and includes some beaver ponds up to six feet deep, approximately. Jack Sinn is perhaps the best rail and marsh bird habitat in the county because some of the best saline wetlands in eastern Nebraska are found here. An old railroad bed allows dry walking in this usually wet environment.

15. **Arbor Lake WMA** (map 38, location 1). 63 acres. Arbor Lake is a 63-acre saline and semipermanent wetland that seasonally supports great-tailed grackles, migrant ducks and shorebirds, and prairie passerines.

C. Other Areas

1. **Boosalis Park** (map 38, location 2). Historically known as Roper's Lake, this little-visited part of Lincoln can be reached only by following 48th Street north to the old city landfill and stopping there for permission to go on to the undeveloped marshes and riparian wooded habitats about a quarter mile beyond. It is well worth the effort; this area is perhaps the best place in Lincoln for seeing large numbers of species (Kaufman, 2003). Red-tailed hawks and great horned owls nest here, coyotes and deer are regularly seen, and the marshy areas attract rails, ducks, geese, cormorants, yellow-headed blackbirds, black-crowned night herons, and many other species. Care must be taken in walking through the area (which is partly old landfill) because the ground has irregularities in some places that one can easily fall into or trip over. Ospreys and shorebirds are sometimes seen along Salt Creek, which borders the area on the north and west.

2. **Nine-Mile Prairie** (map 38, location 3). 230 acres. Owned by the University of Nebraska Foundation, Nine-Mile Prairie is one of the few remaining native tall-grass prairies in Lancaster County and a classic site of early ecological research. Only a small amount of water exists on the prairie, so the bird species are mostly upland passerines, such as grasshopper sparrows and dickcissels. The area is open year round. See also https://grassland.unl.edu/nine-mile-prairie.

3. **Oak Lake Park** (map 38, location 5). 186 acres. Oak Lake Park actually has two lakes, which attract gulls, cormorants, geese, ducks, and other water birds during migration.

4. **Lincoln Saline Wetlands Nature Center** (map 38, location 6). Located on the undeveloped east side of Capitol Beach Lake, this area still supports a good marsh habitat. The Lower Platte South Natural Resources District now owns the area and has provided records of king rails and other uncommon to rare water-dependent birds. To reach the wetlands, turn from Sun Valley Blvd. onto Westgate Blvd.; then proceed west on Lake Drive to a small parking area. Grassy wetland areas are also excellent for sparrows. See also https://www.lpsnrd.org/lincoln-saline-wetlands-nature-center and https://app.lincoln.ne.gov/city/parks/parksfacilities/wetlands/wetlandsnc.htm.

5. **Pioneers Park and Pioneers Park Nature Center** (map 38, location 7). 668 acres. Pioneers Park is the oldest of Lincoln's city parks and one of the largest. It has a few small ponds and some native prairie but is mostly planted to pines and other conifers. These wooded habitats support great horned owls (year round), long-eared owls (in winter), red-tailed and sharp-shinned hawks, and many passerines. A nature trail extends out into prairie and brushland, and through riparian wooded habitats along a branch of Salt Creek, where wood ducks are common. The Prairie Corridor on Haines Branch hiking trail is under construction and will eventually extend south to Spring Creek Prairie Audubon Center. The Chet Ager Building offers views of wintering songbirds that gather near feeders and looks out over a pond. A bird checklist has 237 species. Open a variety of hours, depending where you go in the park or nature center; phone 402-441-7895 or check https://www.lincoln.ne.gov/City/Departments/Parks-and-Recreation/Parks-Facilities/Pioneers-Park-Nature-Center.

6. **Holmes Lake Park** (map 38, location 19). 555 acres. Holmes Lake Park is a city-maintained recreational park surrounding a flood-control reservoir (110 acres) that has a resident flock of Canada geese. During some winters, ducks such as goldeneye, bufflehead, ruddy duck, scaup, and sometimes hooded merganser can be seen among the geese.

7. **Wilderness Park** (map 38, location 16). 1,455 acres. This long, narrow park follows Salt Creek for about 7 miles and has about 20 miles of hiking and horseback trails. There are good stands of mature bur oak and riparian forest, and several species of owls are common (barred,

Prairie coneflowers, Spring Creek Prairie Audubon Center

eastern screech-owl, and great horned owl) as well as several woodpeckers, including the red-bellied. It is probably the best Lincoln location for migrant warblers, and breeding songbirds include tufted titmouse (rare, near its western limits), eastern bluebird, orchard and Baltimore oriole, and Carolina wren (near its northwestern limits). A park checklist has 191 species.

8. **Wyuka Cemetery.** Although not pinpointed on the map, the entrance is at 37th and O Streets in Lincoln. This 140-acre historical cemetery is an excellent location for viewing migrant songbirds such as vireos and warblers, mainly along the eastern edge.

9. **Spring Creek Prairie Audubon Center** (map 38, location 21). 850 acres. Owned by the National Audubon Society, this Audubon Center is located three miles south of the west edge of Denton. Follow 98th St. south from Denton and access the gate on the east side of the highway. Spring Creek has some small wetlands—including a spring—riparian wooded habitats, and hilly prairie uplands. Many hiking trails are maintained, and the Prairie Corridor on Haines Branch hiking trail is under construction and will eventually extend from Spring Creek north to Pioneers Park. Three hundred seventy plant species and 235 species of birds have been recorded. Henslow's sparrows are regular here, and the site is classified as a Nebraska Important Bird Area. Open Monday through Friday 8:30 a.m.–4:30 p.m. and Saturday and Sunday 8:30 a.m.–12:30 p.m. Admission is free (an entrance donation is always suggested), while some events and tours have fees. For more information, phone 402-797-2301 and see also https://springcreek.audubon.org/.

10. **Little Salt Fork Marsh Preserve.** 280 acres. Formerly owned by the Nature Conservancy, Little Salt Fork Marsh is now owned and maintained by the Lower Platte South Natural Resources District. It is a saline wetlands (similar to Arbor Lake) and prairie located two miles east of Raymond (1st Street and Raymond Road). Three other small WMA and LPSNRD saline wetlands are in this immediate area as well. (Not shown on the map.)

11. **Marsh Wren Saline Wetland.** Marsh Wren is a 150-acre Lower Platte South Natural Resources District restoration project preserve located at 40th Street and Arbor Road in north Lincoln. There is a parking lot, trail, and observation deck for birders. Time-lapse photography is being used to track the restoration progress and changes. (Not shown on the map.)

12. **MoPac East Recreational Trail** (map 38, location 20). This 25-mile (so far) rail corridor bike trail—also recommended for hiking, running, cross-country skiing, and wildlife watching—has a parking lot in Lincoln on 84th Street, and from there it travels in an easterly direction to Walton and several other Cass County towns. Maintained by the Lower Platte South Natural Resources District, the trail passes through woodlands, prairie, and farm fields and pastures.

18. Cass County (Map 39)

Cass County is a Platte River and Missouri River valleys county with about 1,800 acres of surface water, 24,000 acres of wooded habitats, and almost 56,000 acres of grasslands or farmlands. Tourist accommodations are available in Greenwood.

A. Federal Areas — None

B. State Areas

1. **Eugene T. Mahoney State Park** (map location 1). 574 acres. Mahoney State Park is a highly developed riverine woodland park, with lodging, cabins, eating facilities, and other popular attractions. It has an excellent population of eastern bluebirds, and borders the Platte River, where riparian deciduous forest is well developed. A tall observation tower built among a stand of bur oaks gives an aerial view, and a 6-mile network of trails is available for hiking. A state park entry permit is required. Phone 402-944-2523 for more information or see http://outdoornebraska.gov/mahoney/.

2. **Platte River State Park** (map location 2). Another popular area, Platte River State Park is quite similar to Mahoney State Park and also to Louisville Lakes SRA. Migrant warblers are abundant, and Kentucky warblers breed here, as probably do scarlet and summer tanagers. There are two observation towers. Cabins and campsites are available, along with miles of trails for hiking, running, biking, and bird watching. A state park entry permit is required. Phone 402-234-2217 for more information or see http://outdoornebraska.gov/platteriver/.

3. **Louisville Lakes SRA** (map location 3). 192 acres. Louisville SRA is much like the two previous parks, offering both primitive and RV camping, various concessions, and some hiking trails as well as river access. Nearby Schramm

Tallgrass prairie, Spring Creek Prairie Audubon Center

Park SRA (see Sarpy County) is less crowded and offers better birding. A state park entry permit is required.

4. **Randall W. Schilling WMA** (map location 4). 1,500 acres. This WMA is a large managed waterfowl area, with 25 acres of water and nearby cropland, mainly designed to attract snow geese. It is open to the public from April 1 to September 30 and used for controlled-access goose hunting during the fall season.

5. **Rakes Creek WMA** (map location 5). 316 acres. This WMA is located approximately three miles east and three miles south of Murray. All the acreage is upland.

19. Otoe County (Map 40)

Otoe County is a Missouri River valley county with 2,500 acres of surface water, more than 15,000 acres of wooded habitats, and nearly 102,000 acres of grasslands or farmlands. Tourist accommodations are available in Nebraska City and Syracuse.

A. Federal Areas — None

B. State Areas

1. **Wilson Creek WMA** (map location 1). 41 acres. Wilson Creek WMA is located 1 mile south and 3.5 miles east of Otoe. It includes a 14-acre reservoir and surrounding grasses and shrubs.

2. **Arbor Lodge State Historical Park** (map location 2). Arbor Lodge is located just west of Nebraska City. In the arboretum are hundreds of planted but mature trees with a half-mile "tree trail" with identification tags. The lodge is worth visiting for historical reasons (it is associated with the establishment of Arbor Day) as well as for learning tree identification.

3. **Missouri River Basin Lewis and Clark Visitor Center and Interpretive Trail** (map location 3). This modern center is located on 80 acres overlooking the Missouri River, at the southeast edge of Nebraska City (off US Hwy. 2). It documents the natural history aspects of the 1803–6 Corps of Discovery Expedition. For more information, see https://lewisandclarkvisitorcenter.org.

4. **Triple Creek WMA** (map location 4). 80 acres. Located three miles south and one mile west of Palmyra, Triple Creek WMA has two intermittent streams and 16 acres of wooded habitats.

20. Saline County

Saline County is in a region of loess and dissected plains, with about 1,900 acres of surface water, almost 11,000 acres of wooded habitats, and about 89,000 acres of grasslands or farmlands. There are tourist accommodations at Crete, Friend and Wilber.

A. Federal Areas — None

B. State Areas

1. **Swan Creek WMA.** 160 acres. Swan Creek is located nine miles south and one mile east of Friend. The WMA has a 27-acre lake, marshland, native prairie, wooded habitats, and cropland.

2. **Walnut Creek Public Use Area.** 64 acres. Walnut Creek is owned and managed by the Lower Big Blue Natural Resources District. It is located three miles north and one mile east of Crete. Various upland habitats and a 20-acre fishing lake are present.

21. Jefferson County

Jefferson County is in a region of loess and dissected plains, with nearly 2,000 acres of surface water, more than 10,000 acres of wooded habitats, and 148,000 acres of grasslands or farmlands. Tourist accommodations are available in Fairbury.

A. Federal Areas — None

B. State Areas

1. **Alexandria Lakes SRA/WMA.** 778 acres. Located nine miles west and six miles north of Fairbury, or two miles east of Alexandria, this WMA has a 43-acre lake, marshes, streams, ponds, and wooded habitats.

2. **Rock Creek Station State Historical Park and SRA.** 350 acres (SHP) and 40 acres (SRA). The adjacent park and recreation area are located about two miles north and three miles east of Endicott. The areas include about 100 acres of native prairie and six miles of trails. A state park

entry permit is required. See also http://outdoornebraska.gov/rockcreekstation/ and http://outdoornebraska.gov/rockcreekstationsra/.

3. **Rock Glen WMA**. 706 acres. Located seven miles east and two miles south of Fairbury, Rock Glen WMA is not far from Rock Creek Station. It includes rolling native upland prairie and tree-lined drainages.

22. Gage County (Map 41)

Gage County is in an area of loess and glacial drift, with nearly 2,000 acres of surface water, 17,000 acres of wooded habitats, and 166,000 acres of grasslands or farmlands. Tourist accommodations are available in Beatrice and Wymore.

A. Federal Areas

1. **Homestead National Historical Park** (map location 2). This park celebrates the Homestead Act of 1862. It includes a visitor center with educational exhibits that feature pioneer history and related artifacts and a 2.5-mile trail that passes through riparian wooded habitats and about 100 acres of restored prairie. A bird checklist contains more than 150 species, and a prairie plant list is available as well. For more information, phone 402-223-3514 or see https://www.nps.gov/home/index.htm.

B. State Areas

1. **Clatonia Public Use Area** (map location 1). 115 acres with a 40-acre reservoir. This area is owned and managed by the Lower Big Blue Natural Resources District.

2. **Iron Horse Trail WMA** (map location 3). More than 20 sites (so far), ranging in size from 1 to 19 acres, are located in Gage and Pawnee Counties on abandoned railroad track right-of-way. In this area, the westernmost unit is between Beatrice and Holmesville, and the easternmost is near Mayberry.

3. **Rockford SRA** (map location 4). 300 acres with a 150-acre reservoir. Rockford is set up for boating, fishing, swimming, picnicking, and camping. The area has a one-mile hiking trail. A state park entry permit is required. See also http://outdoornebraska.gov/rockford/.

4. **Wolf-Wildcat WMA** (map location 5). 160 acres with a 42-acre reservoir. This area is owned and managed by the Lower Big Blue Natural Resources District and provides for fishing, camping, hunting, and bird watching.

5. **Arrowhead WMA** (map location 6). 320 acres with a 67-acre reservoir. The upland habitats are crops, pasture, and woods.

6. **Diamond Lake WMA** (map location 7). 320 acres, including lakes. Diamond Lake, three miles west of Odell, consists of open grasslands and hardwood stands around a 33-acre reservoir. The adjoining **Donald Whitney Memorial WMA** is much smaller (50 acres) and also includes a reservoir (14 acres).

7. **Big Indian Recreation Area** (map location 8). 233 acres with a 77-acre lake. Big Indian Recreation Area, owned and operated by the Lower Big Blue Natural Resources District, is located six miles east of Odell. Facilities for boating, fishing, camping, swimming, and hiking are provided.

23. Johnson County (Map 42)

Johnson County is in a region of glacial drift, with about 500 acres of surface water, 6,800 acres of wooded habitats, and more than 92,000 acres of grassland. Tourist accommodations are available in Tecumseh.

A. Federal Areas — None

B. State Areas

1. **Osage WMA** (map locations 1–3). 778 acres total. Osage WMA is mostly composed of wooded habitats and intervening grassland habitats, plus tree plantings and crops.

2. **Hickory Ridge WMA** (map location 4). 250 acres. This area includes 60 acres of woods, a small pond, and fairly steep grassland and creek-bottom habitat.

3. **Twin Oaks WMA** (map locations 5–7). 795 acres total. Twin Oaks WMA has mostly wooded habitats with some grassland and wildlife food plots.

24. Nemaha County (Map 43)

Nemaha County is a Missouri River valley county with nearly 1,800 acres of surface water, more than 21,000 acres of wooded habitats, and 48,000 acres of grasslands or farmlands. Tourist accommodations are available in Auburn and Brownville.

A. Federal Areas — None

B. State Areas

1. **Indian Cave State Park** (map location 1). See Richardson County.

2. **Brownville SRA.** 22 acres. Located at the southeastern edge of Brownville, this small recreation area allows camping and provides boating and fishing access to the Missouri River. A state park entry permit is required. (Not shown on the map.)

25. Pawnee County (Map 44)

Pawnee County is in a region of glacial till, with less than 1,000 acres of surface water, more than 16,000 acres of wooded habitats, and about 124,000 acres of pasture grasslands, the latter being floristically associated with the Flint Hills prairies of Kansas. Tourist accommodations are available in Pawnee City and Steinauer.

A. Federal Areas — None

B. State Areas

1. **Iron Horse Trail WMA** (map location 1). Iron Horse Trail comprises many short sections of railroad bed that are now being used as a hike-bike trail. See also Gage County and Richardson County.

2. **Burchard Lake WMA** (map location 2, plus enlarged inset). 560 acres with a 150-acre reservoir. Burchard Lake is surrounded by native grasslands and some hardwoods. This area has a small resident flock of greater prairie-chickens, and two permanent blinds are located on the hilltop that has historically been used as a lek by males (see inset arrowhead).

3. **Bowwood WMA** (map location 3). 320 acres. Bowwood comprises wooded areas, croplands, grasslands, and two small ponds.

4. **Pawnee Prairie WMA** (map location 4). 1,021 acres. Pawnee Prairie is mostly native prairie, with some wooded

Greater prairie-chicken, Pawnee County

habitats and a small amount of cropland. It supports a flock of about 20 greater prairie-chickens, which have a lek located near the center of the prairie (about 0.75 mile from the various parking lots, which are at the east, northwest, and southwest corners of the area). No permanent blinds are present, but temporary blinds are permitted. Driving on the prairie is not allowed.

5. **Prairie Knoll WMA** (map location 5). 120 acres. This wildlife management area includes a small reservoir and a mixture of wooded habitats, tree plantings, grassland, and cropland.

6. **Mayberry WMA** (map location 6). 195 acres. Located five miles north of Burchard and 0.5 mile east of state Hwy. 99, Mayberry WMA consists of grassland, trees, and a small reservoir.

7. **Table Rock WMA** (map location 7). Located just east of Table Rock on the north side of state Hwy. 4, Table Rock WMA includes mainly wooded bottomland along the Nemaha River, plus grassland and cropland.

26. Richardson County (Map 43)

Richardson County is a Missouri River valley county with more than 1,600 acres of surface water, nearly 16,000 acres of wooded habitats, and 110,000 acres of grassland. Tourist accommodations are available in Falls City.

A. Federal Areas — None

B. State Areas

1. **Indian Cave State Park** (map location 1). 3,052 acres. Like Rulo Bluffs (see the Other Areas section), Indian Cave State Park has a diverse wooded-habitats flora of southern affinities and supports such southern bird species as summer tanagers, Acadian flycatchers, and chuck-will's-widows. The park is 78 percent mature forest, and the rest is grassland or developed areas, with both modern and primitive camping facilities and about 20 miles of hiking trails, including the approximately 7-mile Hardwood Trail that is moderately difficult. The park is classified as a Nebraska Important Bird Area. A state park entry permit is required. For more information, phone 402-883-2575 or see http://outdoornebraska.gov/indiancave/.

2. **Verdon Lake SRA** (map location 2). 30 acres with a 45-acre lake. This recreation area provides for fishing, electric-motor boating, picnicking, and basic camping. Verdon Lake is spring fed. A state park entry permit is required.

3. **Kinters Ford WMA** (map location 3). 200 acres. Kinters Ford includes river-bottom wooded habitats, grassland, and cropland.

4. **Four-Mile Creek WMA** (map location 4). 160 acres. This wildlife management area has mostly upland habitats along a creek bottom.

5. **Iron Horse Trail WMA** (map location 5). 210 acres. This hiking trail follows an abandoned railroad right-of-way. (See also Gage County and Pawnee County.)

6. **Margrave WMA** (map location 6). 106 acres. Located three miles south and seven miles east of Falls City. This area along the Nemaha River has wooded habitats, cropland, grasses, and marshy areas.

Fall color, Indian Cave State Park

C. Other Areas

1. **Rulo Bluffs Preserve** (map location 7). 444 acres. This important former Nature Conservancy area is located nearly on the Kansas border and has the most southern floral affinities of any Nebraska forest. Ridgetop prairie-savanna is the unique habitat. No bird checklist is yet available, but there should be some southern species in addition to chuck-will's-widow to be found there. Permission to visit must be obtained from the Iowa Tribe of Kansas and Nebraska, which since late 2020 owns the land and plans to establish Ioway Tribal National Park. Phone the Tribal Administrative Office at 785-595-3258; see also https://iowatribeofkansasandnebraska.com/.

MAP 1 — SIOUX COUNTY

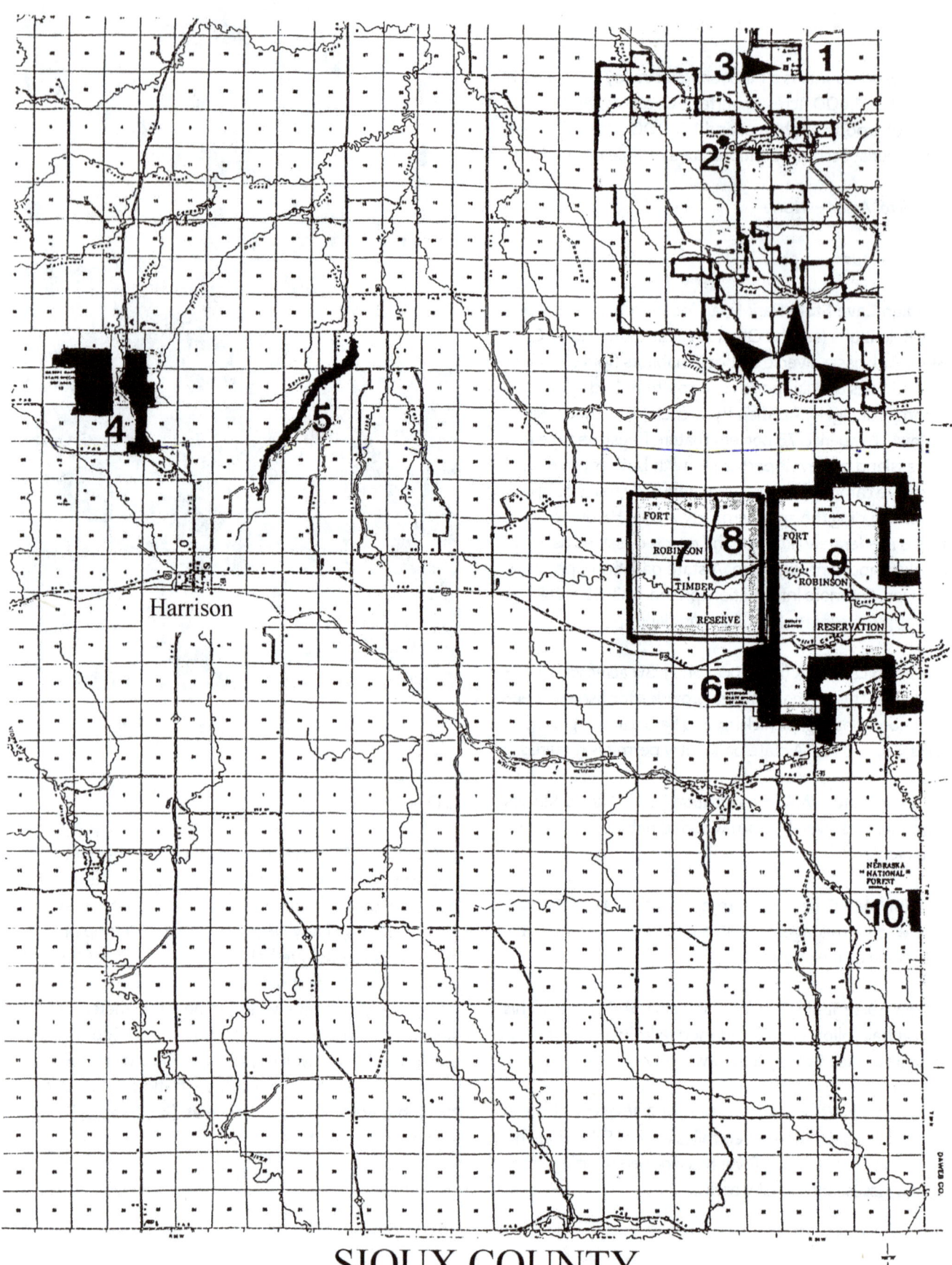

SIOUX COUNTY

1. Sioux County

MAP 2 — DAWES COUNTY

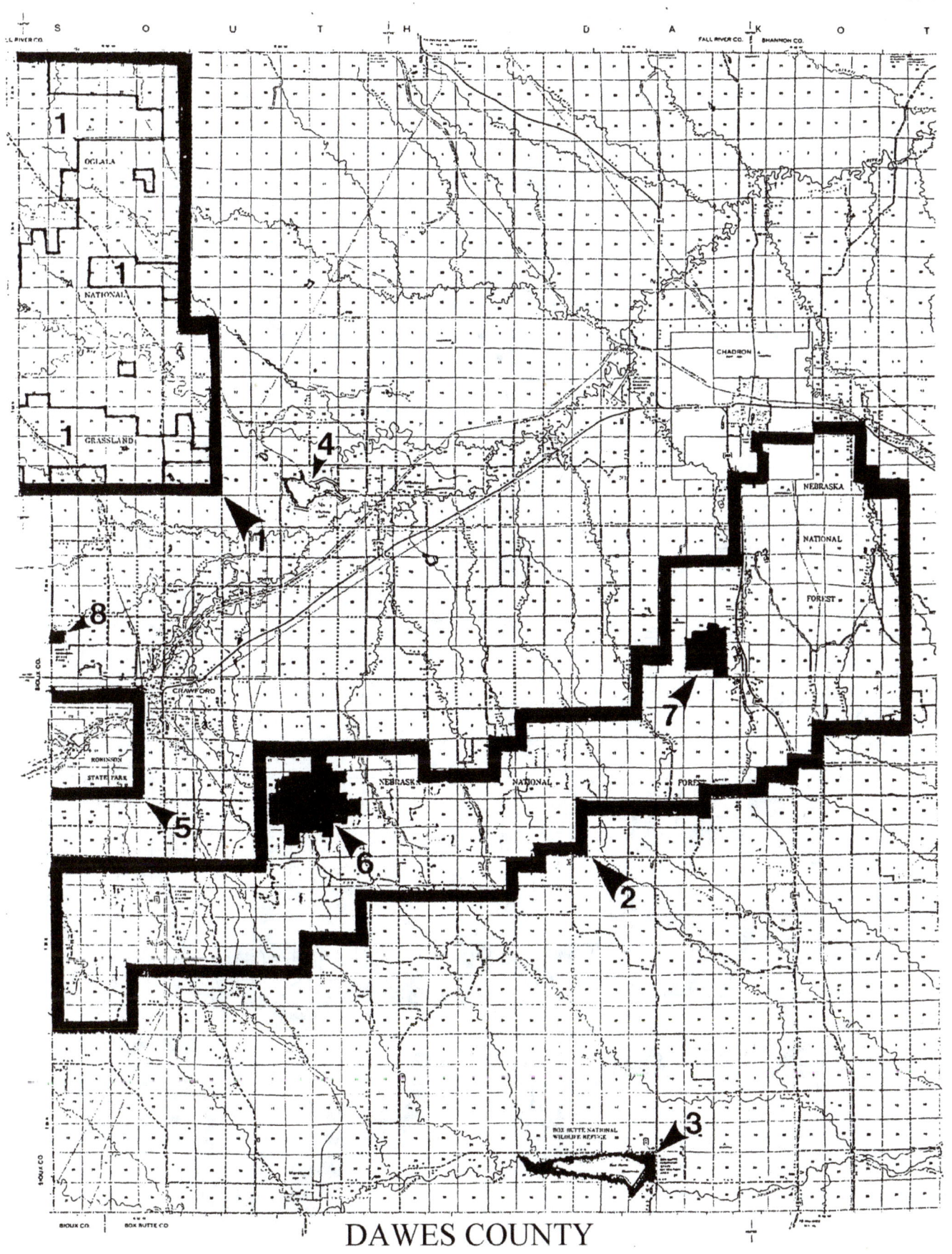

2. Dawes County

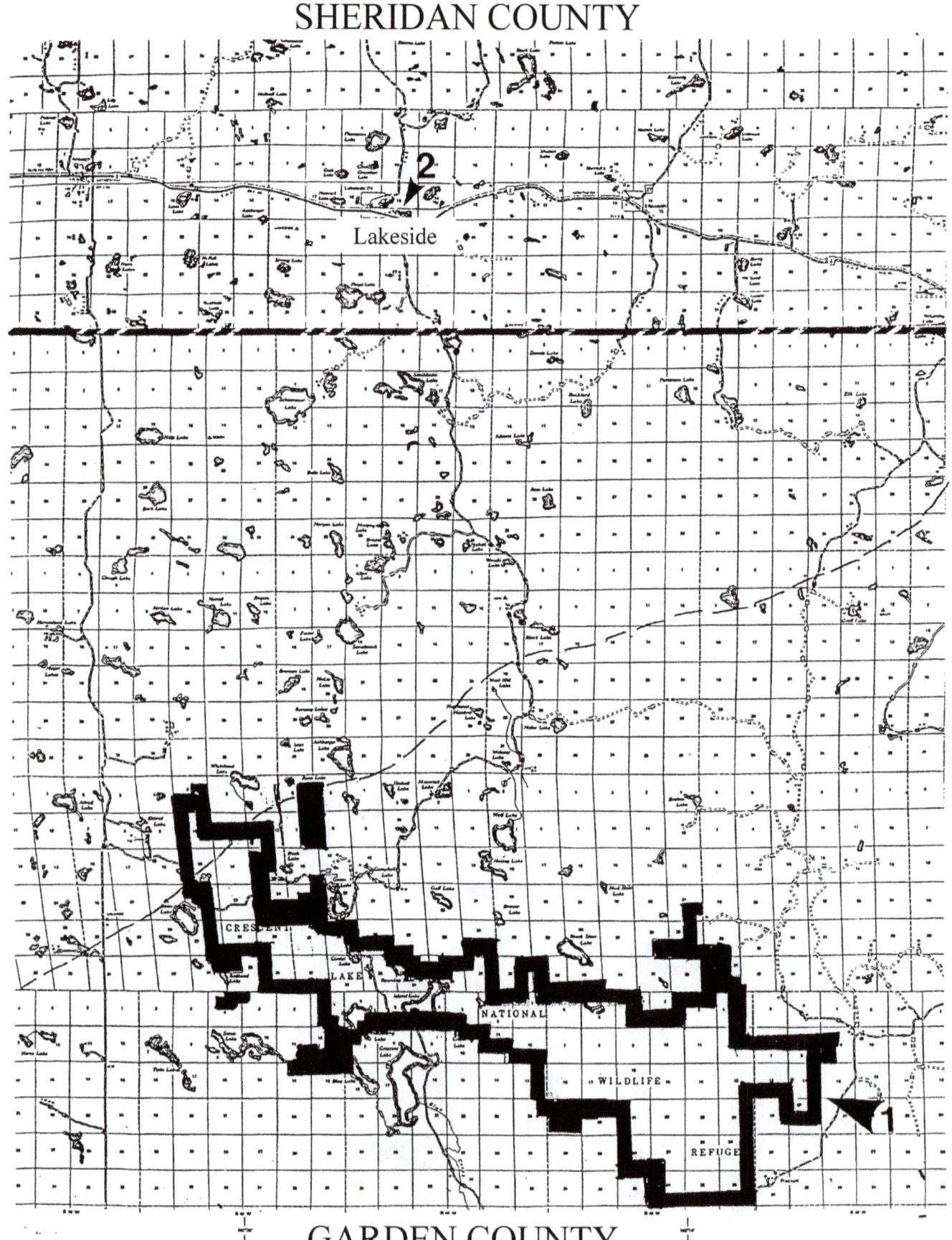

3. Sheridan and Garden Counties

MAP 4 — SCOTTS BLUFF COUNTY

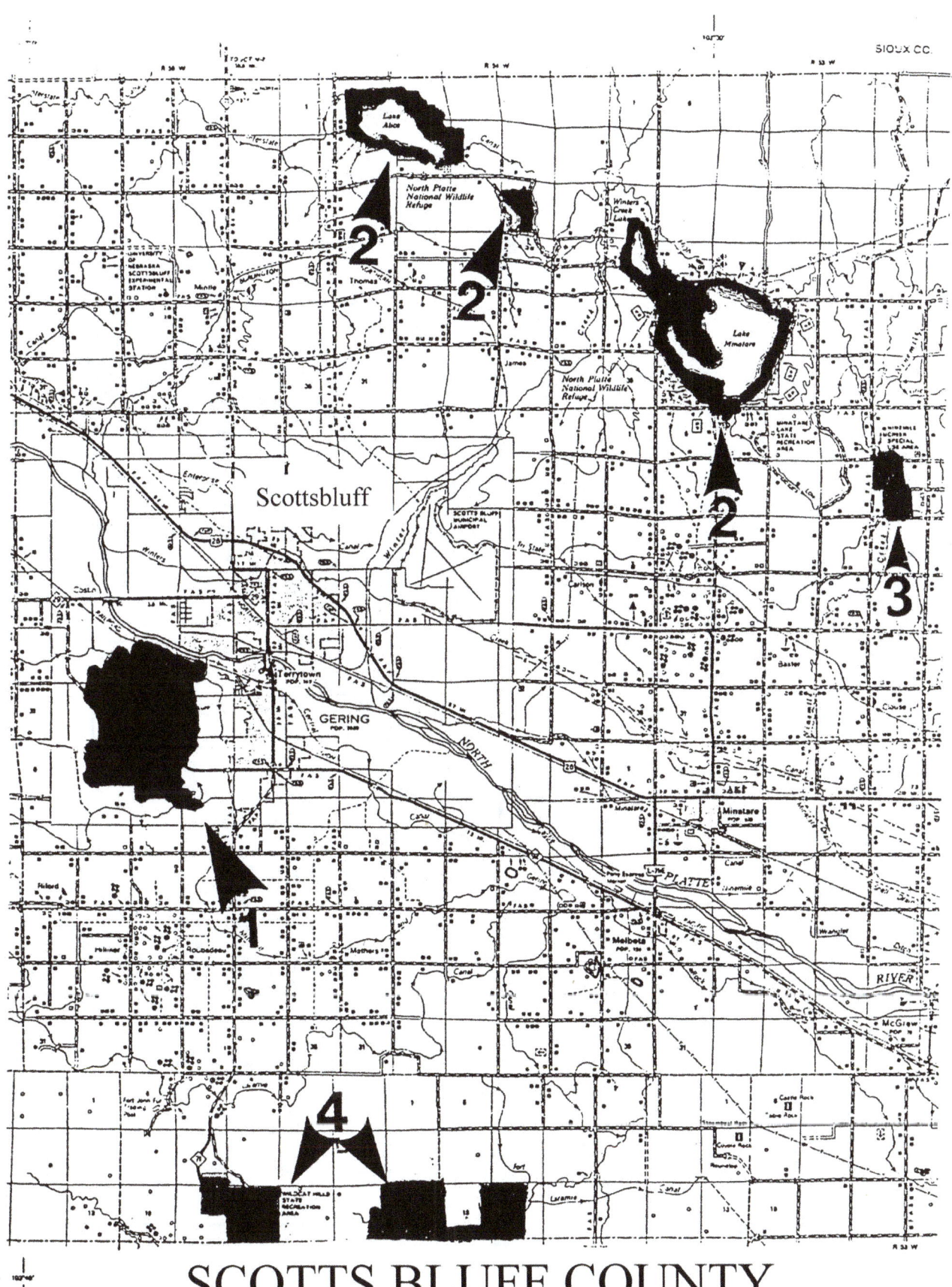

SCOTTS BLUFF COUNTY

4. Scotts Bluff County

MAP 5 — KIMBALL COUNTY

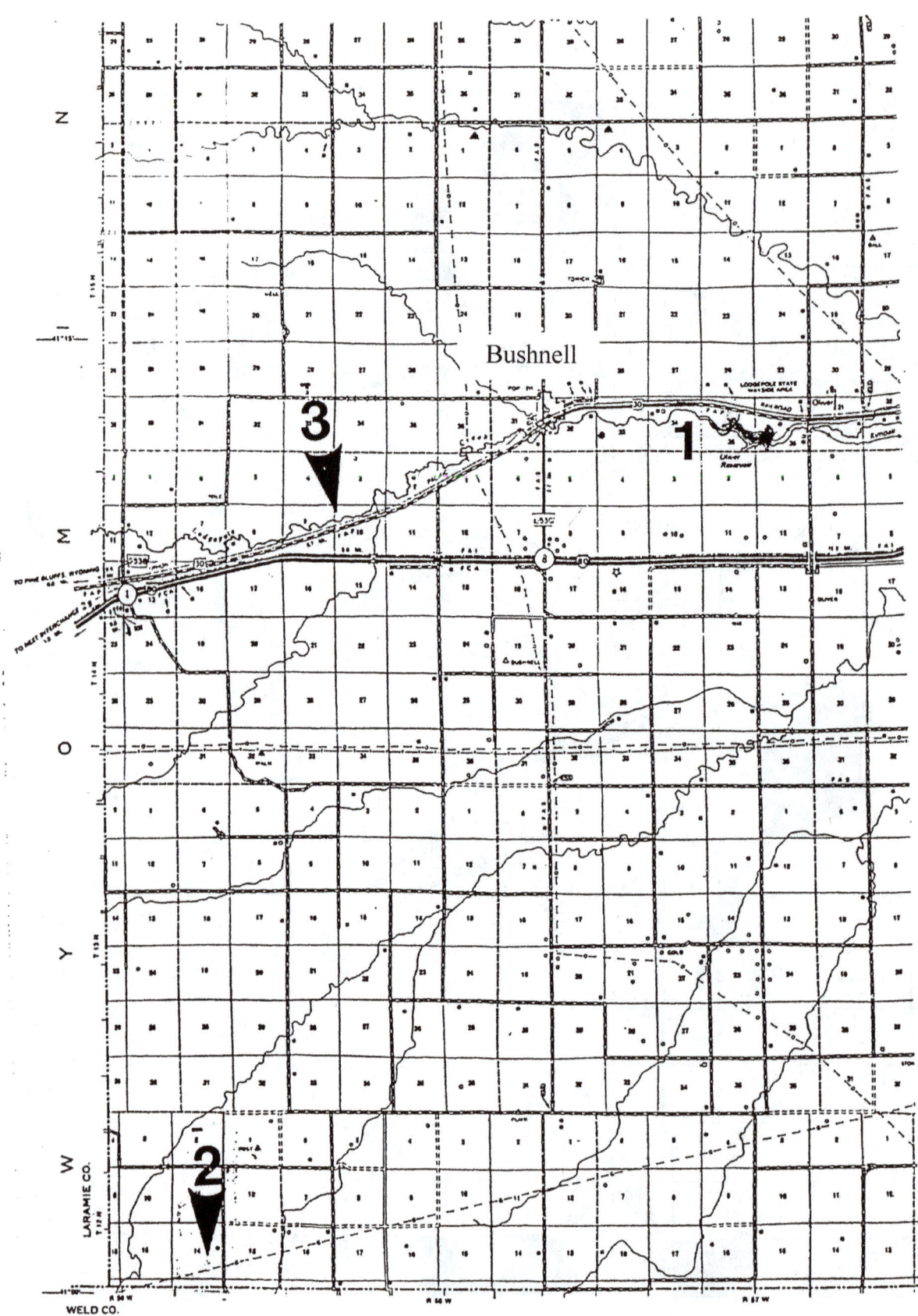

KIMBALL COUNTY

5. Kimball County

MAP 6 — MORRILL COUNTY

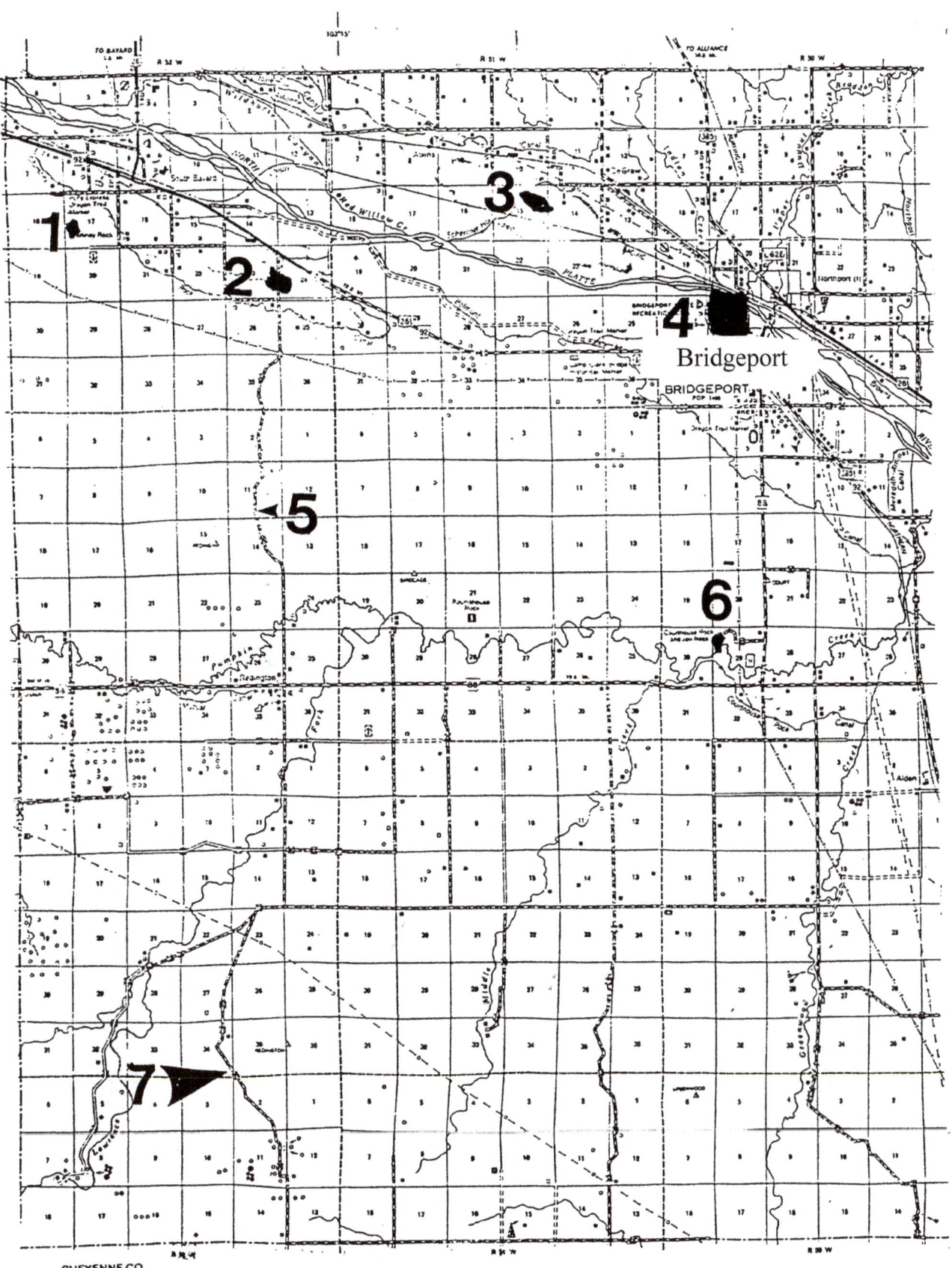

MORRILL COUNTY

6. Morrill County

MAP 7 — GARDEN & DEUEL COUNTIES

GARDEN COUNTY

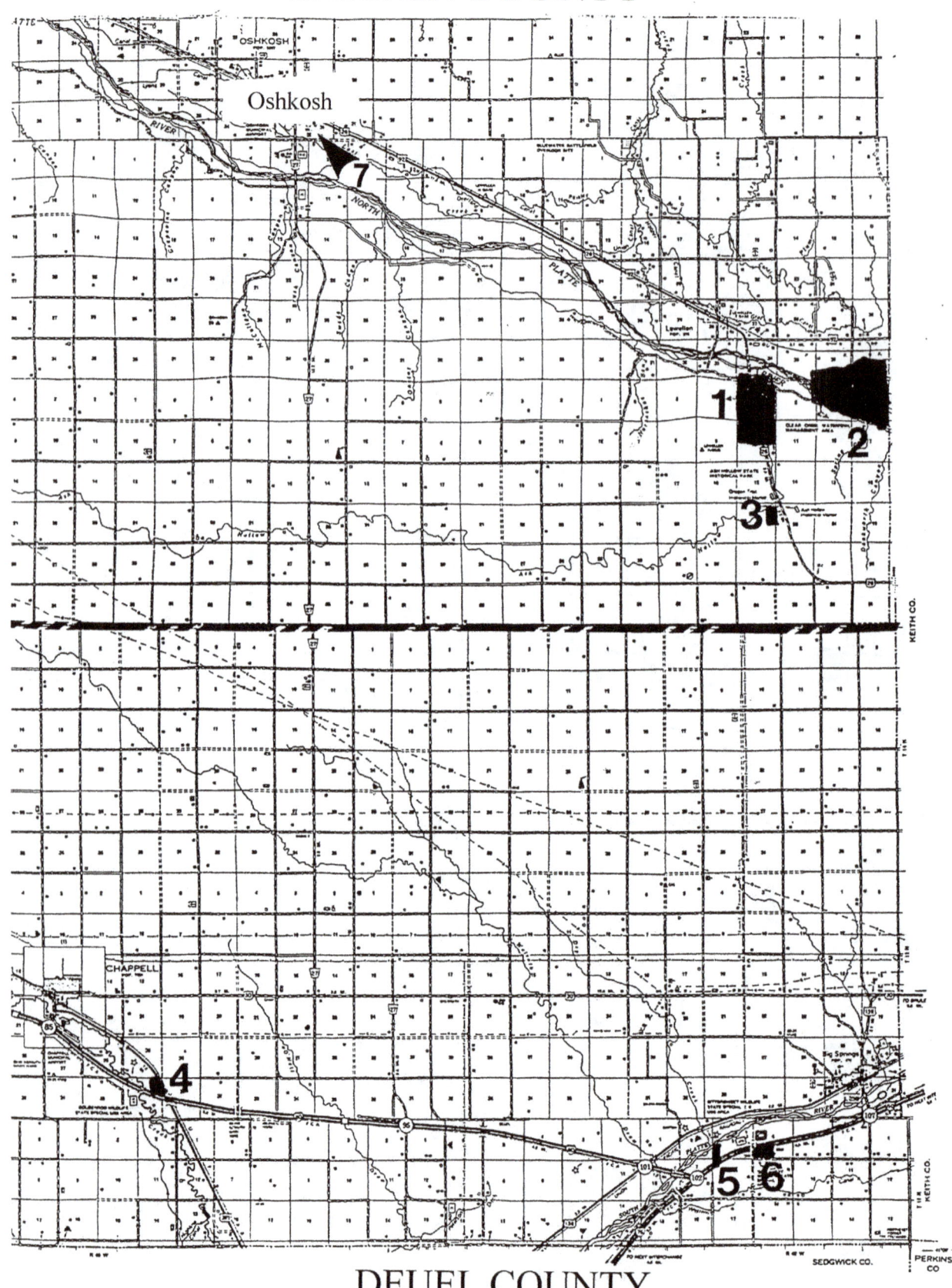

DEUEL COUNTY

7. Garden and Deuel Counties

MAP 8 — CHERRY COUNTY

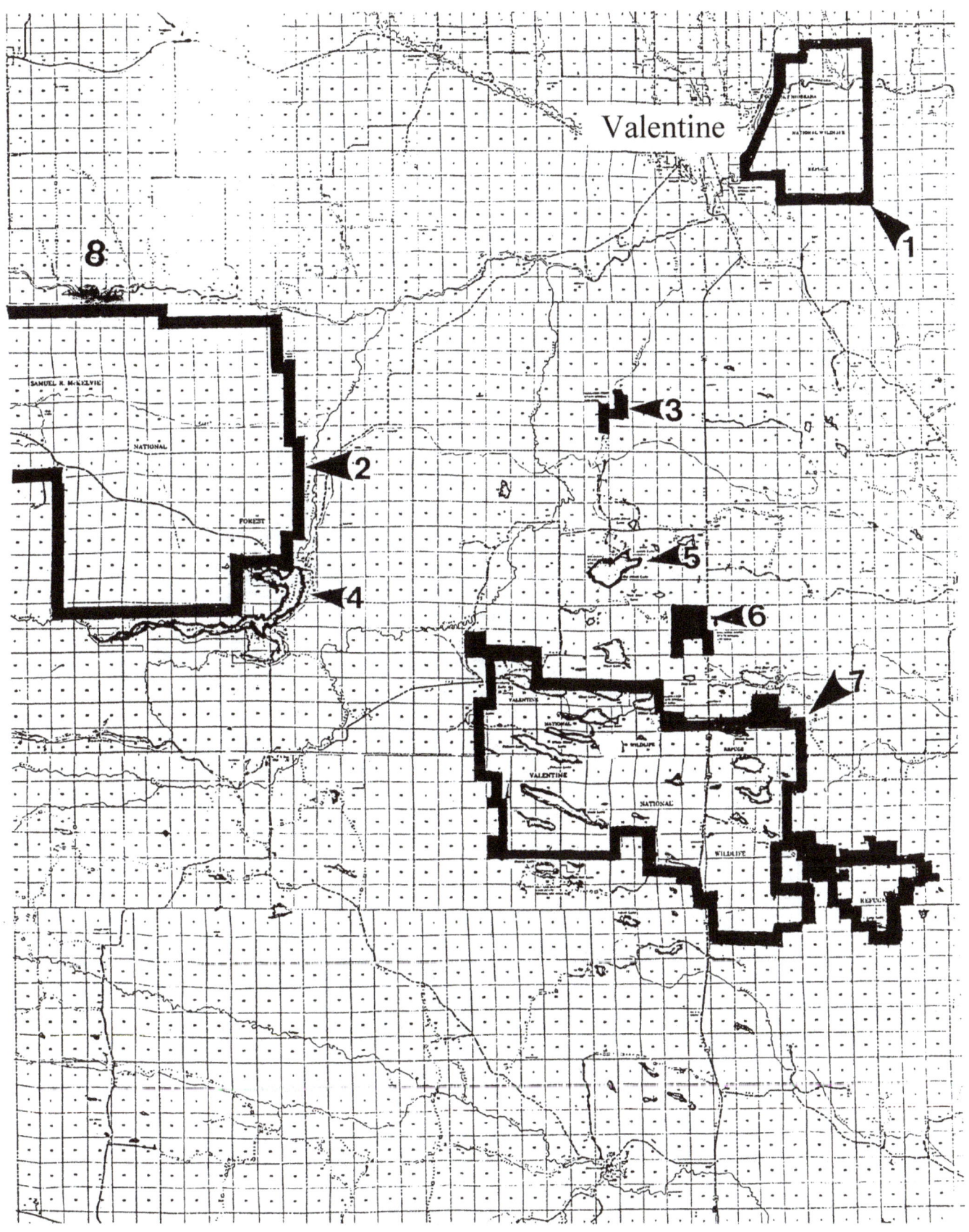

CHERRY COUNTY

8. Cherry County

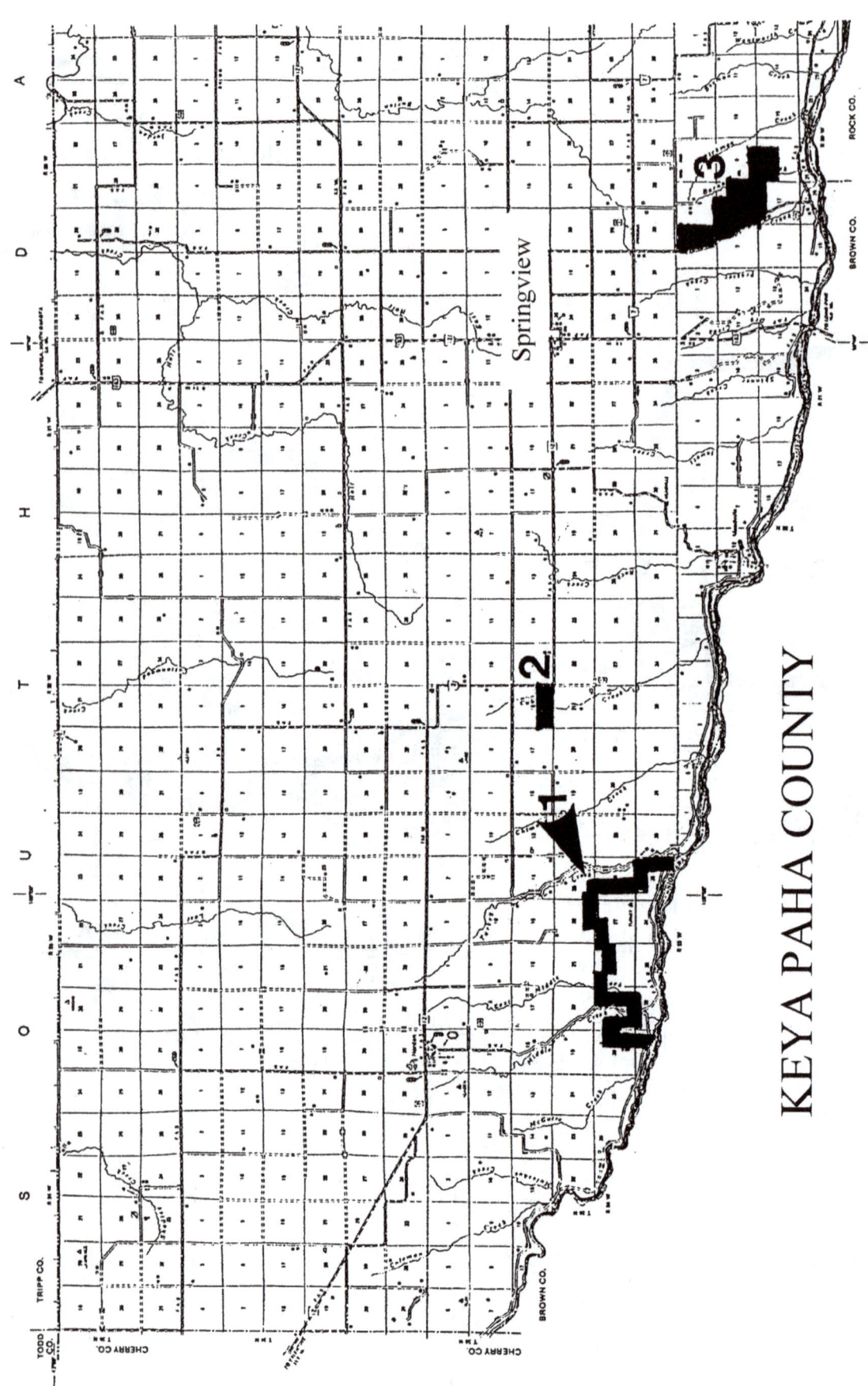

9. Keya Paha County

MAP 10 — BROWN COUNTY

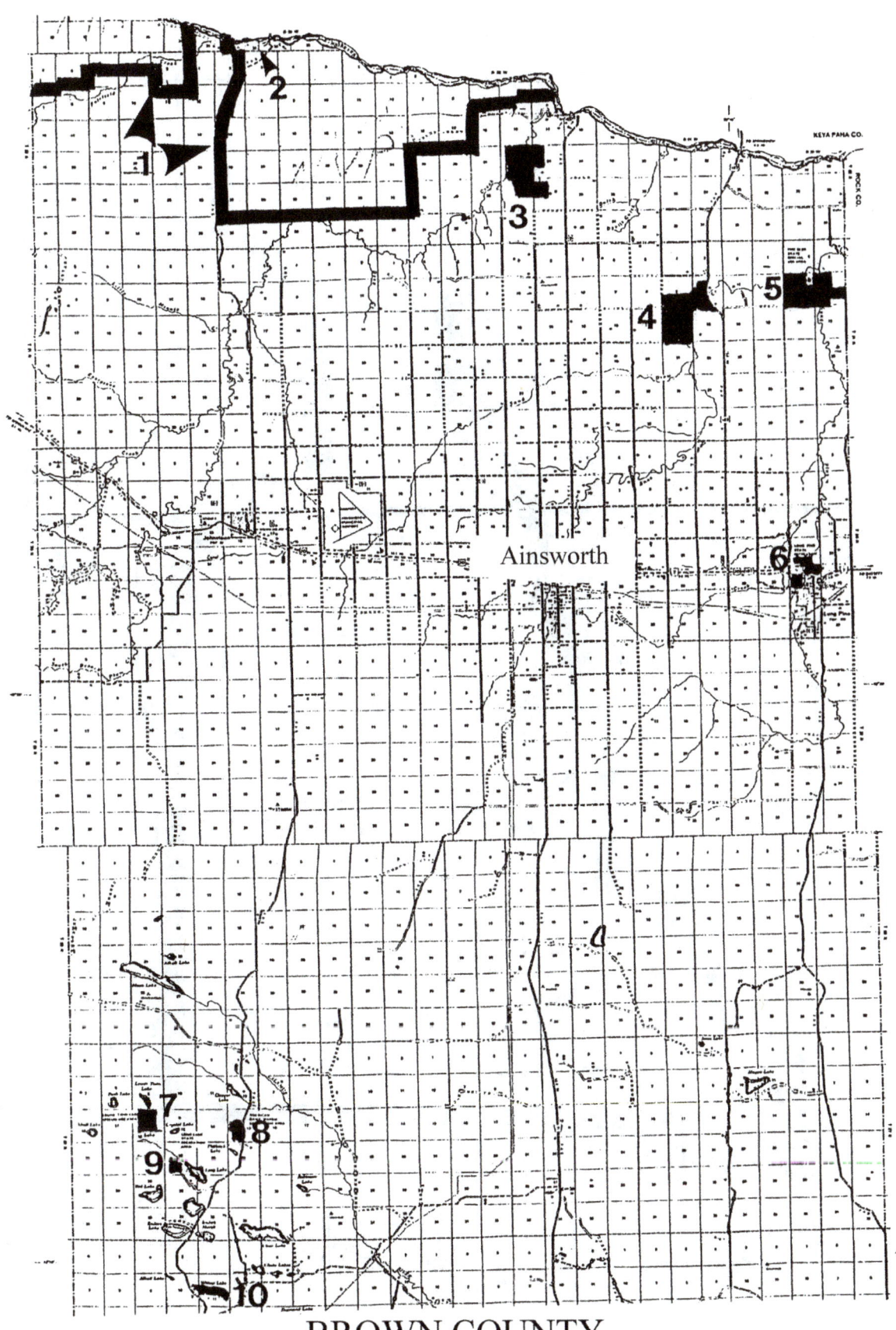

BROWN COUNTY

10. Brown County

MAP 11 — THOMAS & BLAINE COUNTIES

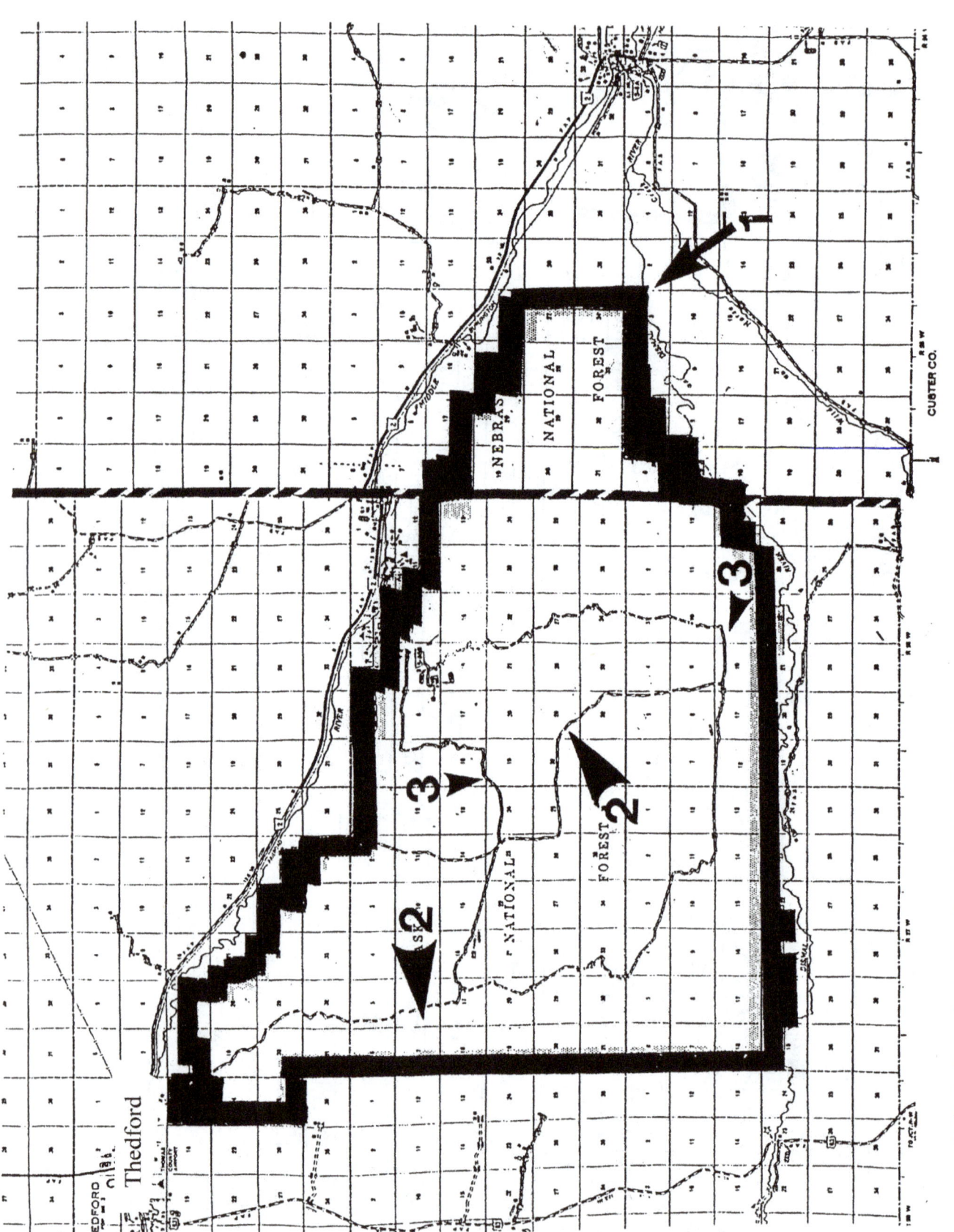

11. Thomas and Blaine Counties

MAP 12 — ARTHUR COUNTY

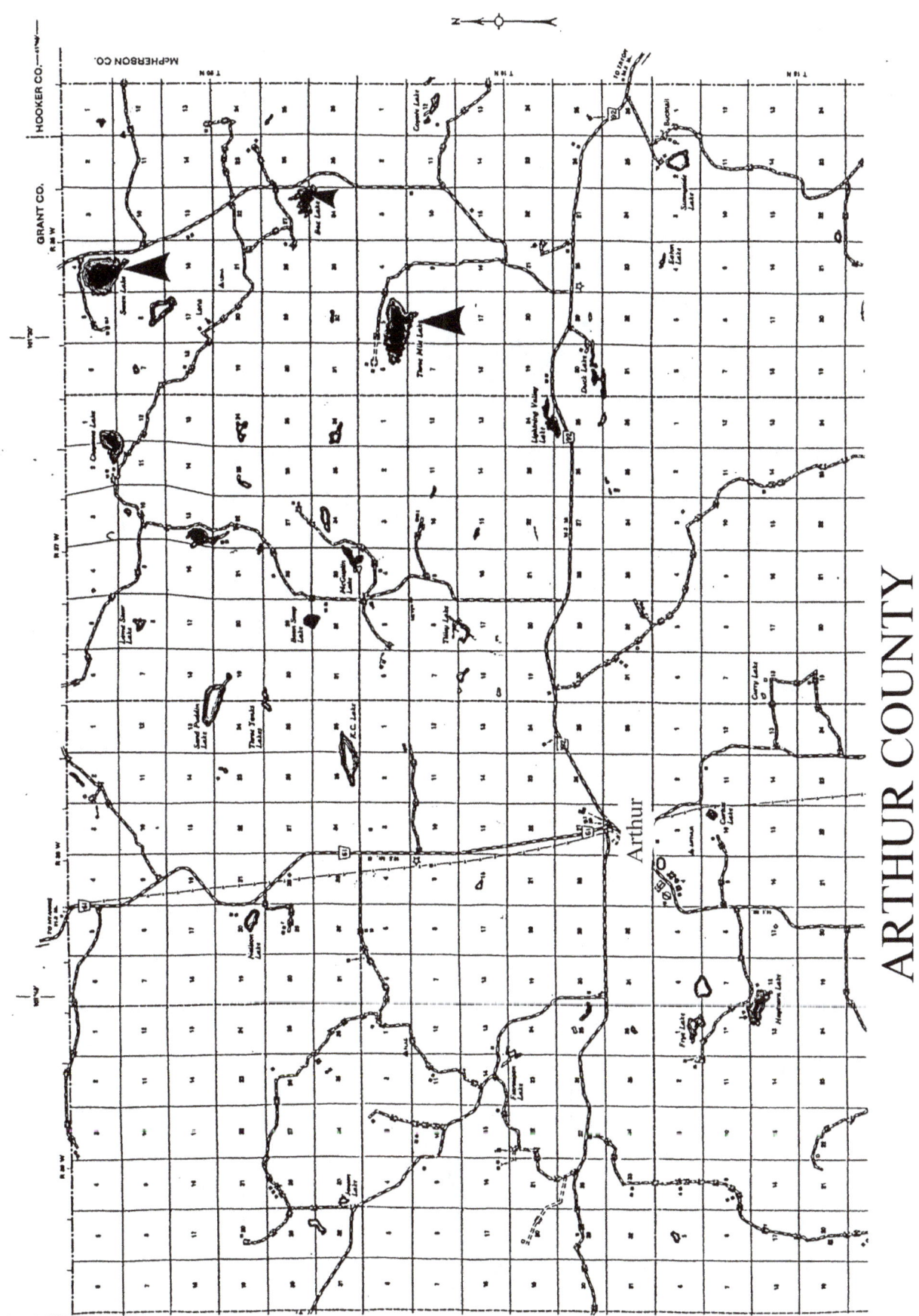

12. Arthur County

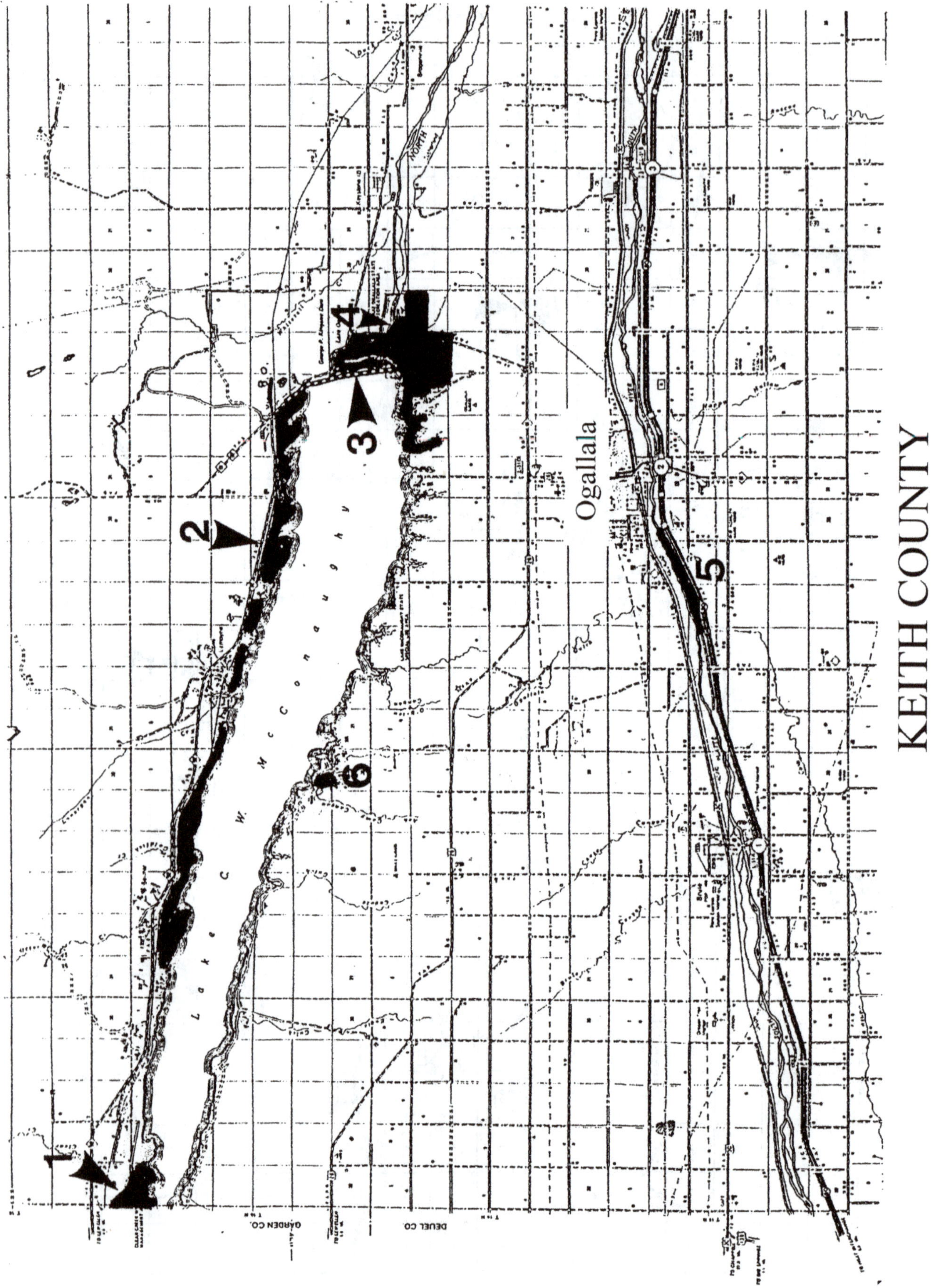

MAP 13 — KEITH COUNTY

13. Keith County

MAP 14 — LINCOLN COUNTY

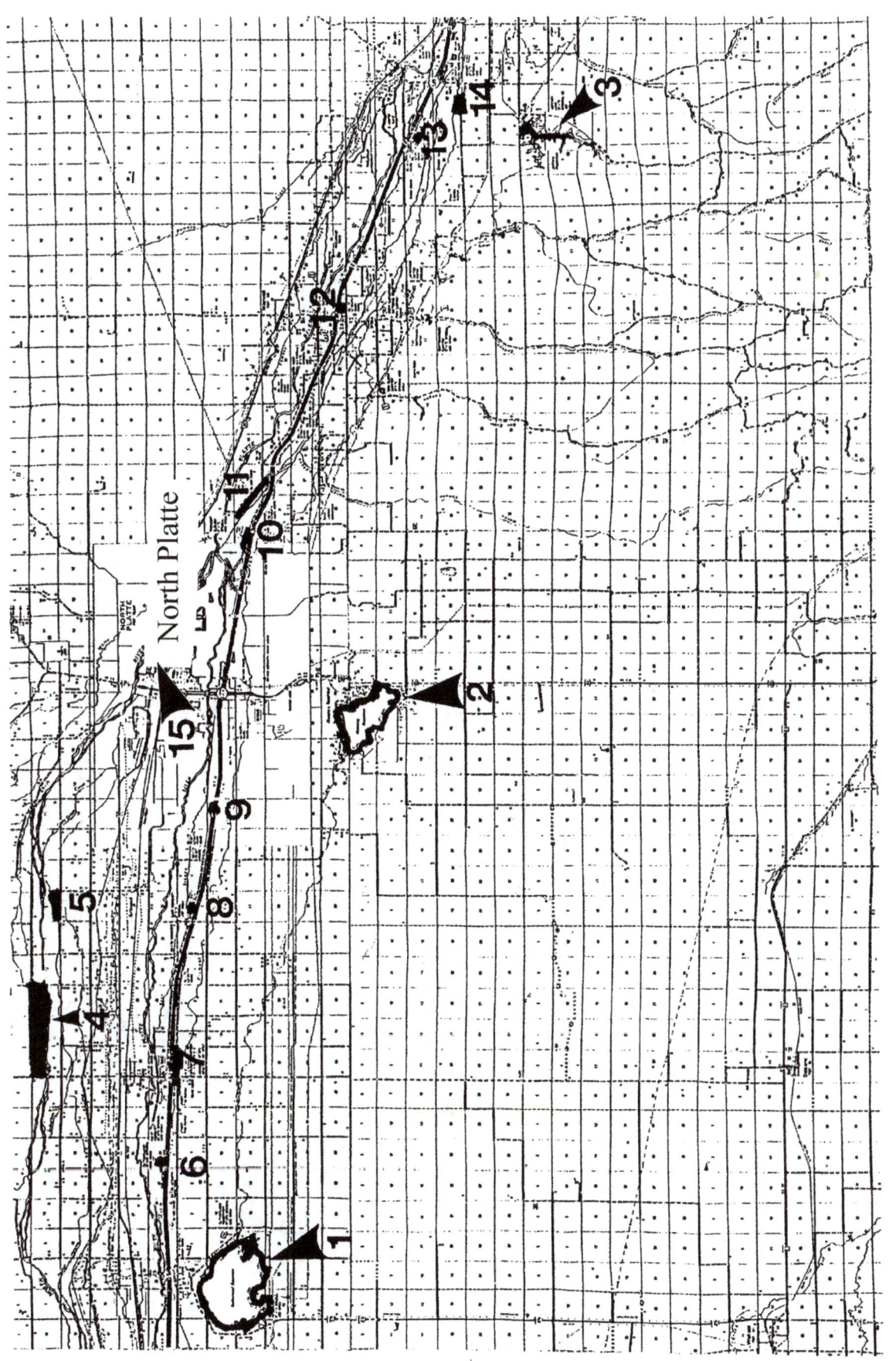

14. Lincoln County

MAP 15 — DAWSON COUNTY

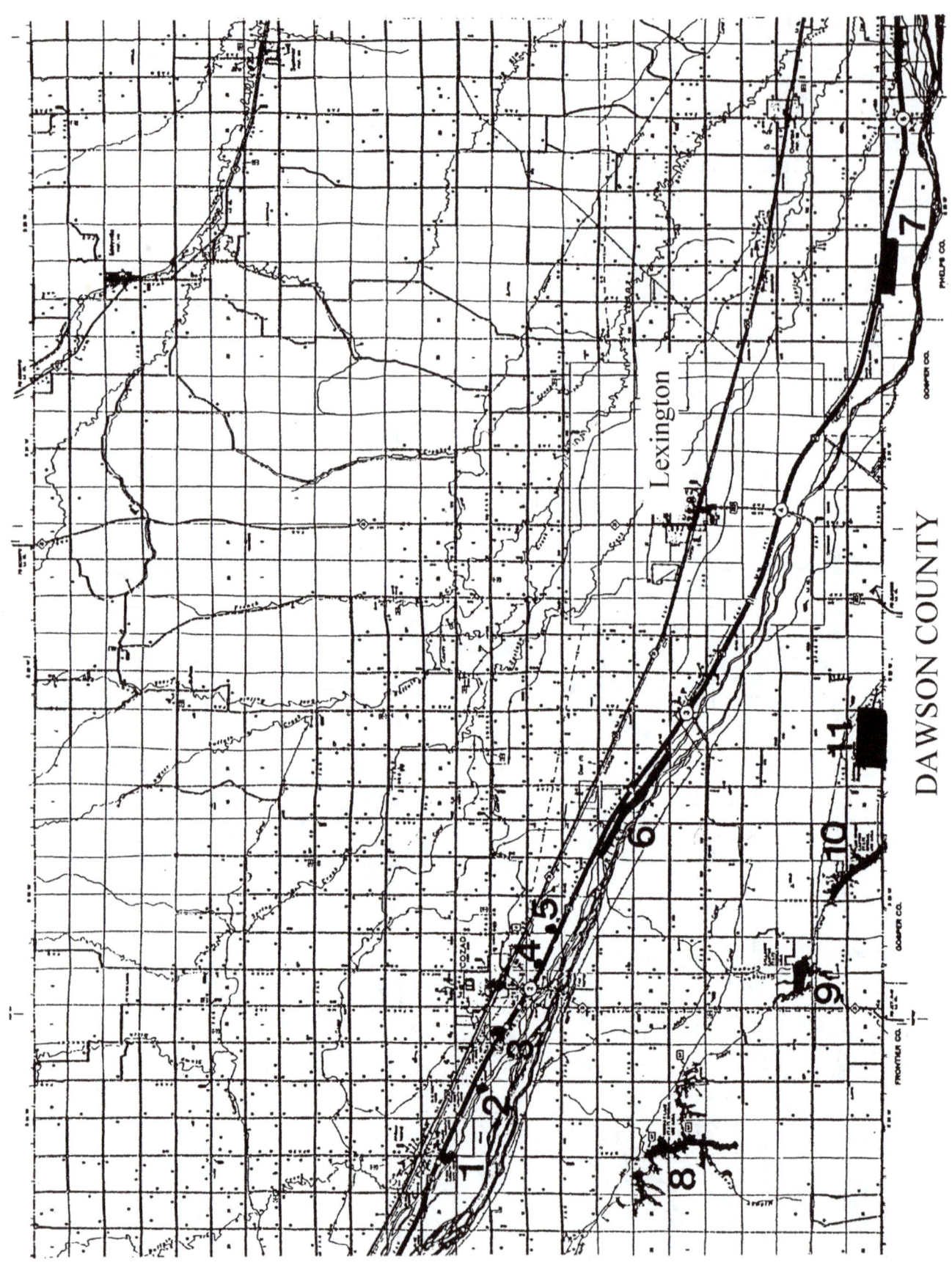

15. Dawson County

MAP 16 — CHASE COUNTY

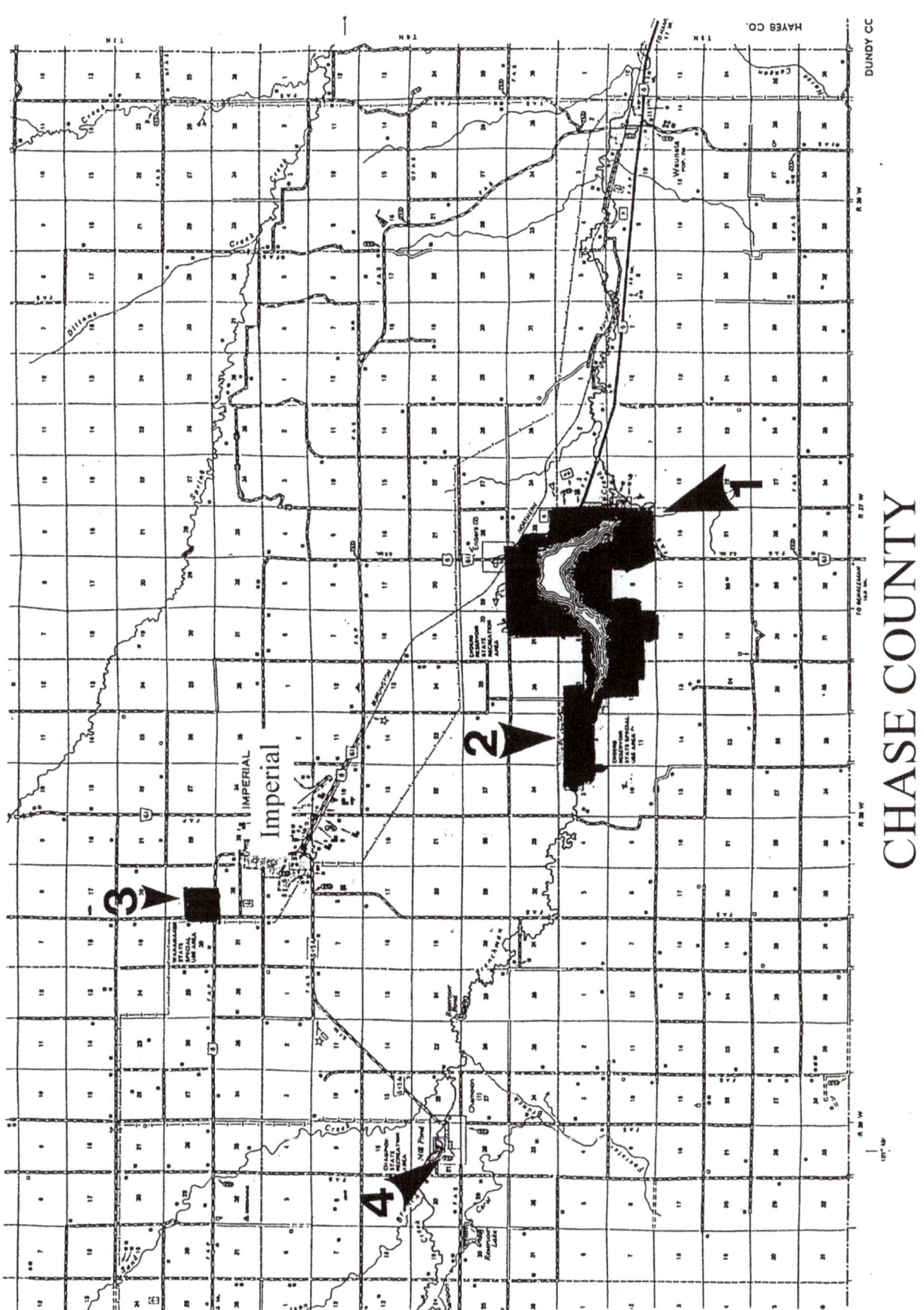

16. *Chase County*

MAP 17 — FRONTIER COUNTY

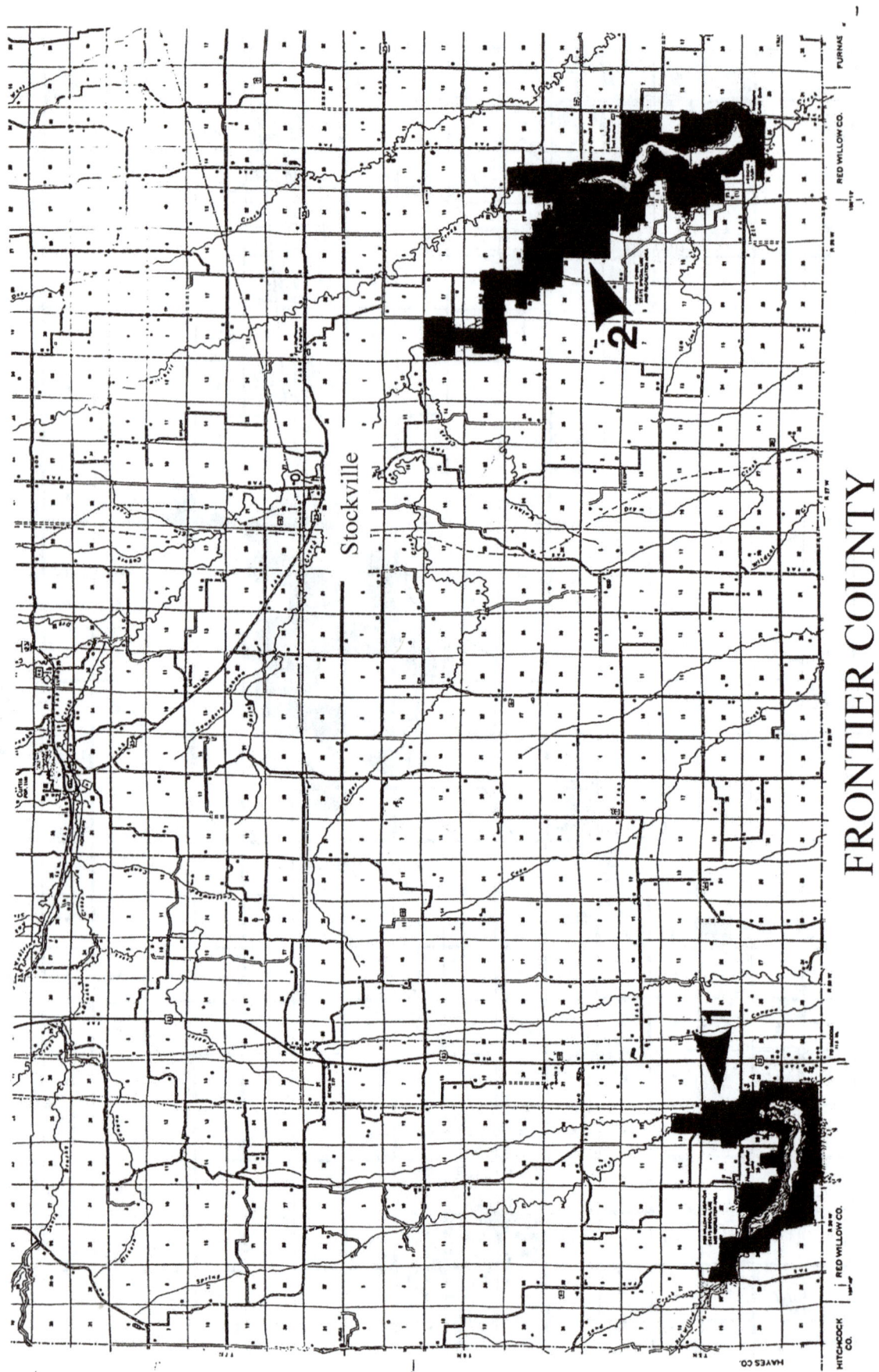

17. Frontier County

MAP 18 — GOSPER & PHELPS COUNTIES

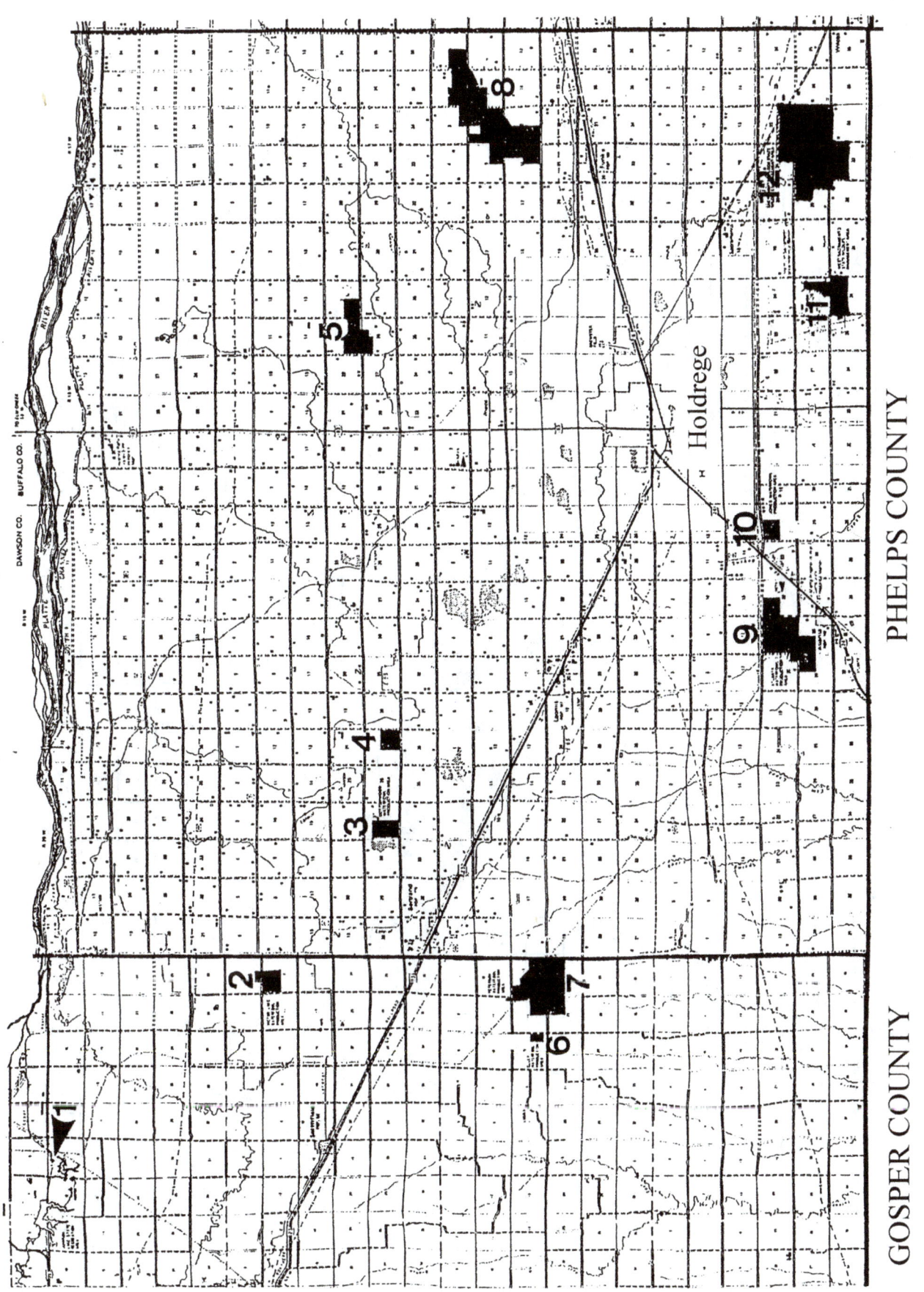

18. Gosper and Phelps Counties

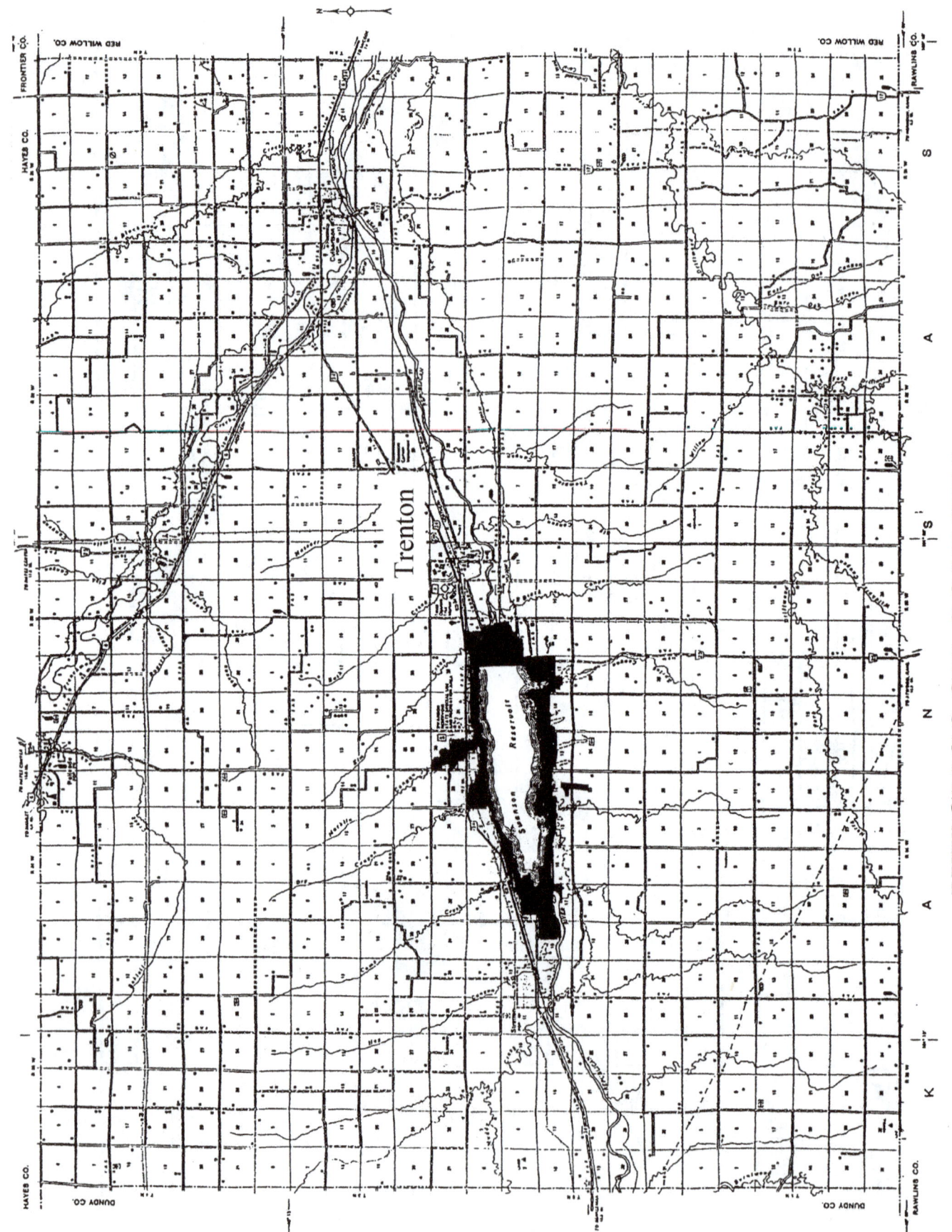

19. Hitchcock County

MAP 20 — HARLAN COUNTY

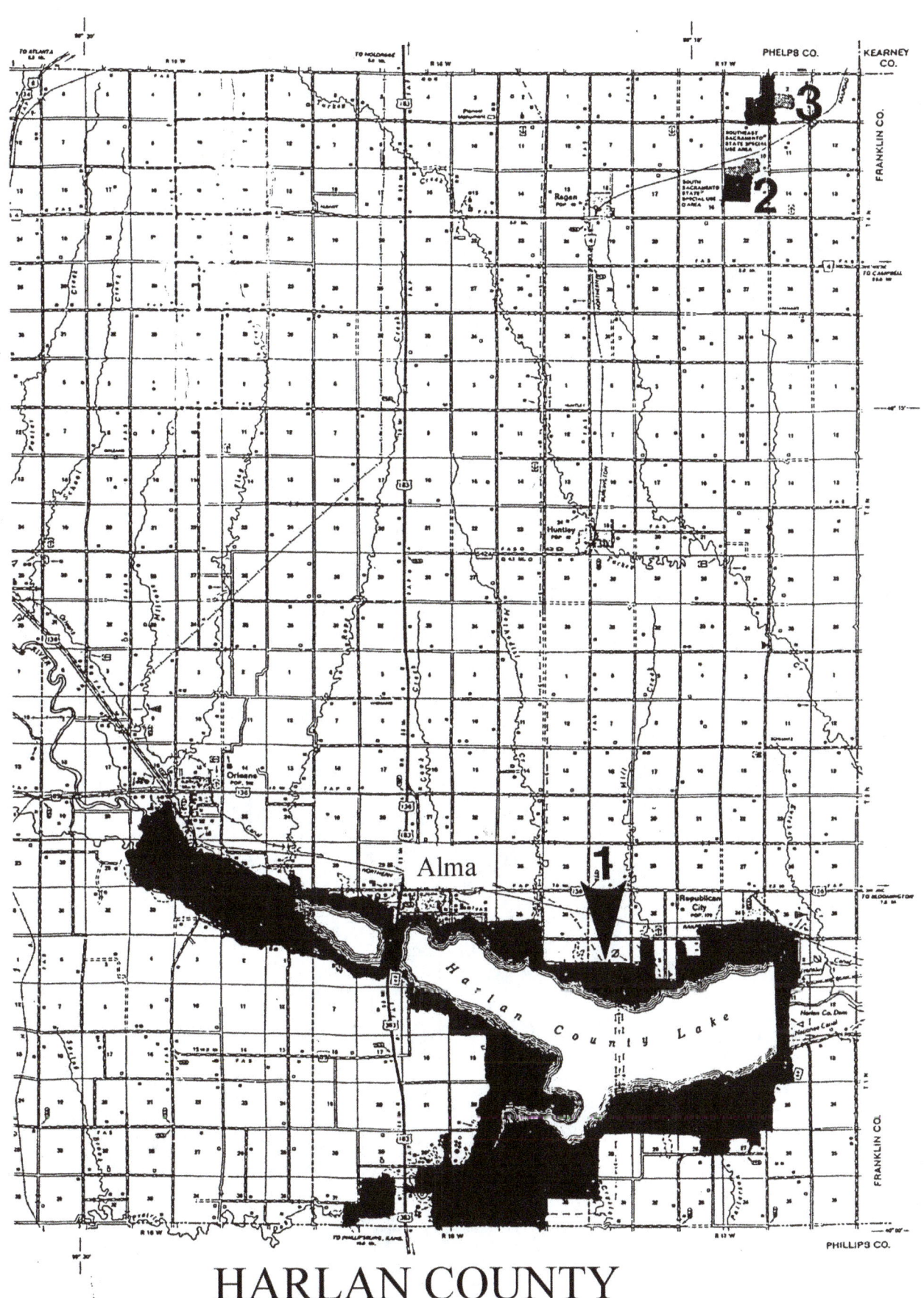

HARLAN COUNTY

20. Harlan County

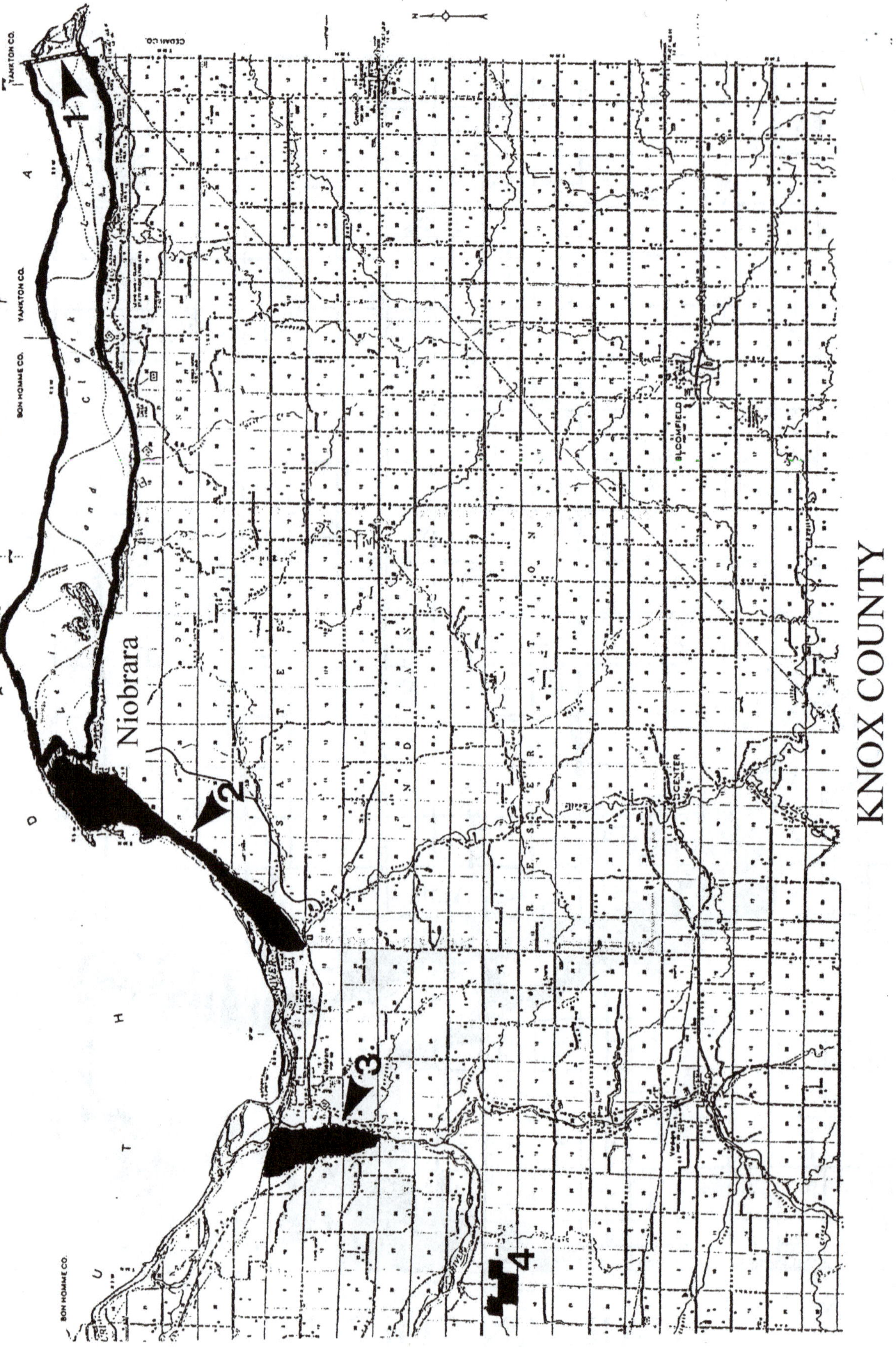

MAP 21 — KNOX COUNTY

21. Knox County

MAP 22 — ANTELOPE COUNTY

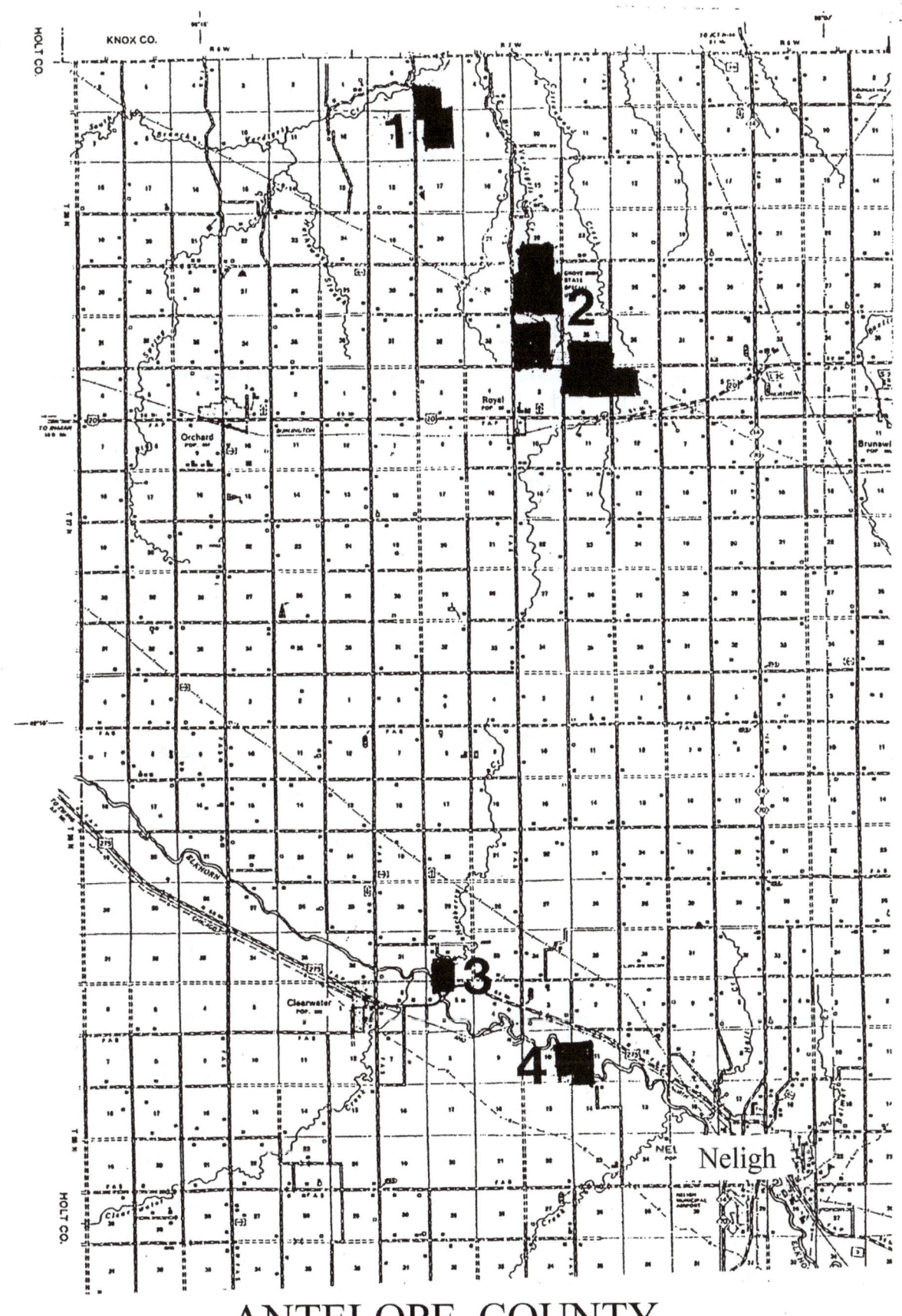

ANTELOPE COUNTY

22. Antelope County

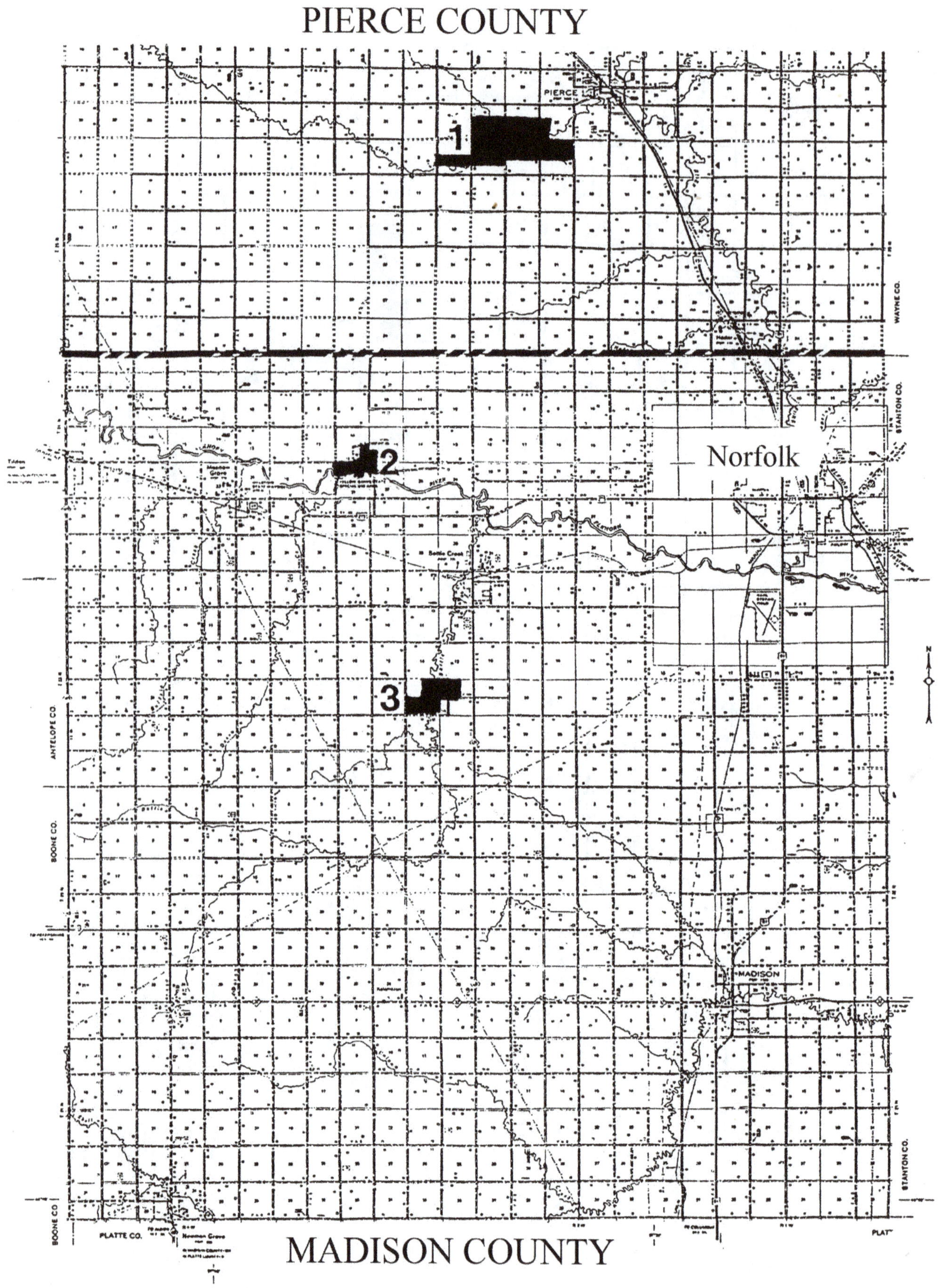

118

MAP 23 — PIERCE & MADISON COUNTIES

PIERCE COUNTY

MADISON COUNTY

23. Pierce and Madison Counties

MAP 24 — PLATTE, NANCE, & MERRICK COUNTIES

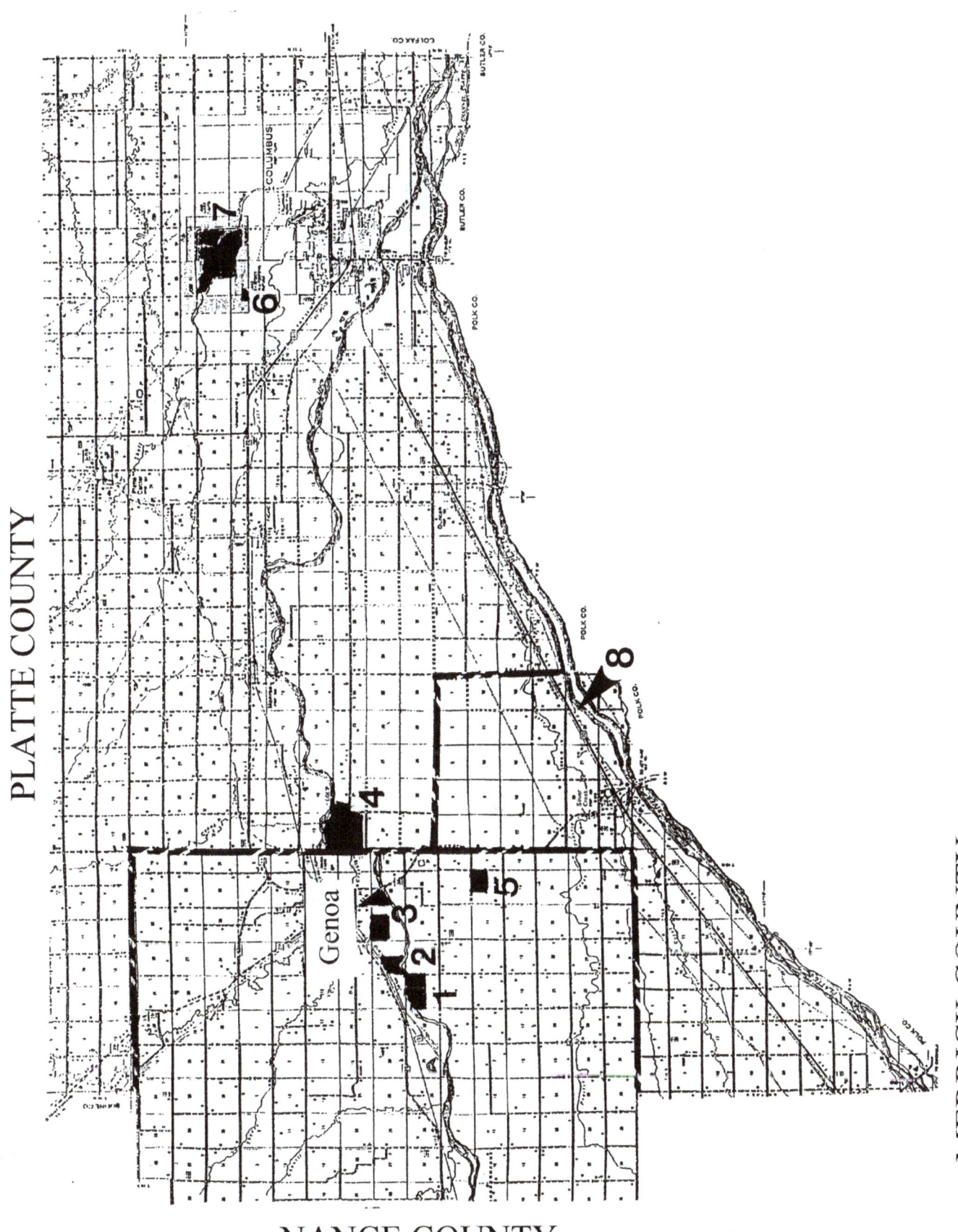

24. Platte, Nance, and Merrick Counties

MAP 25 — SHERMAN COUNTY

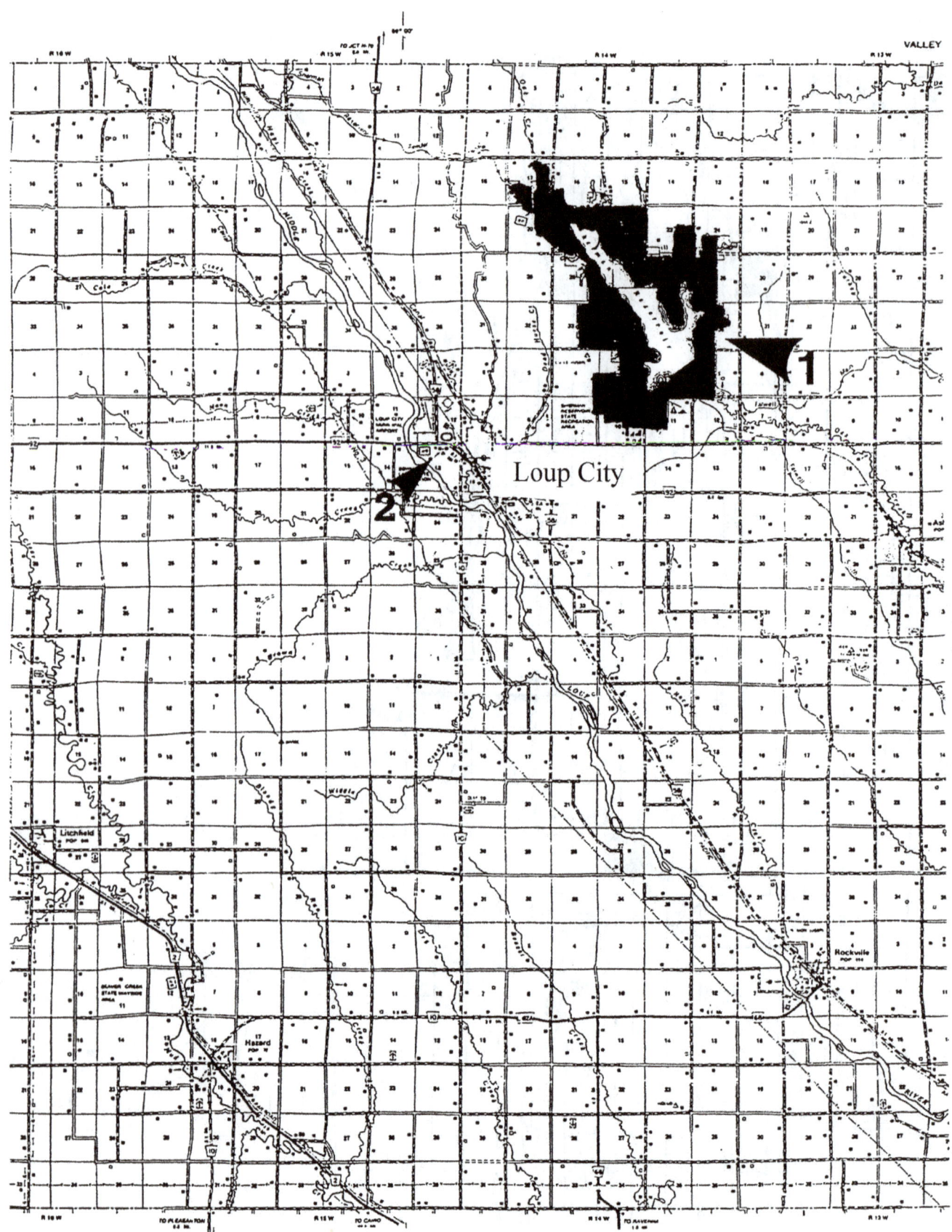

SHERMAN COUNTY

25. Sherman County

MAP 26 — BUFFALO COUNTY

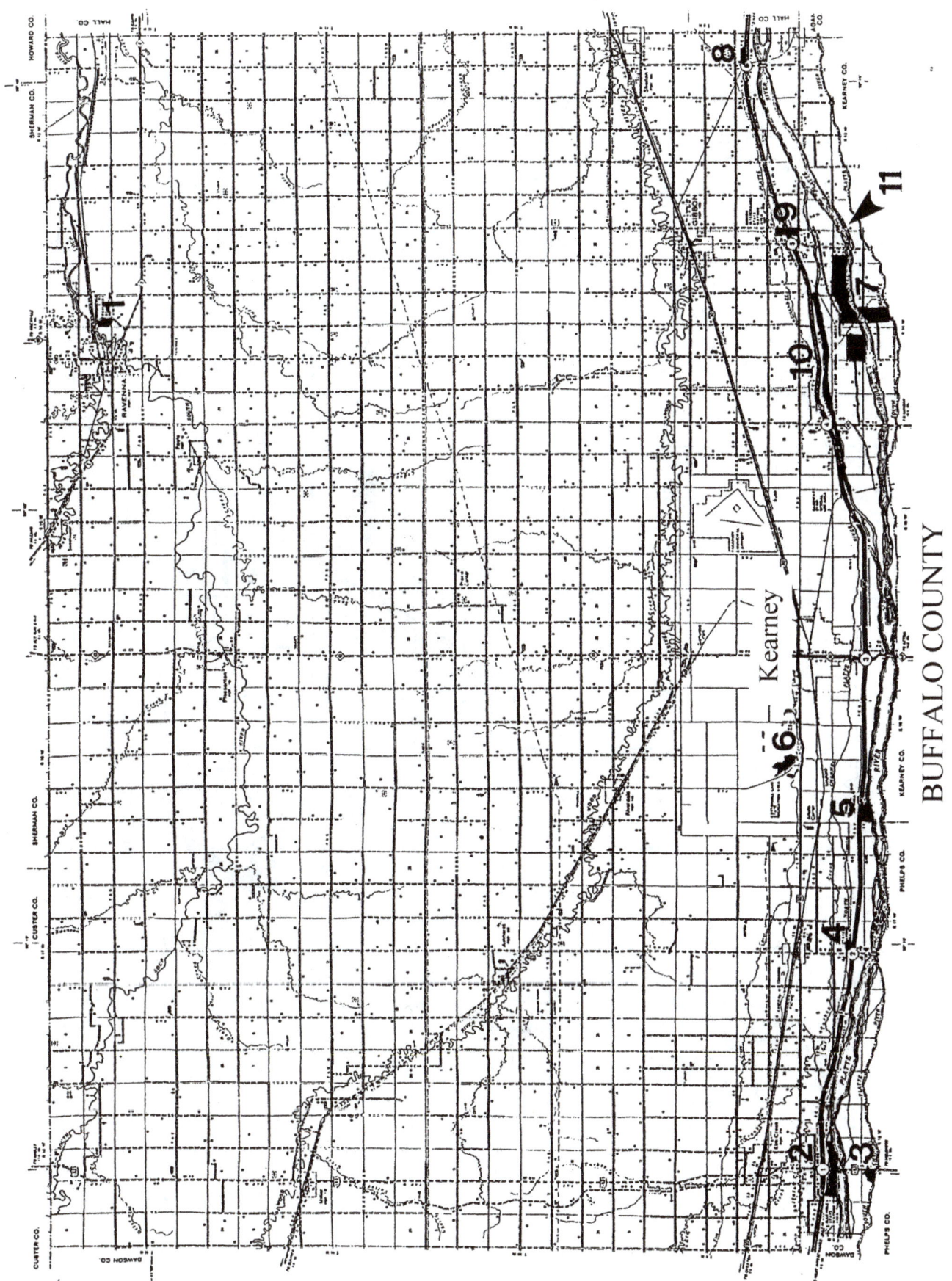

26. Buffalo County

MAP 27 — HALL COUNTY

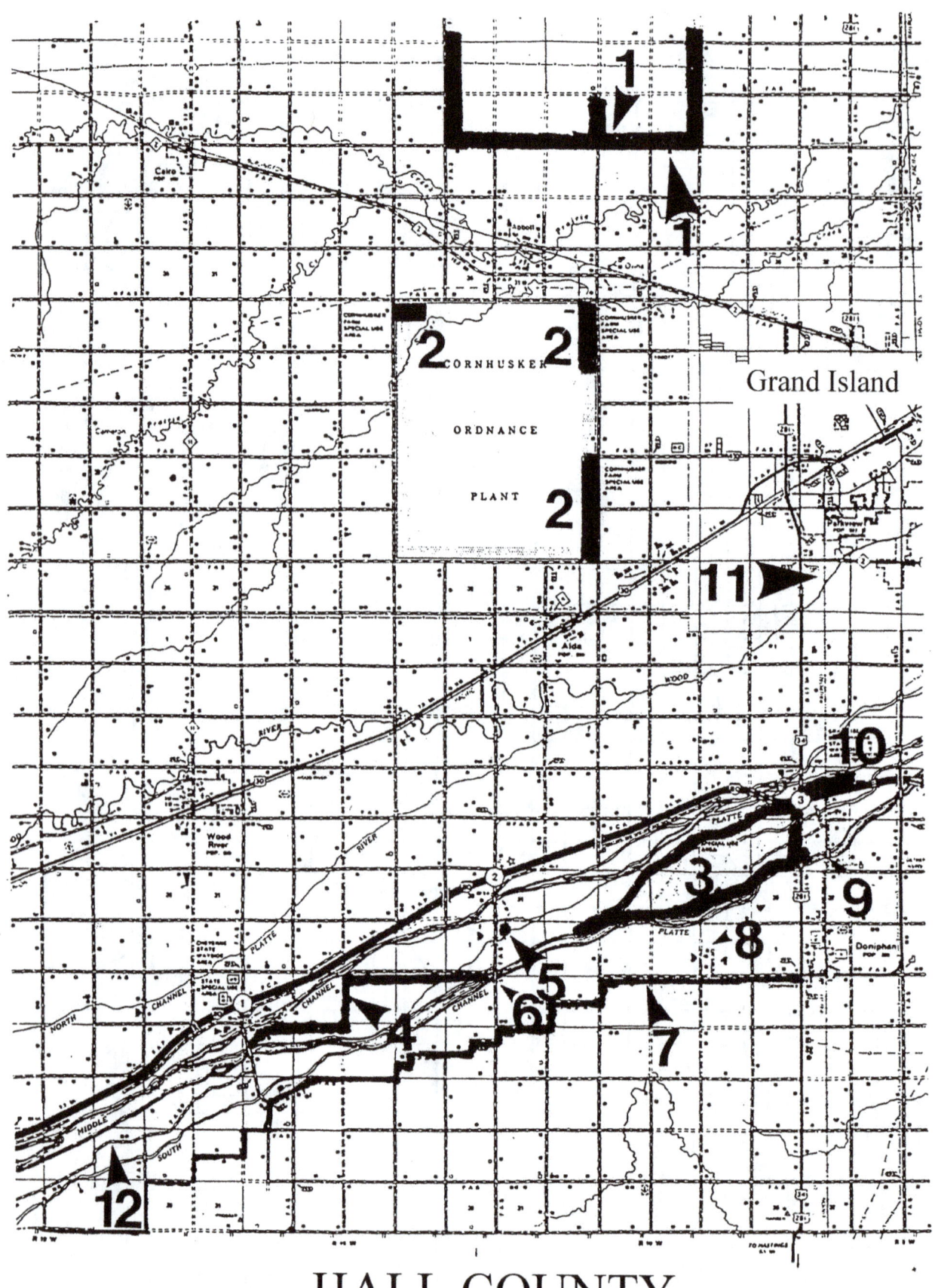

HALL COUNTY

27. Hall County

MAP 28 — HAMILTON & CLAY COUNTIES

HAMILTON COUNTY

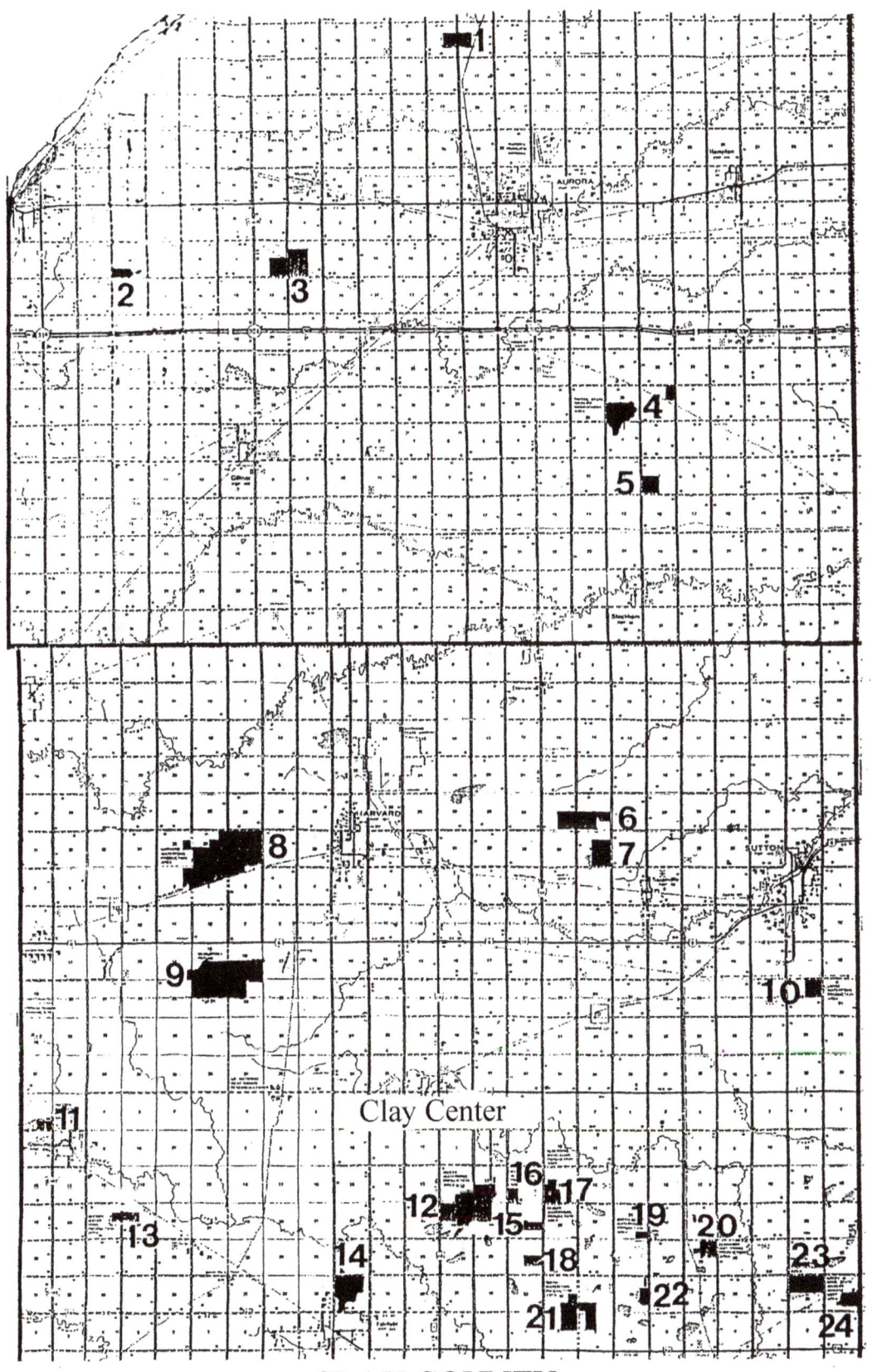

CLAY COUNTY

28. Hamilton and Clay Counties

MAP 29 — YORK, FILLMORE, & SEWARD COUNTIES

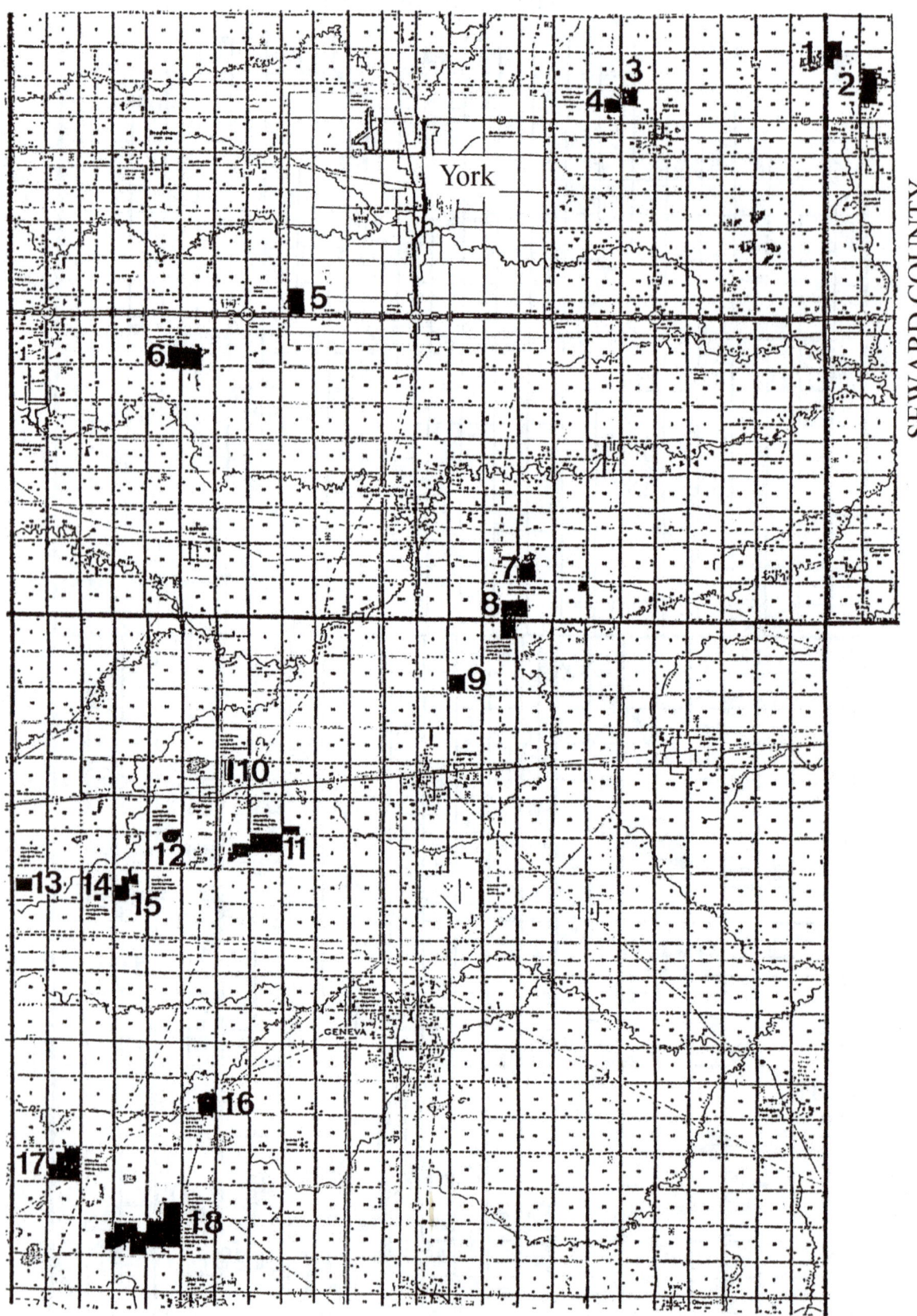

29. York, Fillmore, and Seward Counties

MAP 30 — KEARNEY & FRANKLIN COUNTIES

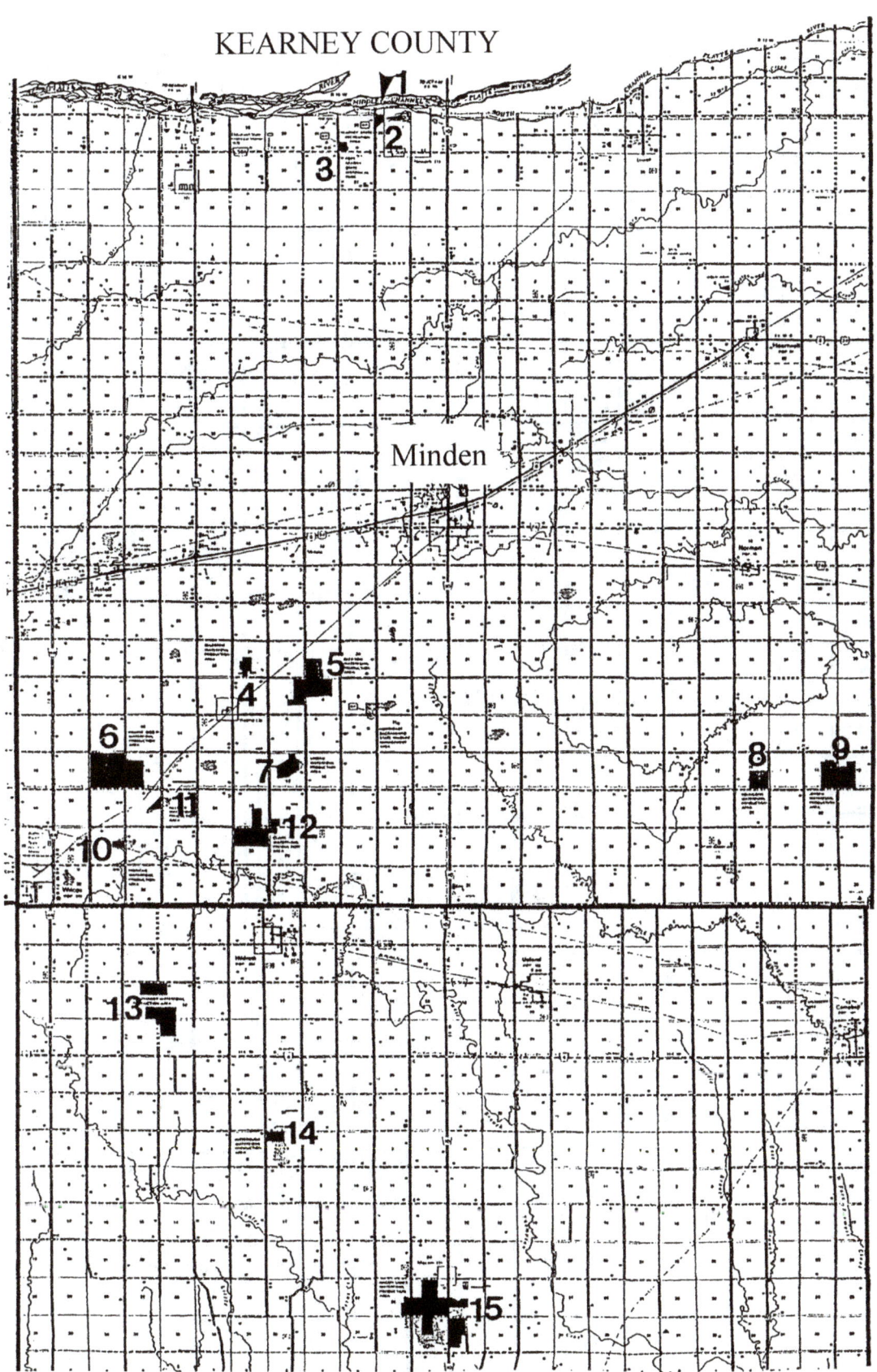

30. Kearney and Franklin Counties

MAP 31 — ADAMS COUNTY

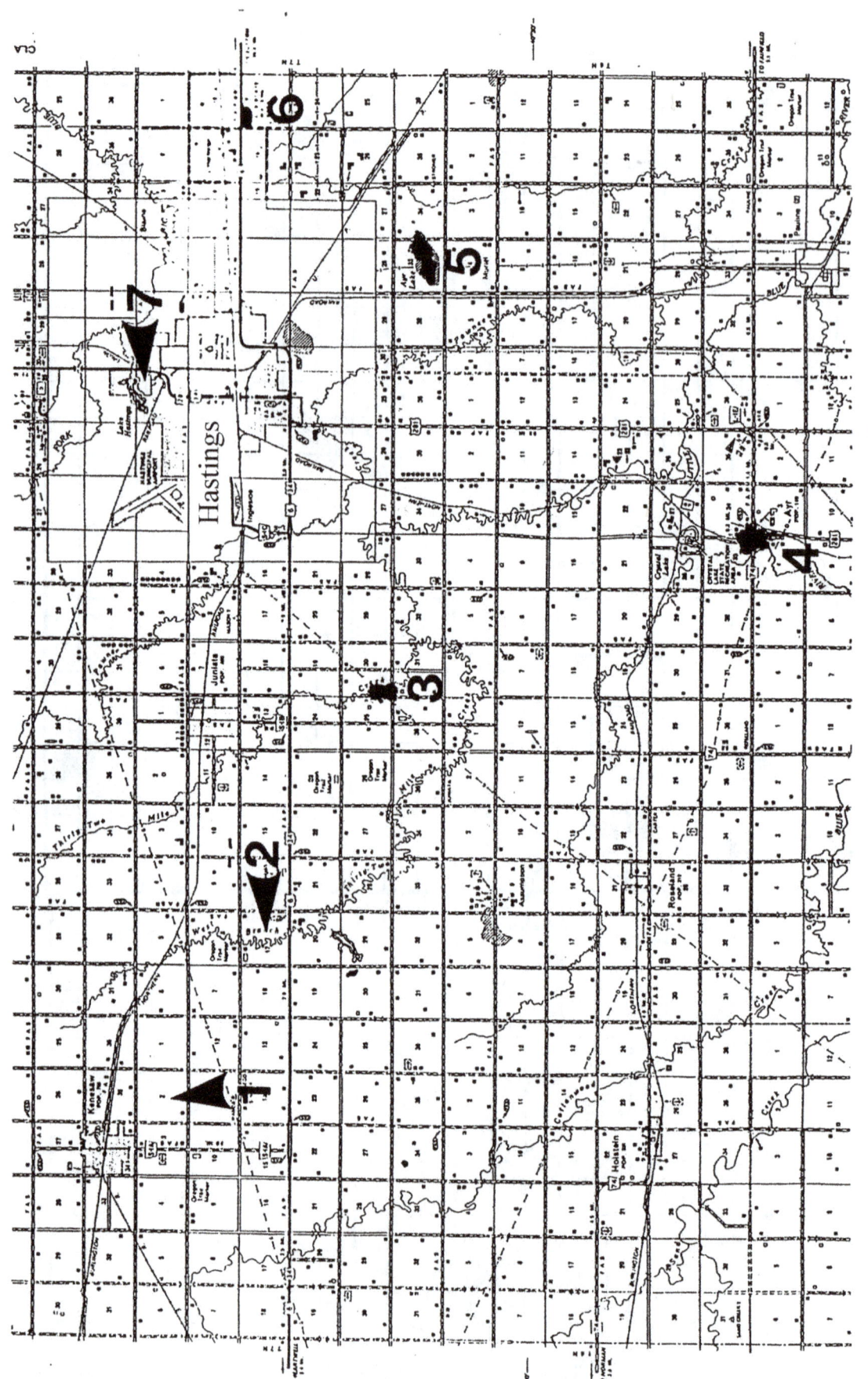

31. Adams County

MAP 32 — DIXON & DAKOTA COUNTIES

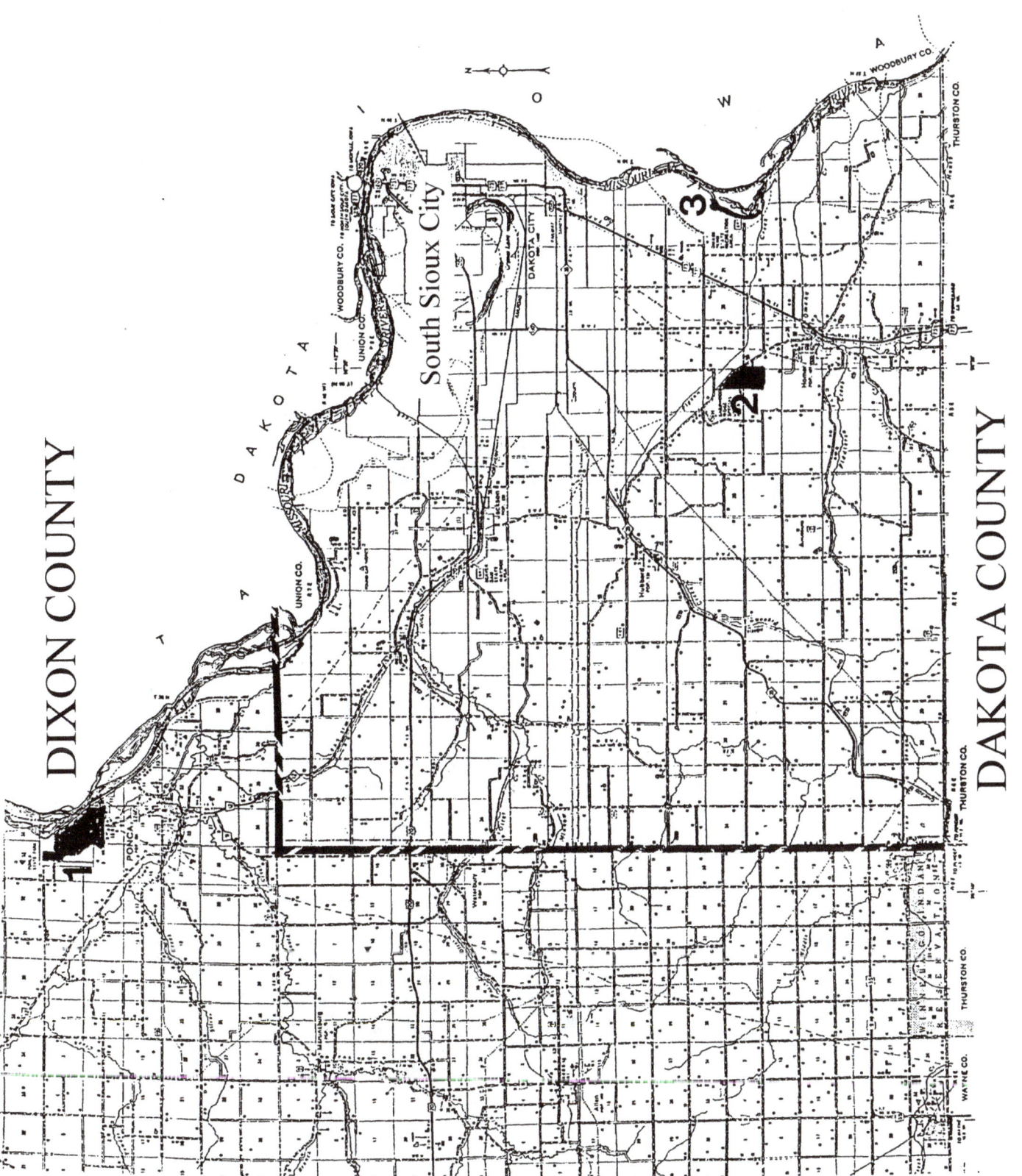

32. Dixon and Dakota Counties

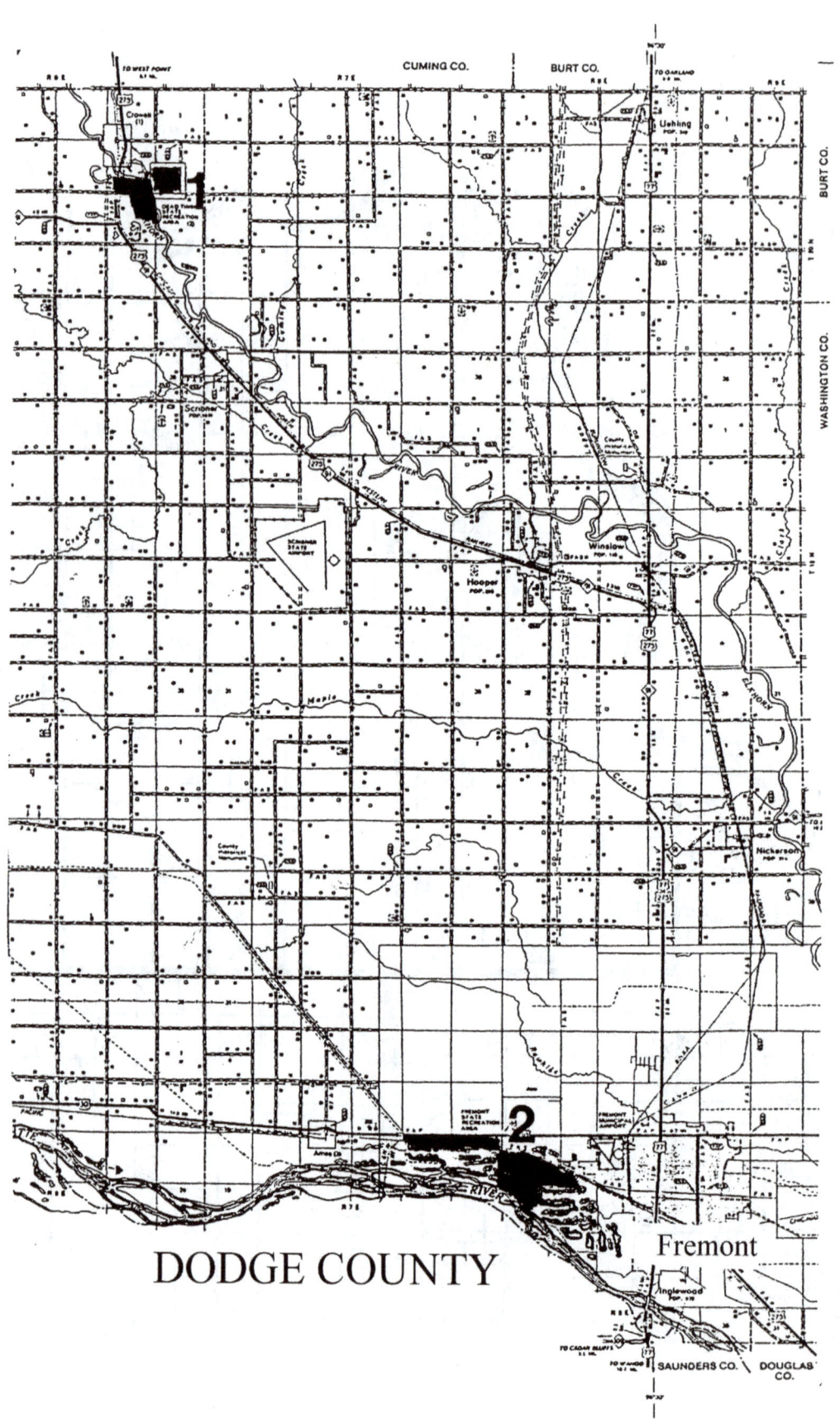

33. Dodge County

MAP 34 — WASHINGTON COUNTY

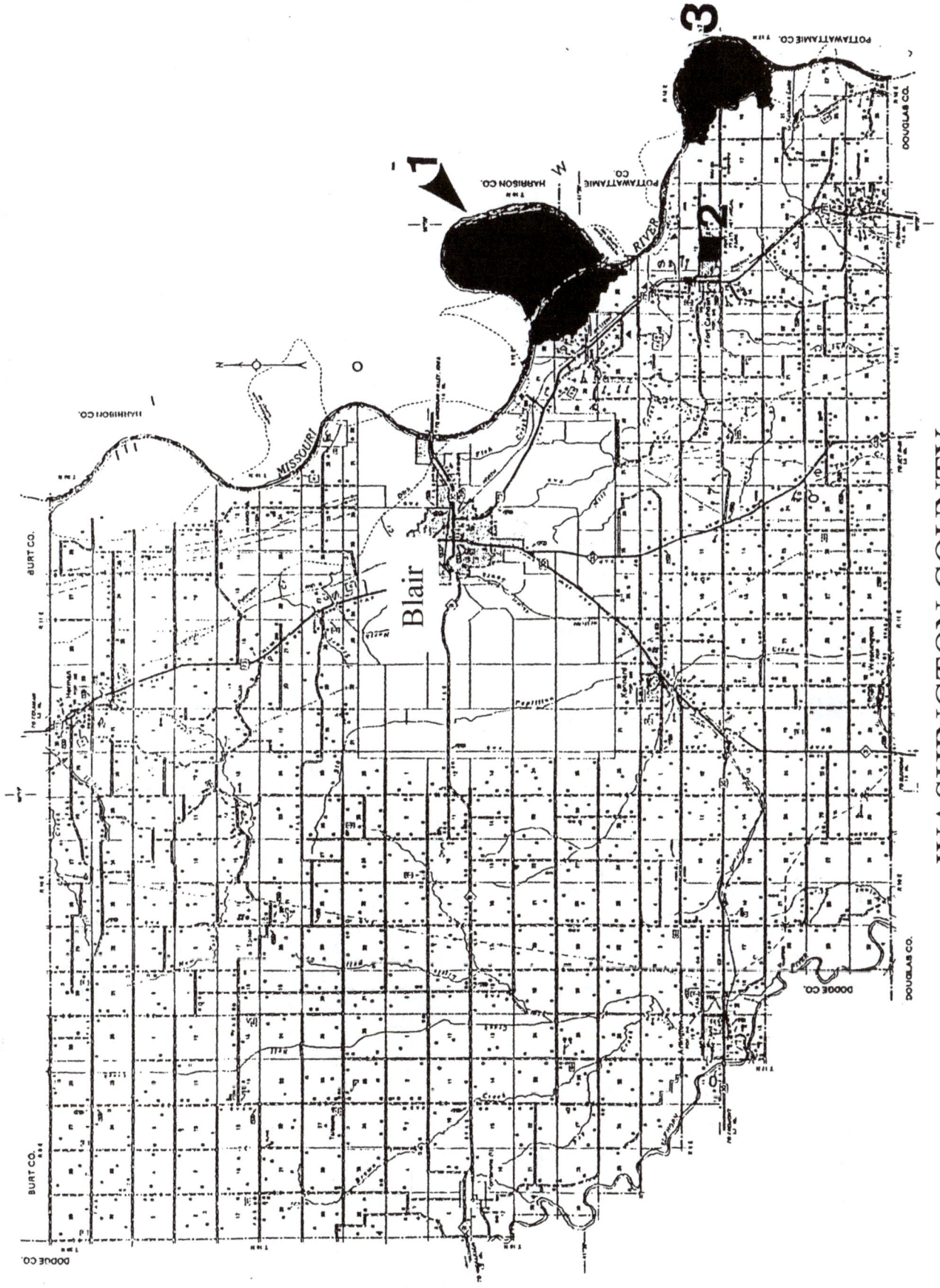

34. Washington County

MAP 35 — SAUNDERS & LANCASTER COUNTIES

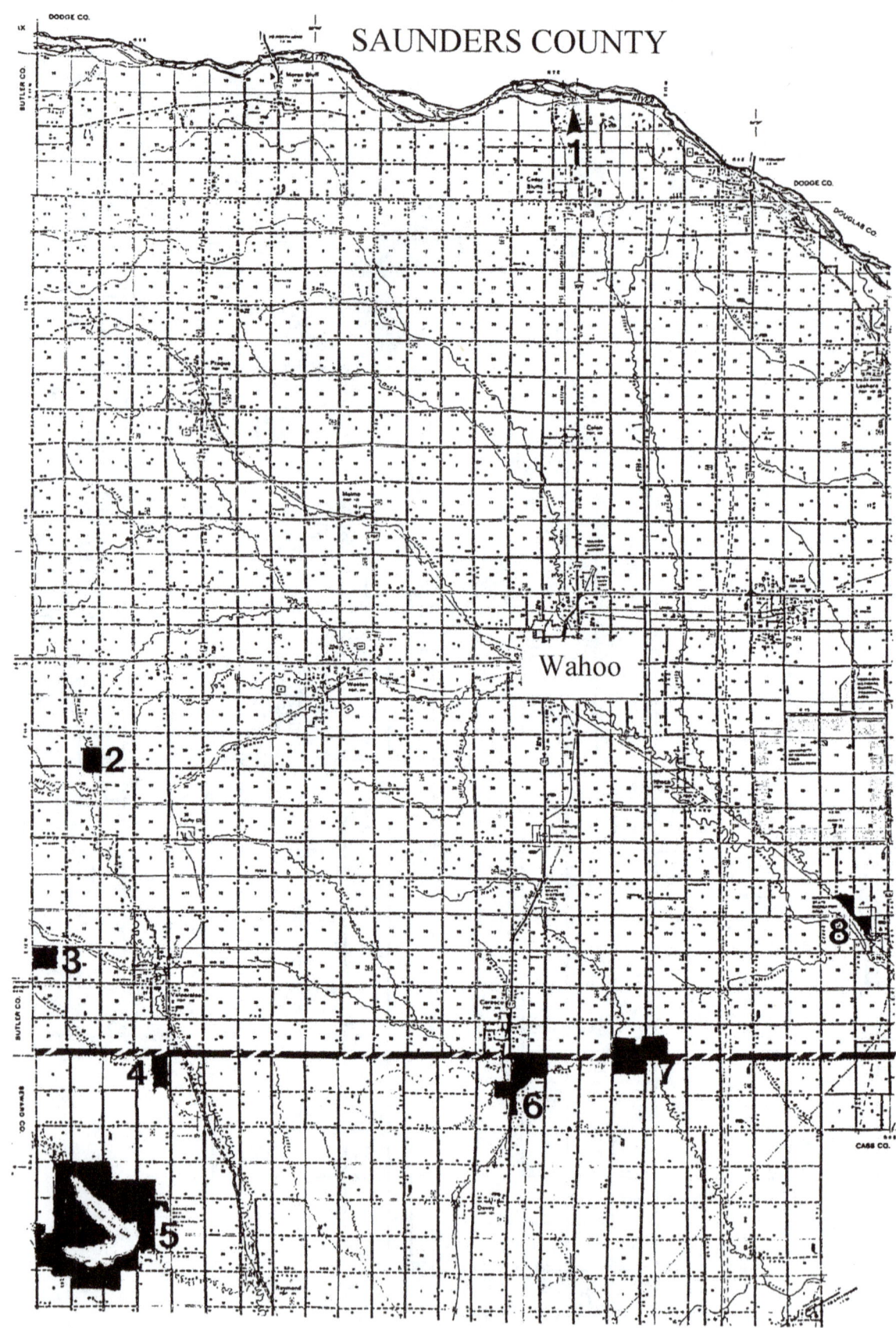

35. Saunders and Lancaster Counties

MAP 36 — DOUGLAS & SARPY COUNTIES

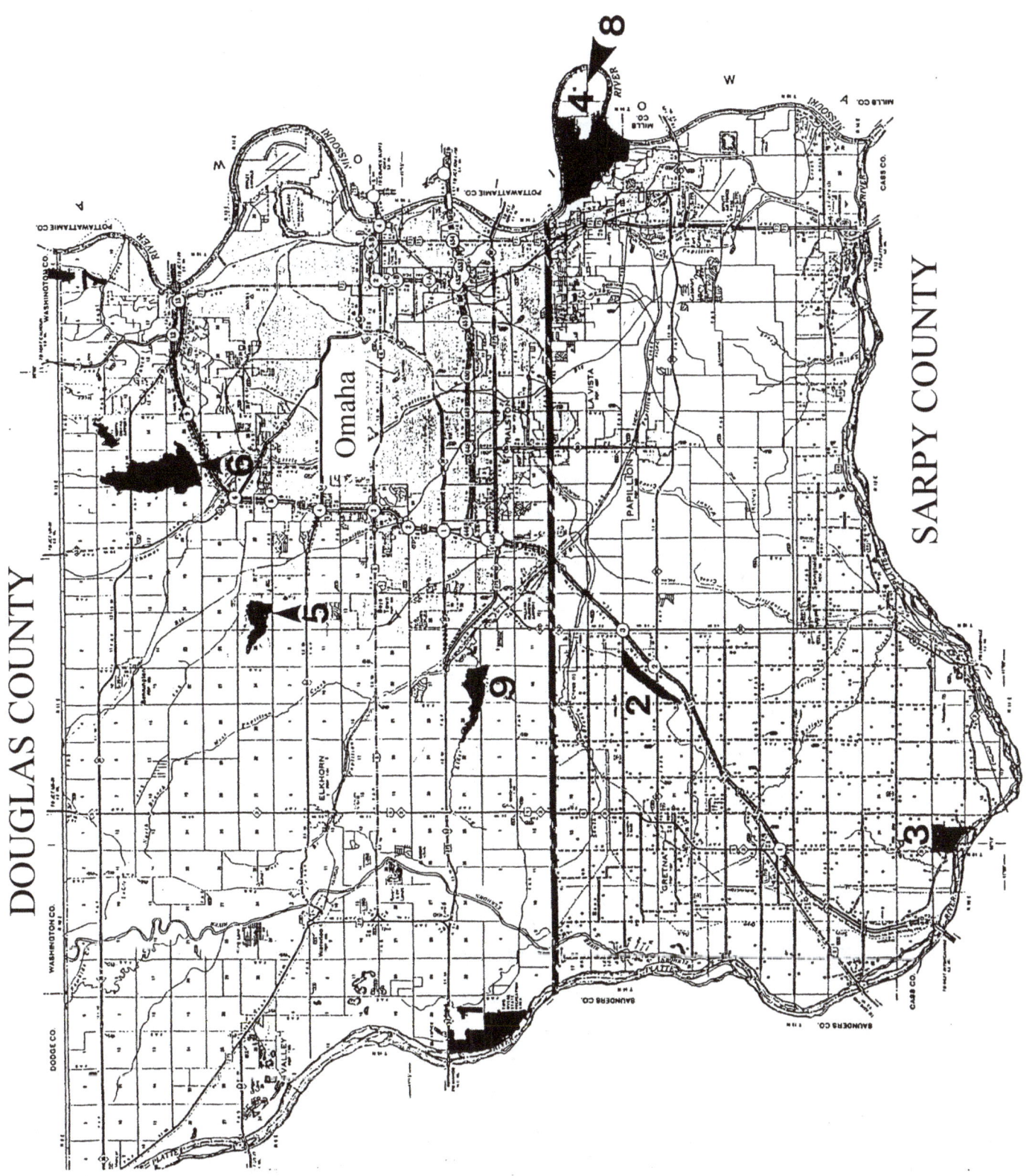

36. Douglas and Sarpy Counties

132

MAP 37 – SEWARD COUNTY

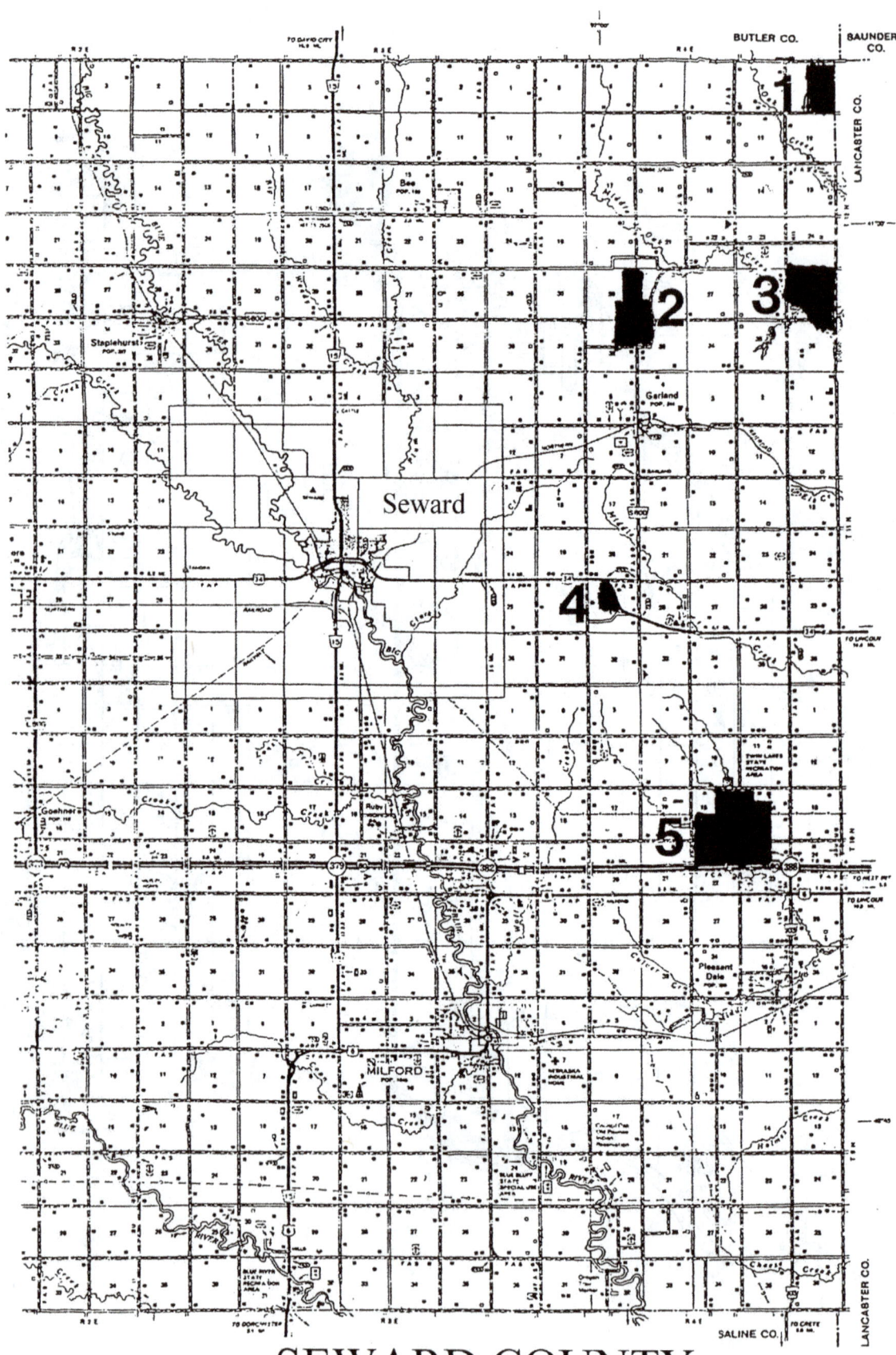

SEWARD COUNTY

37. Seward County

MAP 38 — LANCASTER COUNTY

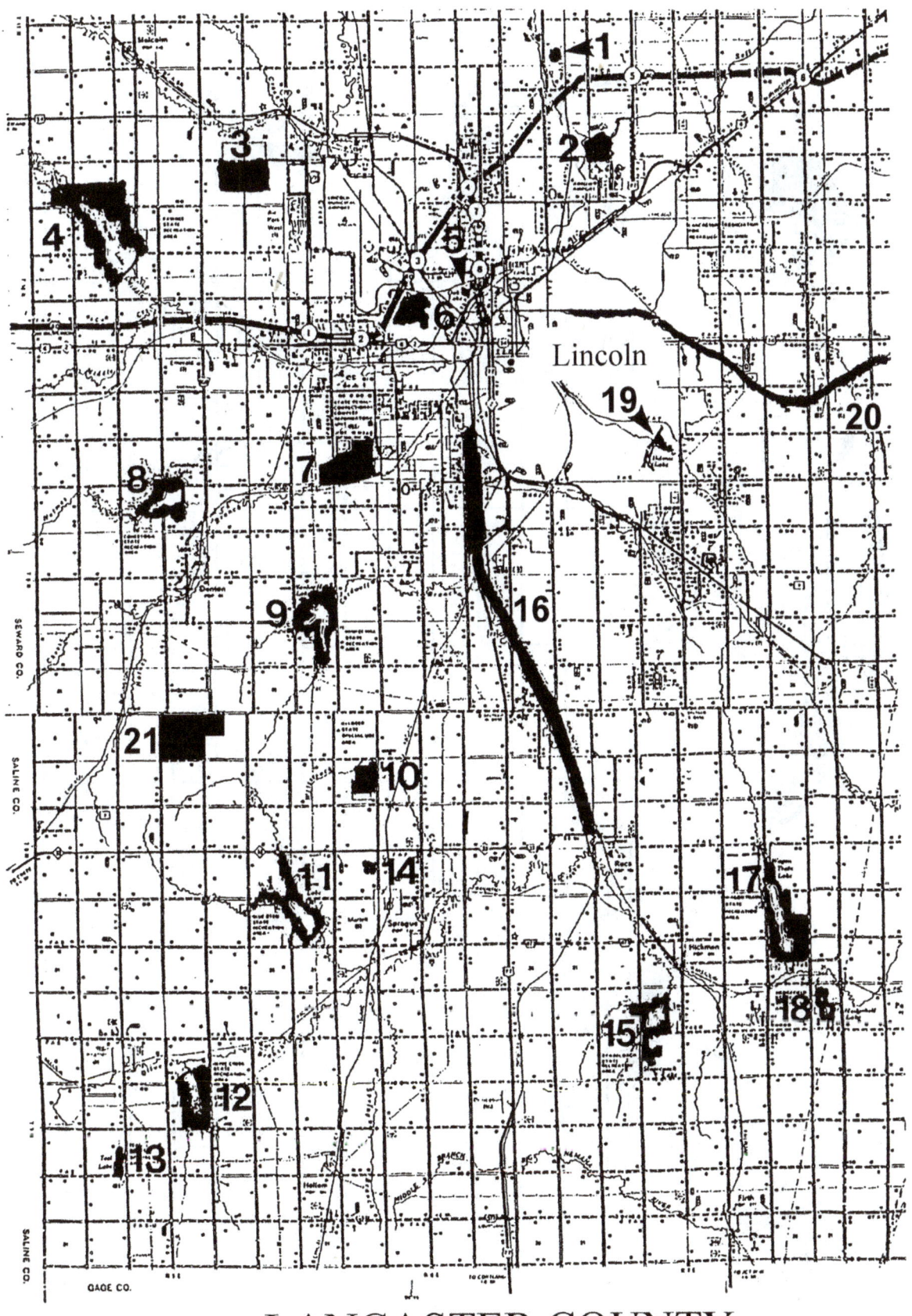

LANCASTER COUNTY

38. Lancaster County

MAP 39 — CASS COUNTY

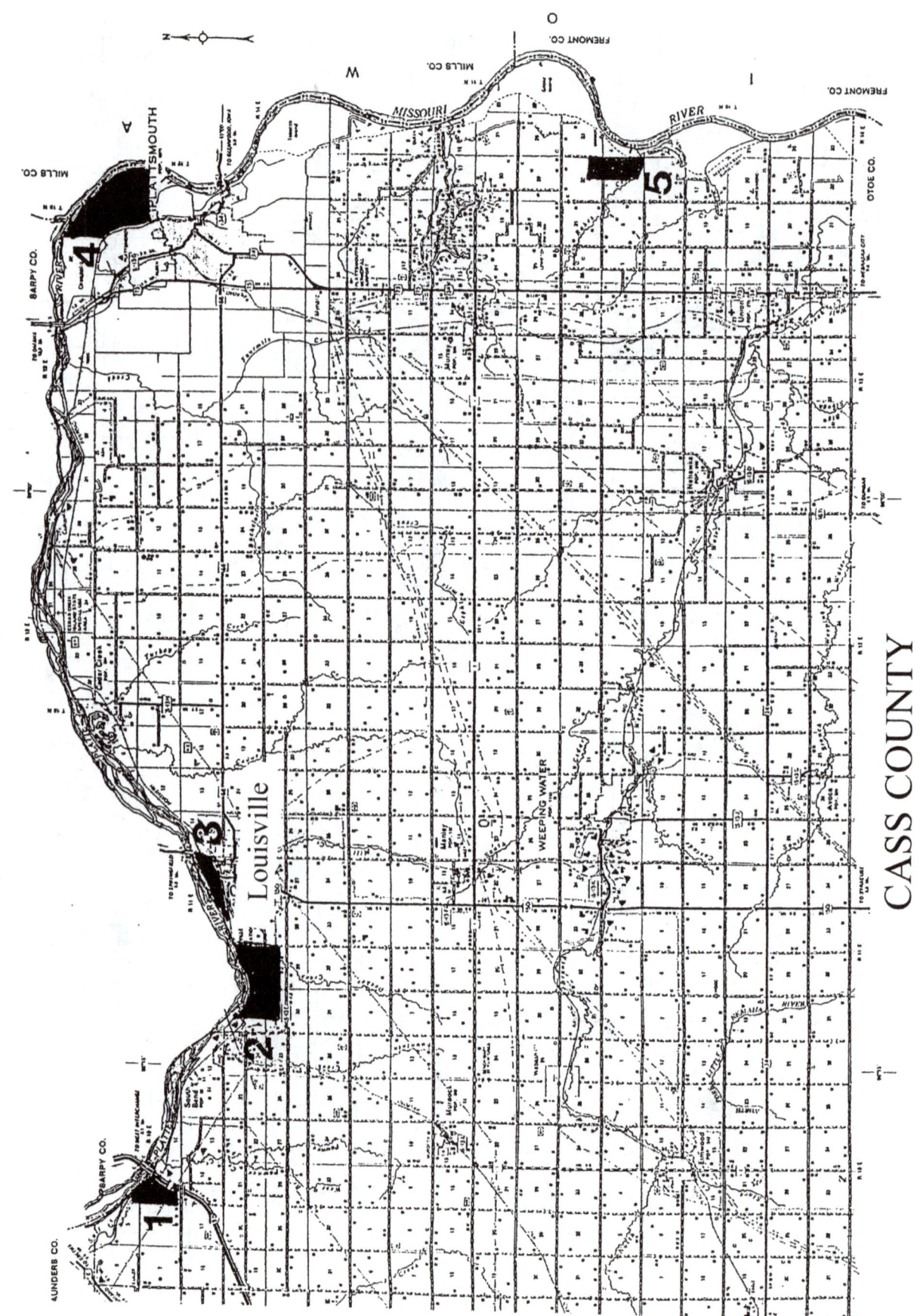

39. Cass County

MAP 40 — OTOE COUNTY

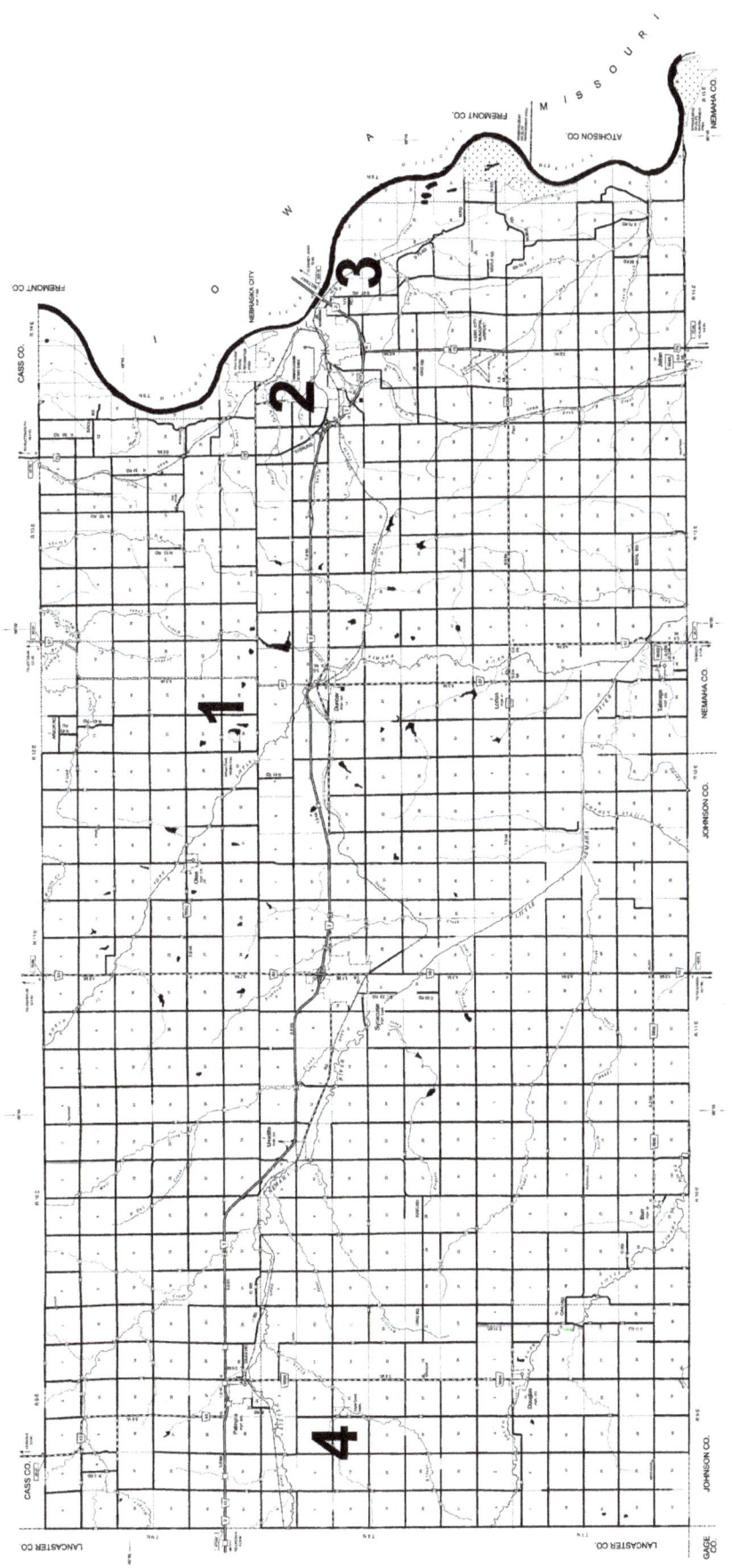

40. Otoe County

MAP 41 — GAGE COUNTY

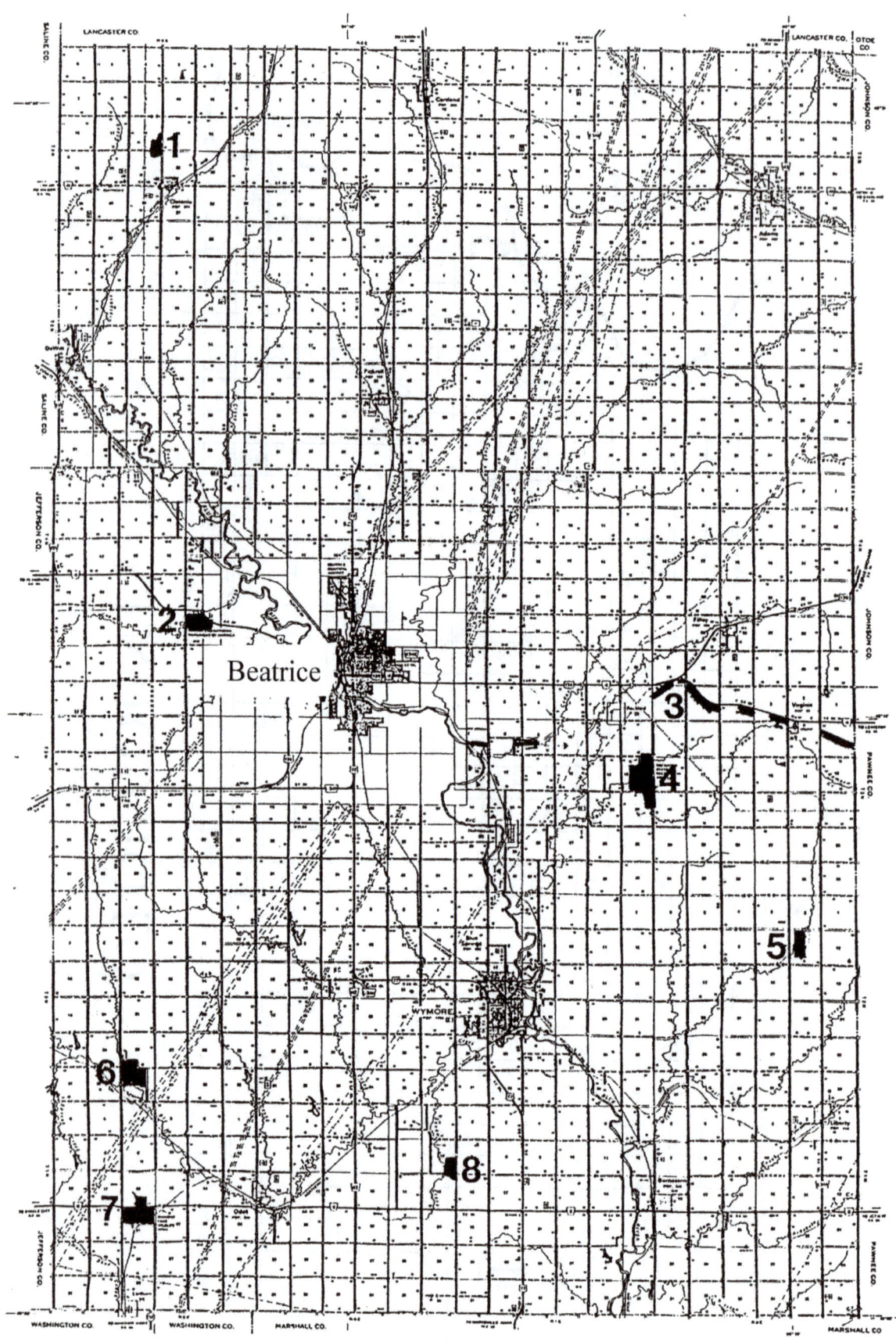

GAGE COUNTY

41. Gage County

MAP 42 — JOHNSON COUNTY

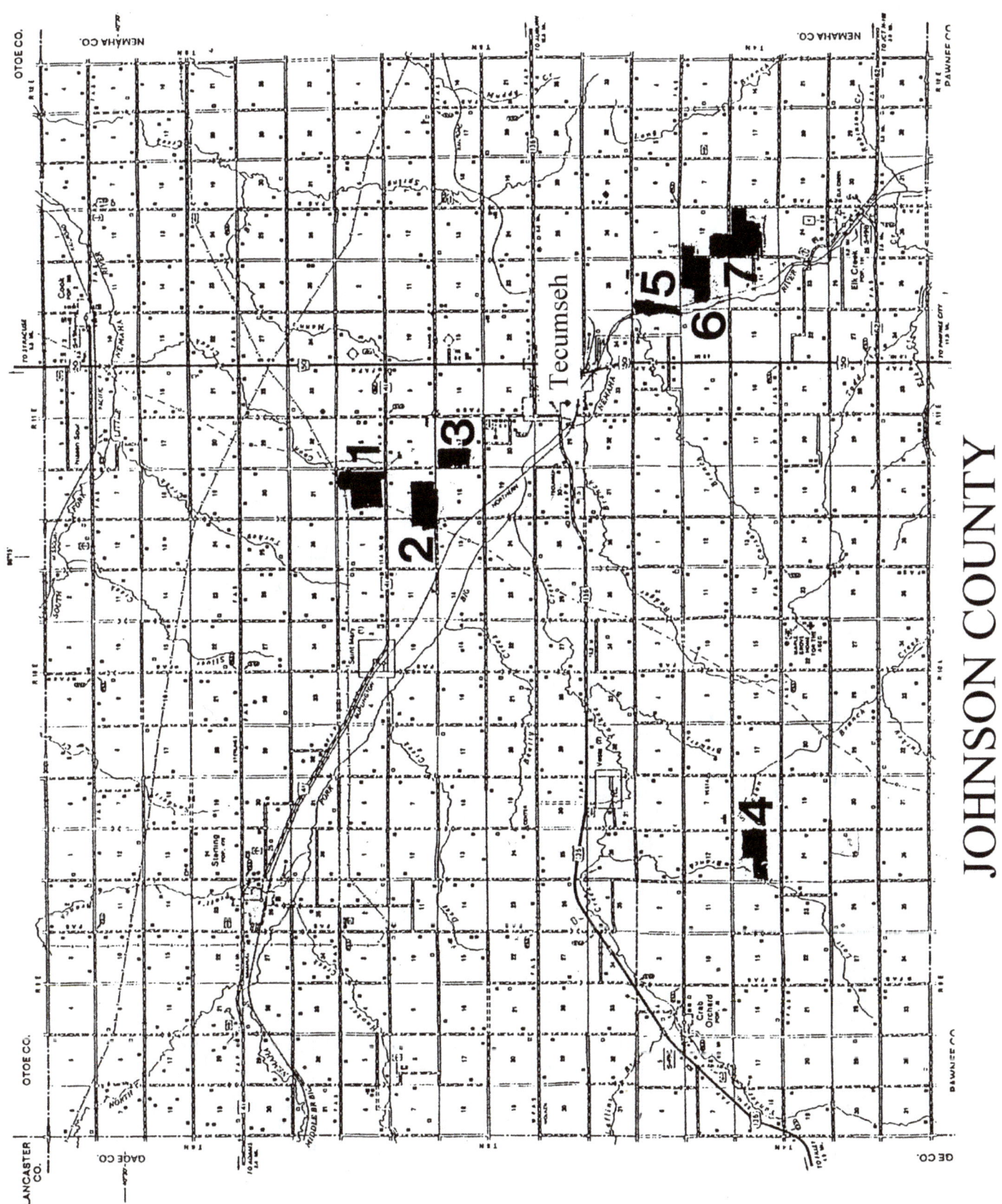

42. Johnson County

MAP 43 — NEMAHA & RICHARDSON COUNTIES

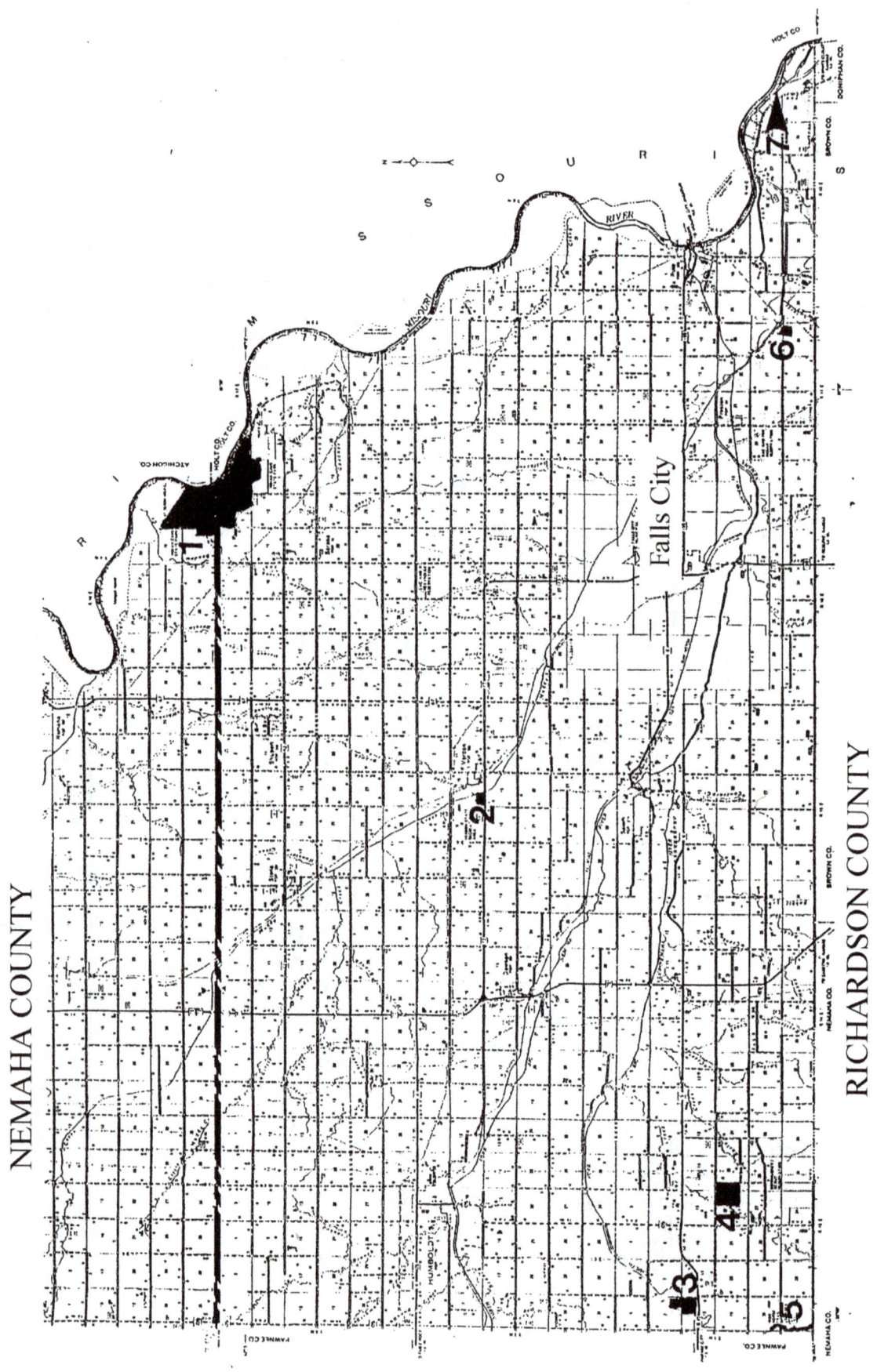

43. Nemaha and Richardson Counties

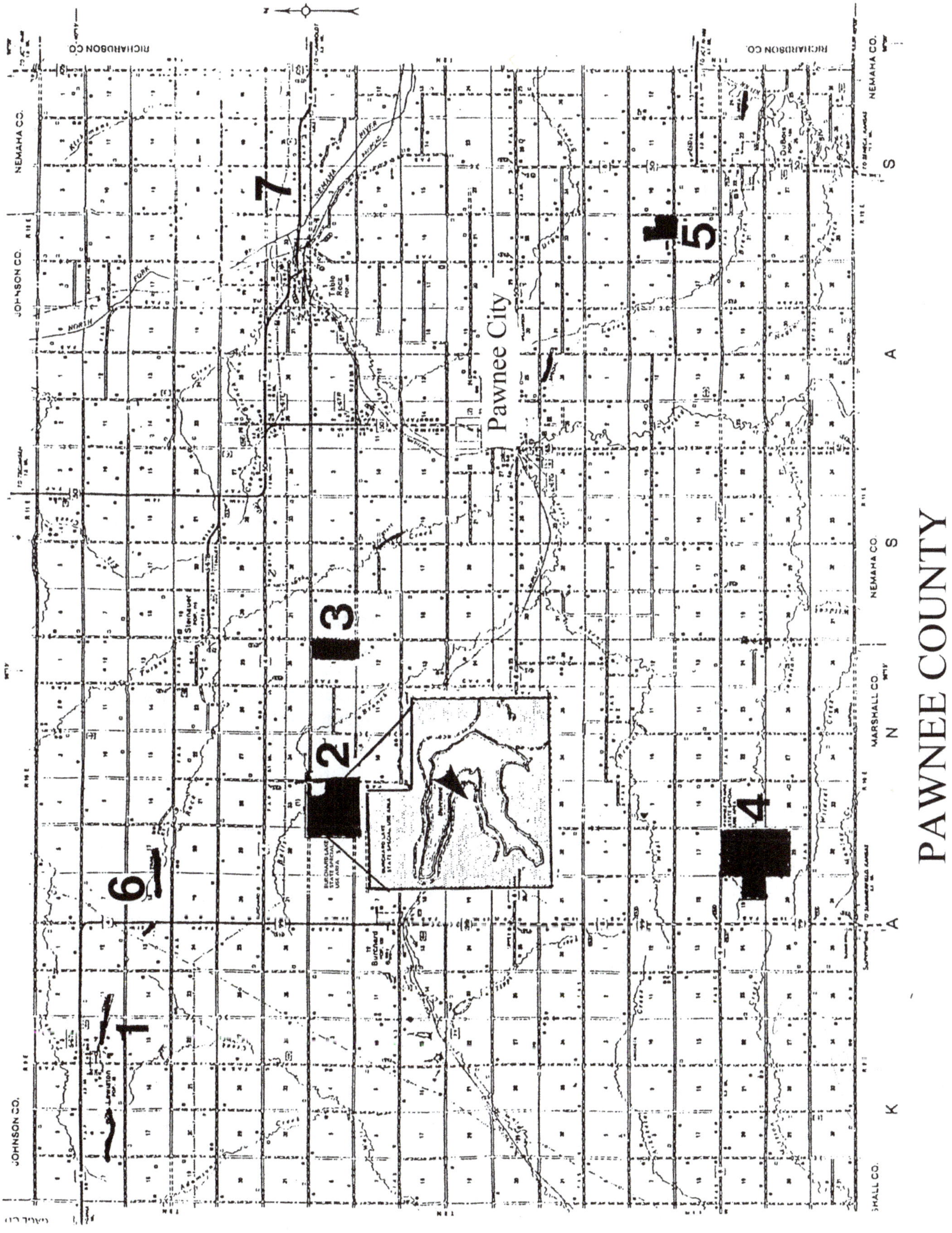

MAP 44 — PAWNEE COUNTY

44. Pawnee County

Tallgrass Prairie Ecology

The tallgrass prairie is one of the most romantic concepts of the American West. The imagined view of endless bison herds plodding through grasses so tall that they half obscured them from sight is a powerful image, and one that today must remain more in the realm of fancy than fact. Quite probably most bison foraged on prairies of shorter stature. The taller grasses that were present were likely soon clipped by the hungry migrants, but at least the vision is a most attractive one. One image that can still be realized is the sight of tallgrass prairie in full bloom from June through September, when dozens of prairie forbs vie for the attention of bees, butterflies, and moths.

As a child, my mother lived on a farm in southeastern North Dakota, situated along the Sheyenne River in northern Richland County. Near her home, the winding, slow-flowing Sheyenne encounters the sandy soils deposited in late Pleistocene times. There, the river once flowed into glacial Lake Agassiz and, depositing its water-carried sand, formed a broad delta. Because the resulting sandy soils were impractical to cultivate, their tall prairie grasses were spared by homesteaders for grazing. As a result, that small region of North Dakota represents the last major remnants of native prairie in the entire state, which now, a century later, is preserved as the Sheyenne National Grassland.

As a further result of this obscure geologic event that occurred 15,000 to 20,000 years ago, my mother came to know the prairie grasses and prairie birds intimately, as she walked or rode her horse through the region's lush big bluestem and Indiangrass meadows. She passed her knowledge of prairie plants and grassland birds on to me when I was a child; it was perhaps the greatest of all the many gifts she gave me. On the warm summer day of her funeral nearly two decades ago, I left the cemetery as soon as possible and drove 30 miles to near where her family's home had been and spent the afternoon alone, amid the sounds and sights of western meadowlarks, upland sandpipers, bobolinks, and our other beloved prairie birds and grasses. I believe that is how mother would have wanted me to respond to her death, by being surrounded by vibrant life.

Today the prairies that have been lovingly preserved by farmers and other landowners who must also have had many similar memories of homesteaders, families, and individuals lucky enough to have learned the quiet beauty of prairies. The family names associated with many of these prairies are a testimony to the pride with which these persons cared for and protected tiny remnants of an earlier time, and of a richer, more wonderful landscape. Preserving these prairies is not only a truly humane and uniquely human act; we are also preserving countless kinds of plants and animals that can and will repay us by their simple presence.

Botanic Characteristics of Tallgrass Prairies

Of all of the grassland types in North America, the tallgrass prairie has been the most ravaged. One estimate of its original extent, based on a map published by A. W. Küchler (1964), was 221,375 square miles, as compared with 218,543 square miles for mixed-grass prairie and 237,476 square miles for shortgrass prairie. At least 95 percent of the tallgrass prairie is now gone, but if the Nebraska Sandhills prairies were classified as tallgrass prairie (they are usually considered to be mixed-grass prairie) they would certainly be the largest remaining remnant in all of North America.

One of the best-studied of all tallgrass prairies is Nine-Mile Prairie near Lincoln, where 392 species of plants (291 native) have been detected over a half-century of study by John Weaver (1965) and more recent botanists (Johnsgard, 2018a). It now comprises only some 230 acres but was about 800 acres when originally studied. Similarly, Audubon Nebraska's Spring Creek Prairie near Denton, an area originally of slightly more than 600 acres, was found by Kay Kottas to support nearly 400 species (Johnsgard, 2018b).

The species diversity of Sandhills prairie plants is much lower than in true tallgrass prairie. In the entire six central Sandhills counties, there are no more than a total of about 450 reported species (Johnsgard, 2001a). By further comparison, a mixed-grass prairie site in south-central Nebraska's Loess Hills that was studied by Steven Rothenberger contained 239 species, whereas a total of 194 plant species were reported from the two-square-mile Arapahoe Prairie in the central Sandhills.

Detailed structure of big bluestem. Adapted from Hitchcock (1935).

Besides big bluestem, Indiangrass, switchgrass, and, in wetter sites, prairie cordgrass, are important high-stature grasses of tallgrass prairie. All are well above three feet tall at maturity and have root systems that extend down 8 to 12 feet for switchgrass, 7 to 8 feet for prairie cordgrass, and 5 to 6 feet for Indiangrass. All of these are warm-season grasses that grow mostly during late-summer heat are strongly rhizomatous, spreading by their roots. Two of the three are also continuous sod-formers, but Indiangrass is a bunch-grass species, mainly spreading from tillers that are produced from late summer rhizomes that overwinter and provide for early spring growth the following year. Seed production estimates for big bluestem, Indiangrass, and switchgrass seem to average substantially less than that of little bluestem, but this statistic seems subject to considerable experimental variability. Additionally, all these species reproduce mainly by rhizomes rather than from seed dispersal.

Such famous plant ecologists as John Weaver and Frederic Clements (1954) studied Nine-Mile Prairie and similar sites in eastern Nebraska for many decades. A study of several such tallgrass prairies established that about 200 species of upland forbs were typically present, and that 75 of these were present in 90 percent of the prairies they examined. The most abundant and most consistently occurring upland forb was lead plant, which has a root system that can be up to more than 16 feet in length and is provided with nitrogen-fixing nodules. The gayfeather, or blazing star, may have roots of comparable length. Many species of goldenrods are also present, with roots up to eight feet long.

John Weaver (1965) calculated that a square foot of big bluestem sod might contain about 55 linear feet and an acre about 400 miles of densely matted rhizomes, from the surface to a depth of only a few inches. The strong roots of big bluestem have individual tensile strengths of 55 to 64 pounds, making prairie sod one of the strongest of natural organic substances. It is indeed strong enough to construct sod-built houses that have sometimes lasted a century or more in the face of Nebraska's relatively inhospitable climate. Weaver also calculated that the big bluestem has root systems up to about three feet in diameter that penetrate to a depth of nearly seven feet. Some 43 percent of its underground biomass is concentrated in the top 2.5 inches of soil and 78 percent is in the top six inches.

The overall underground (root and rhizome) biomass of tallgrass prairies is usually two to four times greater than the aboveground biomass. The root component usually contributes about 30 percent of the annual primary production, or up to nearly 40 percent in the case of grazed prairie. Overall annual primary production of organic matter in tallgrass prairie averages about 300 grams per square meter (or nearly 3,000 pounds per acre). Likewise, the total underground parts of tallgrass prairie may contribute more than a ton of new organic matter per acre annually.

Annual turnover (decomposition) rates for the aboveground parts of tallgrass prairie average about 80 percent, resulting in an average turnover period for the aboveground component of about 1.25 years, whereas turnover periods for underground biomass average about three or four years. As a result, prairie soils are constantly being refertilized by organic matter that has been produced during the past few growing seasons.

The soils of tallgrass prairie are among the deepest and most productive for grain crops of any on earth. They represent the breakdown products of thousands of generations of annual productivity of grass and other herbaceous organic matter. Because of these organic materials and the clays usually present in prairie soils, such soils have excellent water-holding capabilities. In addition to the humus and related organic matter thus produced, many prairie legumes have nitrogen-fixing root bacteria that enrich and fertilize the soil to a depth of at least 15 feet. Earthworms and various vertebrate animals such as gophers make subterranean burrows that mix and aerate prairie soils, in the case of earthworms to a depth of 13 feet or more.

Eastern Nebraska Native Prairie Types

Upland Tallgrass Prairie

The five dominant grasses of upland tallgrass prairie are actually those of medium stature and consist of little bluestem, needlegrass, prairie drop-seed, Junegrass, and side-oats grama (the scientific names of all the prairie plants mentioned in this book are not included here but can be found in Johnsgard [2018a]). All are bunchgrasses, and of all these perennial native grasses little bluestem is easily the most important. It alone may compose 60 to 90 percent of the total vegetational cover, and on very favorable sites it may lose its bunchlike form and produce a continuous sod of interlocking roots. In most cases, though, the major upland grasses occur in clumps spaced about a foot or more apart, with roots extending downward at least four to five feet.

John Weaver once calculated that a strip of prairie sod 4 inches wide, 8 inches deep, and 100 inches long held a tangled network of roots with a total length of more than 20 miles! In tallgrass prairie, the total weight of

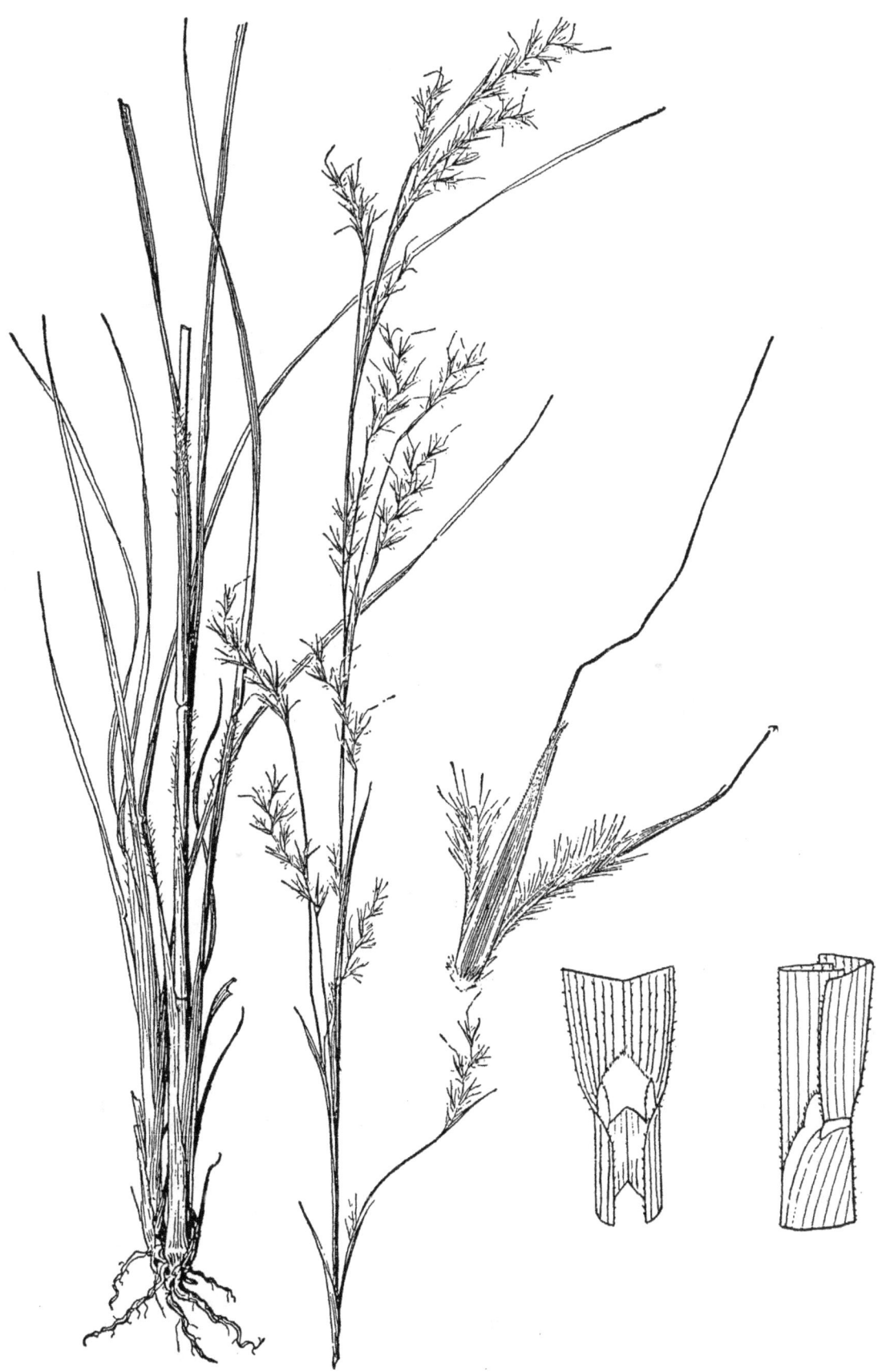

Detailed structure of little bluestem. Adapted from Hitchcock (1935).

underground vegetation in the form of roots is likely to be as great as the aboveground parts, and much of this is recycled back into the soil on a yearly basis.

In contrast, forests and woodlands store most of their productivity as woody above-ground parts, which recycle back into the soil only when the trees eventually die, or perhaps are burned. Most of the important grasses of the tallgrass prairie are from three to six feet tall, with the higher slopes having a greater proportion of mid-stature species.

One of the few large and bushy shrubs of significance on the uplands is wild plum, although the smaller lead plant is widely distributed, and both prairie rose and New Jersey tea are likely to exist as scattered plants. On the uplands, the leguminous lead plant is usually the most important forb, although it has a woody base and might well be classified as a half-shrub. Other important prairie half-shrubs include prairie rose and New Jersey tea.

Forbs (entirely nonwoody broad-leaved plants) of the tallgrass prairie are very numerous. The stiff sunflower is one of the most widely distributed upland forbs in upland Nebraska prairies, and it also extends to many lowlands. Other regular forb participants are prairie goldenrod, prairie flax, wild alfalfa, heath aster, bastard toadflax, and daisy fleabane. Several sunflowers, such as the sawtoothed sunflower, Maximilian's sunflower, and Jerusalem artichoke are important tallgrass prairie forbs, especially in moister situations, and the Jerusalem artichoke has enlarged starchy tubers that can be eaten raw or cooked in various ways. Another perennial legume, prairie turnip, was also an important food source for Native Americans.

Wet Mesic Prairie

If the plants of upland tallgrass prairie are impressive, those of the lowland prairie are even more visually memorable. In this situation, big bluestem may comprise 80 to 90 percent of the overall prairie vegetation, and together with little bluestem the two species represent at least 75 percent of all true lowland prairie communities. Big bluestem is substantially taller than little bluestem, and where both occur together the shorter species may be shaded out. However, on slopes and drier hilltops the smaller species has an advantage over the larger one.

The roots of big bluestem grow about six to eight feet deep, and those of little bluestem are about five feet deep, so big bluestem has an advantage in moister sites. However, its roots tend to grow directly downward, whereas those of little bluestem and other bunchgrasses tend to spread widely, intercepting a much broader area than the aboveground parts of the plant.

Like many prairie perennials, both bluestem species are believed to be very long-lived, probably for many decades. Both species are warm-season grasses that grow primarily through the summer. Big bluestem may rarely reach a height of 8 to 10 feet on some lowland sites by about September, when it finally bursts into full flower.

Other very tall grasses of lowland sites are prairie cordgrass, Canada wild rye, Indiangrass, and switchgrass. An additional 20 or more grass species are of importance in lowland prairie. In typical lowland prairie big bluestem is dominant, but Indiangrass, switchgrass, and Canada wild rye may also be abundant, and on wetter sites prairie cordgrass may take the place of big bluestem as the dominant species.

Typical wet mesic prairie shrubs include wild plum, rough-leafed dogwood, and wolfberry. There are many late summer- and fall-flowering composites, such as sunflowers, goldenrods, and asters, and the rare prairie fringed orchid is likely to bloom earlier, and in slightly moister ravines before disappearing into the rapidly growing summer mantle of green.

Many taller forbs are also part of the low prairie flora. Among these is a remarkable composite, the compass plant, which grows to nearly 10 feet tall and has leaves that may be nearly two feet long. Younger plants especially have their leaves twisted vertically, and the leaf axis is oriented almost perfectly north-south (thus the plant's common name). This trait allows them to take advantage of early morning and late afternoon sunlight but not to become too desiccated during midday hours. A related species, the cup plant, has opposite leaves united at the base in such a way that a small cuplike structure is formed that holds water after rains.

Sumac-Dogwood Shrubland

Over much of eastern Nebraska, a shrubby community dominated by smooth sumac, rough-leaved dogwood, and sometimes also wild plum, wolfberry, and coralberry, is fairly common. It occurs along the edges of woodlands, or in ravines of tallgrass prairies, over well-drained soils. The shrubs may be fairly open or quite dense, even to the point of restricting human passage, but in the more open stands an understory of typical prairie plants may be present. Recurrent prairie fires once restricted this community, but fire suppression in recent times has encouraged its growth. Fire reduction has also encouraged the proliferation of eastern red cedar, the growth of which in eastern Nebraska is a much more serious threat to prairie survival than are sumac and dogwood.

Detailed structure of Indiangrass. Adapted from Hitchcock (1935).

Bur Oak Woodland

Bur oak woodland is a transitional upland community type that sometimes occurs near, or is interspersed with, tallgrass prairie, forming a savanna-like community, especially where recurrent burning or grazing helps to control the understory.

Profiles of Some Typical Tallgrass Species

Big Bluestem

Big bluestem is a warm-season perennial grass that often grows to a height of six feet or more during the hot summer months and finally blooms in September. By October it starts to shed its seed crop, which in natural stands might reach 100 pounds per acre, and much more in planted stands. By then its rather rank foliage is not so attractive to large ungulates, but earlier in the season it is a highly preferred food for most grazing mammals. Its generic name, *Andropogon*, translates as "man's beard," a fair description of its flowering head, which includes an equal mix of somewhat hairy and sessile but fertile spikelets and adjacent stalked but infertile ones.

Although the undisputed dominant of moist tallgrass prairie, big bluestem has an overall range extending east to the Atlantic coast, north in eastern Canada almost to James Bay, and south well into Mexico. Other species of this genus have similar ranges, and little bluestem, which is sometimes placed in the same genus, is also a warm-season grass with a range similar to that of big bluestem. Sand bluestem is an extremely close relative of big bluestem that is more sand- and arid-adapted but is otherwise nearly identical, and sometimes the two forms hybridize where their ranges overlap in Nebraska.

Little Bluestem

Little bluestem is the "shaggy" prairie grass of which Willa Cather wrote lovingly, whose English name refers to a bluish cast that is present on the lower leaves and stem nodes of growing plants. However, by midsummer much of the entire visible plant starts to turn a rich Indian red, and by fall it is easily recognizable by its combination of bunchlike (or "shaggy") shape and its wonderful overall coppery red color, which almost matches the colors of an autumnal prairie sunset. It and side-oats grama have equally distinctive florets that hang down one side of the plant stem—like the feathers fastened to a Lakota warrior's lance, and thus was called "banner-waving-in-the-wind grass"—and so they are two of the most easily recognized and highly distinctive grasses of mixed-grass prairies.

Little bluestem is by far the most important plant of mixed-grass prairie, and it also extends eastward to share dominance with big bluestem in tallgrass prairie. It likewise penetrates the entire Nebraska Sandhills region, and locally may even find opportunities for survival in moist depressions of shortgrass prairie. Like big bluestem, it is a warm-season perennial species, putting on much of its growth in the warmest summer months and sending out graceful feathery flowering stalks in early fall, typically in late September and October. Its abundant seeds are soon dropped, but the upright stems and leaves persist over the winter. Cattle are not as fond of using little bluestem for winter forage as are bison. In good years little bluestem may produce 200 or more pounds of seeds per acre, or at least as much as big bluestem. This compares with about 100 pounds of seeds per acre produced by side-oats grama, and 100 to 180 pounds for blue grama.

Western Prairie Fringed Orchid

The western prairie fringed orchid is a lovely, all too ephemeral orchid that may remain hidden for years but suddenly appear in full bloom during late June or early July for a week or so, and then disappear as quickly and quietly as it had materialized. Thus, one must watch closely for it, usually in the wetter swales of tallgrass prairie. A farmer-photographer friend told me of once haying in a prairie meadow and seeing the orchid's blooms just as the plant was about to be mowed down. Before he could stop the machine the flower had gone into the mower. Going back in following summers, he wasn't able to find the plant again.

These plants often remain unseen for several years, in a dormant, subterranean state, nourished by fungal micorrhizae. They may then suddenly exhibit mass blooming, possibly stimulated by fire or by shifts in soil moisture that are associated with varied rainfall patterns. There are many other orchid species of the genus *Platanthera*, most of which have whitish or greenish flowers and are pollinated by nocturnal or crepuscular moths.

The white blossoms of the fringed orchid show up well under low-light conditions and no doubt help attract moths. The enlarged and strongly fringed lower petal and sepals also might draw attention to the blossoms. Studies on the pollination biology by Charles J. Sheviak and Marlin L. Bowles (1986) have filled in the details for this species and a closely related but smaller one, the eastern prairie fringed orchid, which is fairly widespread in more eastern states.

Both species have blossoms that are creamy white to white, and in both the blossom fragrance is very sweet,

Western prairie fringed orchid and a visiting white-lined sphinx moth

intensifying after sunset. The blossoms of the western form are somewhat creamier, and their fragrance spicier, than in the eastern species. Their petal and sepal shapes also differ, and in the western species the blossom heads are shorter and denser, with fewer but larger individual blossoms.

Both species are specifically adapted to pollination by sphinx moths, being nocturnally fragrant, deeply fringed, with extruded reproductive columns, and extremely long nectar-bearing spurs. There is a very limited entrance access to the spur, and the pollen-bearing pollinaria are situated in such a way that they will adhere either to the proboscis or eyes of the visiting moth. After these structures have deposited their pollen on a moth, the columns rotate, so that they fully expose their stigmas, ready to receive pollen from the next moth that visits. Sheviak and Bowles estimated that any pollinating moths of the western species must have a notably long proboscis length (between 35 to 45 mm) and must also have an across-the-eyes distance that approximates the distance between the pollen-bearing viscidia.

Five prairie-ranging sphinx moths, all of which are native to Nebraska, seem to meet these requirements: the achemon sphinx, white-lined sphinx, wild cherry sphinx, laurel sphinx, and vashti sphinx. Of these, the head measurements of the vashti sphinx do not quite "fit" the proper requirements, and it may instead be a nectar thief, able to obtain nectar without carrying away pollen. The same is possibly true of the wild cherry sphinx.

Although it historically occurred all across eastern Nebraska, the current known distribution of the western prairie fringed orchid is now limited to Lancaster County, eastern Seward County, Hall County, and east-central Cherry County. In 1989 the species was listed federally and concurrently by the State of Nebraska as a threatened species.

Small White Lady's-slipper

The beautiful small white lady's-slipper orchid once had a range similar to those of the eastern and western prairie fringed orchids combined. It extended west into eastern Nebraska and east to the southern New England states. It favors damp soil but full sunlight, often occurring in wetter meadows than where the prairie fringed orchid might also occur. This lady's-slipper blooms fairly early, in May and June, or about the same time as the yellow lady's slipper, and before the white prairie fringed orchids. The blossoms may open before the leaves are fully unfurled, the flowers being mostly yellowish green except for the lower lip, which is glossy white, with some flecks and narrow lines of purple.

The conspicuous stamen-bearing structure is golden yellow, with noticeable crimson spots, the colors of which probably serve as insect attractants. There is usually only a single blossom per stem but sometimes two. However, the plants often grow in clumps, with stems up to 12 inches tall and their long, oval leaves wrapped around the stem at their bases. The white slipper-shaped pouch is up to an inch in length, and the two lateral petal-like sepals are long, narrow, and rather twisted; the dorsal hood is formed by a sepal that is also elongated and somewhat twisted.

The pollination ecology of this species is still little known but is probably much like that of a close European relative (*Cypripedium calceola*) that probably was separated from it during glacial periods. This species was one of the many orchids studied by Charles Darwin. He discovered that orchid flowers of this pouch-like type act as "conical traps, with the edges inwards, like the traps which are sold to catch beetles and cockroaches."

Insects are perhaps attracted by scent or by the conspicuous white color of the pouch, with the crimson spots on the yellow staminode attracting further attention, and the purple lines leading inward along the pouch perhaps acting as false nectar guides.

The plant produces a variety of fragrances, some of which are similar to sex-attractant pheromones used by bees for attracting females. Insects that crawl into the pouch become trapped and can escape only by exiting through one of two rear openings. To do that they must first brush the surface of the stigma and later one of the anthers. This sequence prevents self-pollination of the flower.

Most of the orchid's visitors are bees, especially solitary bees of various genera such as *Andrena*, a large and widespread group of bees that dig nesting burrows in soil and are thus called mining bees. Bumblebees may alight on the pouch but cannot enter, and some small bees and flies that do enter are too small to effect pollination. Once very common in the wet meadows of eastern Nebraska, this orchid is now rare and currently known only from Howard, Pierce, Platte, and Sherman Counties. It is on the list of Nebraska's threatened species.

Western and Eastern Meadowlarks

Nebraska is a bit unusual in that over much of the state both western and eastern meadowlarks can be seen and heard. Where they commonly occur together in the eastern quarter of the state, the eastern meadowlark is likely to be found in lower, moister sites and the western on uplands and in drier habitats. But often both can be heard

Detailed structure of switchgrass. Adapted from Hitchcock (1935).

singing almost simultaneously, and it is the difference in the advertising songs of the males that make field identification easiest. The western has a complex, melodious, and trumpetlike series of many short notes, uttered too rapidly to count them easily. The eastern has a more trombonelike series of a few more obviously sliding-scale notes.

If the singers are visible, it may be apparent that the lower cheek ("malar") area of the western is more tinged with a yellowish color, like the chin, whereas in the eastern this area has little if any yellowish color present. Intermediate songs, as well as intermediate-looking birds, are sometimes present and may leave the observer in doubt as to their identity.

Individual male western meadowlarks sing a variety of unique song types, usually ranging from about 3 to 12. Some of these song types may be shared with other males in the local population, but no two males exhibit the exact same repertoire. A male may repeat one of his song types several times but will switch to a different type upon hearing a rival, perhaps to reduce the likelihood of this other male becoming less responsive to a particular rival's song type.

Song-switching may also be important both in territorial defense and in achieving mate attraction. Males that have the largest song repertoires also tend to be among the first to obtain mates and have greater reproductive success than do less-gifted males, suggesting that song is one of the effective ways to attract a mate, as humans have also much more recently discovered.

The nests of meadowlarks are always extremely well hidden; those I have found have been more the result of accident than design. When walking through prairies and looking for flowers or other things, I have at times been startled by the eruption of a meadowlark at my feet. A careful parting of the grasses will then reveal a roofed-over nest with four or five speckled eggs inside. Such nests are best left alone and carefully covered over again, for in spite of their concealment they are often lost to egg predators.

Greater Prairie-chicken

Greater prairie-chickens are well named. They are indeed closely linked to true prairie, and they are "great," not only in terms of relative size (at least compared to the lesser prairie-chicken) but also in their aesthetic appeal.

In few other places in North America can one live within about a hundred miles of the state's largest cities and yet be able to secrete oneself in a blind on a predawn spring morning and experience what is one of the most

Greater prairie-chicken, male in display

exciting avian shows imaginable. Some of the most pleasurable memories of my life have been formed in such locations. It is like being a first-row spectator at a play whose general plot is known almost by heart. Yet with every such experience there is enough uncertainty about its outcome to make each such viewing like attending an opening-day performance, where the performers' roles may be unexpectedly altered and the morning's outcome unknown (Johnsgard, 2010b, 2016a).

Add to the panorama the sight of a golden sunrise on the eastern horizon and the sounds of meadowlarks and distant coyotes greeting the dawn, and the scene is complete. Or, with the approach of a thunderstorm, sudden strong winds, or the visit of a coyote or prairie falcon, the whole performance may suddenly disappear before one's eyes. They are truly "such things as dreams are made on."

Like the sharp-tailed grouse, prairie-chickens display sexually on traditional sites called arenas, or leks, in which the social status of each male is the sole factor that influences his opportunity for mating successfully. This is Darwinian sexual selection in its clearest form; even a minor setback in status relative to that of neighboring males, such as repeated losses in fights over territorial boundaries, might be enough to exclude a male from hierarchical advancement toward the status of "master cock."

The master cock is the "glue" that holds together the entire social structure in a working, coherent group. Should he suddenly be removed from a stable lek, the resulting fights over new territorial boundaries and associated disruptions over who might replace the dominant male will result in reduced fertilization rates among the females and a possible disintegration of the entire lek structure.

The sounds and postures of the greater prairie-chicken in display are quite different from those of the sharp-tailed grouse. A low-pitched, dovelike "booming" replaces the sharptail's "cooing" and a stately erect posture, with two earlike pinnae erected vertically and lowered wingtips brushing the ground, replaces the frenzied dances and outstretched wings of the sharptail.

Hybrids sometimes occur, however, in areas where both species coexist. This is most likely to happen when females visit a mixed lek and, for whatever reason, allow themselves to be mated by a master cock of the wrong species. Once the females have been mated, the males play no further role in assuring the species' successful reproduction. The females make their nests, lay their eggs, and tend their broods all alone, probably not encountering the adult males again until fall flocks begin to assemble.

Massasauga Rattlesnake

Rattlesnakes of any type are not particularly appealing animals to most people, although their danger to humans is considerably overrated. While I taught nearly 20 summers at the university's biological field station, I knew of only two students who were bitten by snakes, both by prairie rattlesnakes, a larger species than the massasauga. One student was grazed after picking up a snake that had been run over and appeared to be dead. Another student, a young man, was bitten during a show of foolhardy machismo; his hormones seemingly had drowned out any good sense that might have otherwise been there. (Both victims recovered rapidly.)

Fewer people are killed by snake bites each year in the United States (about a dozen out of 6,000 to 7,000 bitten each year) than are killed as a result of being stung by bees, wasps, or ants. In part because of the universal human persecution of rattlesnakes, and partly because of habitat loss in this species' original prairie range, this little rattlesnake has nearly disappeared from Nebraska.

Ferruginous hawk with rattlesnake

One of the massasauga's very few remaining haunts is around Burchard Lake WMA in Pawnee County, where greater prairie-chickens also survive in small numbers. When George Hudson (1985) did a survey of Nebraska's reptiles and amphibians, he was aware of records from Lancaster, Fillmore, Gage, and Nemaha Counties. Five records were from Lancaster County, including one from the prairie remnant near Lincoln called Nine-Mile Prairie.

A more recent survey by John Lynch produced a few more locations, but only in Pawnee County (Pawnee Prairie and Burchard Lake) is the species likely to still be present and receiving some degree of protection. It was recently added to the list of Nebraska's threatened species.

Some Remnant Tallgrass Prairies of Nebraska

The locations given in this tallgrass prairie section are minimal, so refer to the county maps as needed to reach a few of the sites, some of which are also described earlier in the text. Unless otherwise indicated, these prairies are open to the public, with the proviso that many of them contain rare species, and the sites should be treated with great care.

Antelope County

Grove Lake WMA. 2,009 acres. Located 3 miles north of Royal. Mostly mixed-grass upland and Sandhills prairie and riparian hardwoods along East Verdigre Creek. A stand of tallgrass prairie on sand and gravel is located 100 yards northeast of the parking area. Open to the public.

Boone County

Olson Nature Preserve. 112 acres. Located eight miles northwest of Albion on Hwy. 14, then west one mile. Sandhills prairie and oak woodlands. For more information, contact the Prairie Plains Resource Institute by phone at 402-694-5535 or see https://www.prairieplains.org/.

Buffalo County

Lillian Annette Rowe Sanctuary and Iain Nicolson Audubon Center. Six miles of river frontage with 1,000 acres of native prairie. Located two miles south of the Gibbon I-80 exit and two miles west on Elm Island Road (turn west about 100 yards south of the Platte River bridge). Phone 308-468-5282.

Cedar County

Wiseman WMA. 365 acres. Located one mile north and five miles east of Wynot. Virgin upland prairie on ridges and hilltops. Just south of the Missouri River, this area includes steep wooded loess bluffs of bur oak with grassy ridges. Open to the public.

Colfax County

Clarence and Ruth Fertig Tallgrass Prairie. 43.35 acres of Platte River floodplain prairie near Richland. Open to the public. Owned by Wachiska Audubon Society, phone 402-486-4846.

Frank L. and Lillian Pokorny Memorial Prairie. 40 acres (20 acres of virgin tallgrass prairie and 20 acres of restoration). Located 2.5 miles west of Hwy. 15 at "P" Road (about 11 miles north of Schuyler). For more information, contact the Prairie Plains Resource Institute by phone at 402-694-5535 or see the website https://www.prairieplains.org/.

Dixon County

Buckskin Hills WMA. 340 acres. Located two miles west and two miles south of Newcastle. Some virgin prairie is present in the several hundred acres of grassland and woods, as is a 75-acre lake. Open to the public.

Ponca State Park (892 acres) and **Elk Point Bend WMA.** Both sites are located about three miles north of Ponca. Small stands of virgin prairie are present on ridges and hilltops. Mostly forested with mature stands of bur oak, walnut, hackberry, and elms. A state park entry permit is required, phone 402-755-2284.

Douglas County

Allwine Prairie Tract. 140 acres. Located 12 miles northwest of Omaha within Glacier Creek Preserve. From I-680 in west Omaha, drive west on West Dodge Road to 144th St., turn north and go to State St., and then proceed west 0.5 mile to the preserve entrance. For permission to visit, call the Department of Biology at the University of Nebraska Omaha, phone 402-554-3378.

The Audubon Society of Omaha Prairie Preserve (formerly known as Jensen Prairie). 20 acres, about half virgin prairie, half restored. Located at 6720 Bennington Road, near the intersection of 72nd St. and Hwy. 36 (or 72nd and McKinley Streets). Obtain permission to visit from the ASO, phone 402-445-4138. Also see https://audubon-omaha.org/conservation/aso-prairie.html.

Bauermeister Prairie. 40 acres. Owned by the city of Omaha and part of Zorinsky Lake Park (770 acres). The eastern park entrance is on 156th St. midway between Q St. and West Center Road. There are two marked entrances from 156th St., but go to the south entrance and follow the park road to the parking areas near its end. The prairie lies to the south and west, beyond an arm of Zorinsky Lake, via a walking trail.

Neale Woods Nature Center. About 30 acres of restored loess prairie and 520 acres of hardwoods. Located north of Omaha at 14323 Edith Marie Ave. The owner and operator is Fontenelle Forest Nature Center, phone 402-731-3140. Admission fee.

Stolley Prairie. 21 acres. Located along the eastern side of 168th St., midway between Blondo and Dodge Streets. Owned by the City of Omaha and located within the 147-acre Bluestem Prairie Preserve.

Fillmore County

Clyde and Thelma Gewacke Prairie. 11.36 acres of lowland prairie. Located three miles west and one mile north of Ohiowa. Open to the public. Owned by Wachiska Audubon Society, phone 402-486-4846.

Gage County

Homestead Prairie. 100 acres. Located 4.5 miles west of Beatrice on Hwy. 4 within Homestead National Historical Park. The prairie is about 100 acres of locally sourced restored tallgrass on the historic Daniel Freeman homestead site. A 2.5-mile trail winds through riparian wooded habitats and the prairie. A local plant list is available. Free entry. Phone 402-223-3514, website https://www.nps.gov/home/index.htm.

Wildcat Creek Tallgrass Prairie. 32 acres of upland and lowland prairie. Located 5 miles south, 1 mile west, and 1 more mile south of Virginia, then west 0.25 mile on a dirt road. Alternatively, drive 2 miles west and 5 miles north of Liberty, then west 0.25 mile (section 4, on the north side of the road). Open to the public. Owned by Wachiska Audubon Society, phone 402-486-4846.

Hall County

Crane Trust. 6,500 acres. Located about 1.5 miles south of the I-80 Alda exit and about 1 mile east on Whooping Crane Dr. The Crane Trust prairie has about 6,500 acres of native and reseeded wet meadows, with more than 560 plant species reported from Mormon Island. Permission to visit is required, phone 308-382-1820. See also https://cranetrust.org/.

Hamilton County

Gjerloff Prairie. 390 acres of loess prairie and Platte River frontage. Drive 4 miles west of Hwy. 14 south of Marquette on West 22nd Road (41C) and then 0.5 mile north. Owned by Prairie Plains Resource Institute, permission to visit is needed. Phone 402-694-5535; see also https://www.prairieplains.org/.

Lincoln Creek Prairie and Trail. 16 acres. Located in Aurora at N St. and McCollough Lane. The 16 acres include tallgrass prairie and prairie restorations, with more than 100 plant species, and a free-access trail. Owned by Prairie Plains Resource Institute.

Marie Ratzlaff Prairie Preserve. 40 acres of upland prairie (30 virgin acres). Located 6 miles south of the Hampton I-80 exit on the west side of the road. Owned by Prairie Plains Resource Institute. Permission to visit is not required.

Jefferson County

Rock Creek Station State Historical Park and SRA. 550 acres. Virgin tallgrass prairie on hilltops and wooded ravines. Located six miles east of Fairbury. A park entry permit is required.

Rock Glen WMA. 706 acres. Nearly 500 acres of virgin upland and restored prairie. Located seven miles east and two miles south of Fairbury, or four miles northeast of Endicott. Open to the public.

Rose Creek WMA. 200 acres. Located eight miles southwest of Fairbury, this site has about 200 acres of oak savanna. Open to the public.

Johnson County

Ivan A. and Ivan F. Lamb Tallgrass Prairie. 4 acres. Located three miles west and two miles south of Sterling

(NE corner of section 5, west side of the road). Open to the public. Owned by Wachiska Audubon Society, phone 402-486-4846.

Louis and Grace Bentzinger Tallgrass Prairie. 13.5 acres. This upland and lowland prairie is a conservation easement located 0.75 mile north of Cook or 9 miles south of Syracuse via Hwy. 50 (NE corner of section 4, west side of the road). The property is privately owned; the owner allows responsible visits.

Knox County

Bohemia Prairie WMA. 600 acres. This wildlife management area has nearly 600 acres of virgin prairie, with some woods and two ponds. From Verdigre go five miles west on Hwy. 84 and then five miles north. Free access.

Greenvale WMA. 70 acres. This site is nearly all virgin prairie among Middle Verdigre Creek woodlands. It is located 10 miles west and 3 miles south of Verdigre. Free access.

Niobrara State Park. 1,632 acres. Grasslands and riparian woods are at the western edge of the park. A state park entry permit is required. Ask at the park office for prairie site locations.

Lancaster County

Branched Oak SRA. 200 acres. Located four miles west of Raymond. This site has about 200 acres of virgin prairie, plus additional reseeded prairie. Most of the prairie occurs south of the dam near the main south entrance. A state park entry permit is required.

Lincoln Saline Wetlands Nature Center. About 30 acres. These wetlands are the site of a historic saline lake. The eastern edge of Capitol Beach still supports a saline marsh habitat and associated low tallgrass prairie. Turn onto Westgate Blvd. from Sun Valley Blvd. and then proceed west on W. Industrial Lake Dr. to the parking area. Owned by the Lower Platte South Natural Resources District. (Four other preserved saline wetlands—two WMAs and two NRD sites—with possibly some more typical prairie occur east of Raymond. Contact the Nebraska Game and Parks Commission or Lower Platte South NRD for locations and information.)

Nine-Mile Prairie. 240 acres. Drive four miles west on West O St. from downtown Lincoln, then north on NW 48th St. to W. Fletcher Road, and one mile west; walk south about 100 yards from the parking area to the prairie. The total plant list is about 400 species. Owned by the University of Nebraska Foundation and open to the public.

Pawnee Lake SRA. Several acres of native prairie exist on the east side of Pawnee Lake, just south of W. Superior St. Located five miles west and two miles north of Lincoln. A state park entry permit is required.

Pioneers Park. 668 acres. A Lincoln municipal park, Pioneers Park is located southwest of W. Van Dorn St. and Coddington Ave. The park's nature center has a large restored prairie and a native plant garden. A nature trail extends southwest from the Chet Ager Building into restored and native prairie, and a hiking trail (Prairie Corridor on Haines Branch) will eventually extend south to Spring Creek Prairie Audubon Center. A third area of fine prairie is located east of the golf course (west of the parking area near the elk statue). Open to the public.

Spring Creek Prairie Audubon Center. 850 acres, with about 600 acres of prairie. Drive three miles south from the western edge of Denton on SW 100th St.; the entrance gate is on the east side of the road. The site includes native tallgrass prairie uplands, some small wetlands—including a spring—and riparian woods. The plant list approaches 400 species. A donation is expected. (Nearby cemeteries at Emerald, Firth, and Roca also have small areas of prairie that are worth visiting.)

Wilderness Park. This Lincoln municipal park encompasses a seven-mile stretch of riparian woodland along Salt Creek on the southwest side of Lincoln. It includes a small area of prairie on sandstone outcrops at the western edge, 0.2 mile south of Pioneers Blvd. and on the east side of S. 1st St. The park has stands of mature bur oak and hickory, especially at the south end, and riparian forest, with about 20 miles of trails. A great blue heron nesting colony is near the best bur oak stand. Open to the public.

Madison County

Oak Valley WMA. 640 acres. This area is mostly hardwood forest along Battle Creek with prairie uplands. Located 2.5 miles south and 1 mile west of Battle Creek (town). Open to the public.

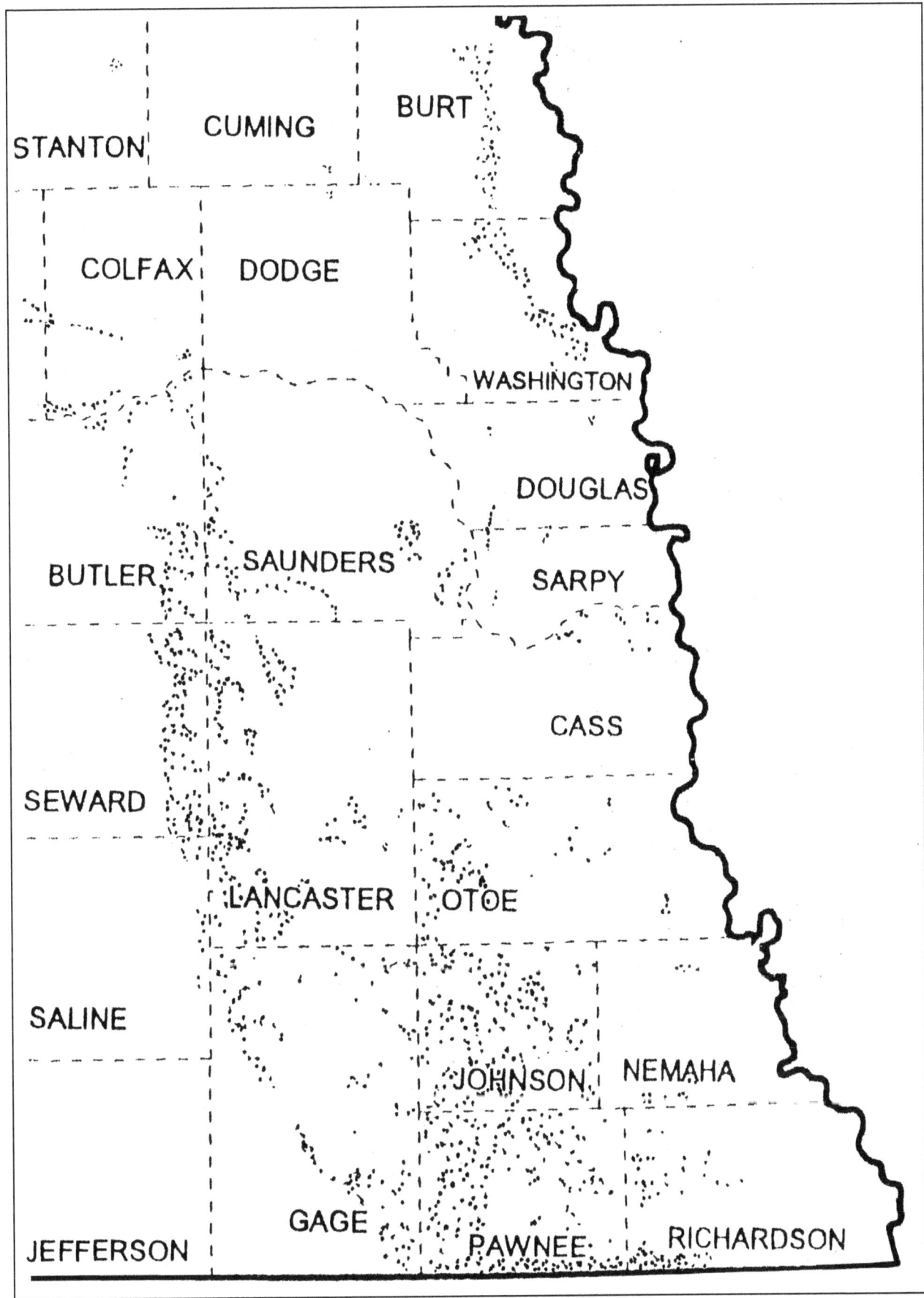

Locations of remnant tallgrass prairies in southeastern Nebraska. From Johnsgard (2007a).

Merrick County

Bader Memorial Park Natural Area. 270 acres. The park is located at the west end of the Chapman Bridge over the Platte River. It includes about 120 acres of grassland (some under restoration) as well as riparian forest and shrubland. Admission fee.

Nance County

Sunny Hollow WMA. 160 acres. Located five miles south and one mile west of Genoa via country roads. This site is mostly lowland virgin prairie, plus two marshes and an excavated wetland. Open to the public.

Nemaha County

Berg Prairie East. 9.88 acres. This lowland prairie is located one mile east of Talmage. Open to the public. Owned by Wachiska Audubon Society, phone 402-486-4846.

Berg Prairie West. 11.7 acres. This prairie has both lowland and upland components and is located 0.5 mile south of Talmage. Open to the public. Owned by Wachiska Audubon Society, phone 402-486-4846.

Otoe County

Henry Dieken Tallgrass Prairie. 14.3 acres. From the western end of Unadilla, drive 1.5 miles south on Road 20 and then 0.75 mile west (section 15, south side of the road). Open to the public. Owned by Wachiska Audubon Society, phone 402-486-4846.

Pawnee County

Burchard Lake WMA. 400 acres. Drive 3 miles east of Burchard and then 1 mile north, or go east 3 miles on Hwy. 4 from the junction of Hwys. 99 and 4 (junction 3 miles north of Burchard) and then 1.5 miles south. Burchard Lake surrounds about 400 acres of rolling prairie over limestone. A prairie-chicken lek has traditionally been active here, but its current status is uncertain. The rare and elusive massasauga rattlesnake is also present. Open to public visits.

Elmer Klapka Farm. 400 acres in four tracts. The farm has about 30 acres of native prairie among 170 acres of farmland/pasture and 200 acres of native pasture. It is located 2.5 miles south of the east side of Table Rock, in sections 9 and 16. The native prairie areas are scattered among brome-dominated pastures. Open to the public. Owned by Wachiska Audubon Society, phone 402-486-4846 (contact for specific locations of prairie areas).

Pawnee Prairie WMA. 1,120 acres of prairie, the largest in southeast Nebraska. Located 8 miles south of Burchard via Hwys. 8 and 99 and then 1 mile east; also accessible by driving 10 miles south of Burchard and 1 mile east. The prairie is to the east of these access points. Two or more prairie-chicken leks are present but unmarked. Open to the public.

Platte County

Wilkinson WMA. About 80 acres of wet virgin prairie, plus upland grassland and wetlands. Located on the east side of 295th Ave. north of the Loup Canal, northwest of Columbus and west of Hwy. 81. Open to the public.

Richardson County

Indian Cave State Park. 3,052 acres. Located five miles east and one mile north of Shubert. About 40 acres of virgin prairie on hilltops and hay meadows exist in the southeast part of the park and also along Trail 10 from the top of the bluffs to the Adirondack shelter. The park is about 80 percent mature hardwood forest, with the rest grassland. A state park entry permit is required.

Rulo Bluffs Preserve. 445 acres. Located about 1.5 miles south and 4 miles east of Rulo, along the southwest bank of the Missouri River. The preserve has ridgetop tallgrass prairie savanna and hardwood forest on high loess bluffs. The terrain is very steep and difficult. For permission to visit, contact the Iowa Tribe of Kansas and Nebraska, phone 785-595-3258.

Saunders County

Bur Oak WMA. This WMA is mostly mature bur oak woods, with about 40 acres of prairie in oak savanna. Located five miles east of Seward along US Hwy. 84. Open to the public.

Knott Tallgrass Prairie (also known as Yutan or Storm Prairie). 21 acres. Located 1 mile north, 1 mile east, and 0.5 mile north (on an often very muddy dirt road) of Yutan (section 24, east side of the road). Owned by Wachiska

Audubon Society, phone 402-486-4846 (call for specific locations of prairie areas).

Madigan Prairie. 23 acres. Located between Valparaiso and Weston, one mile east of the Butler County line and two miles south of Rte. 92. This native prairie is owned by the University of Nebraska Foundation and used by the UNL School of Biological Sciences for research. Contact Biological Sciences for permission to visit.

Red Cedar Lake. 175 acres. Located six miles north and two miles west of Valparaiso, this area is managed by the Lower Platte South Natural Resources District. The 51-acre lake is surrounded by grassland areas and woods. Free access. (The Valparaiso cemetery also has a small area of prairie that can be respectfully visited.)

Seward County

Twin Lakes WMA. 1,300 acres. Located 0.5 mile north and 0.5 mile west of the I-80 Pleasant Dale exit. Twin Lakes includes about 600 acres of grasslands, two lakes, marshes, wooded bottomlands, and upland prairie. The best prairie is southwest of the smaller lake, on the west side of the WMA. Open to the public.

Stanton County

Wood Duck WMA. 668 acres. Located about two miles south and four miles west of Stanton. This site has both virgin prairie on sand-gravel soils and restored prairie as well as riparian wooded habitats and oxbow lakes bordering the Elkhorn River. Open to the public.

Thayer County

Meridian WMA. 190 acres. Located 3.5 miles north of Gilead. Both virgin tallgrass and mixed-grass prairie exist at this WMA. Open to the public.

Washington County

Boyer Chute NWR. 3,500 acres. Boyer Chute is located three miles east of Ft. Calhoun on County Road 34, along the Missouri River. The refuge includes about 2,000 acres of reseeded prairie and riparian woods. Phone 712-388-4800.

Cuming City Cemetery. 11 acres. From the intersection of US Hwys. 30 and 75 in Blair, go north 3.5 miles on Hwy. 75 to County Road 14 and turn left; travel 600 feet to the cemetery entrance (on the left). Owned by Cuming City and open to the public for respectful visits.

DeSoto NWR. 8,362 acres. Located five miles east of Blair on Hwy 30. DeSoto has about 1,900 acres of restored prairie among riparian woods, an oxbow lake, and wetlands. Entrance fee.

Fort Atkinson State Historical Park. 157 acres. Located just east of the town of Fort Calhoun. The park includes some restored prairie with a hiking trail present. Entrance fee.

Wayne County

Thompson-Barnes WMA. 18 acres of restored prairie. From Wayne, go 3.5 miles north on Hwy. 15 and then 1 mile west. Open to the public.

Loggerhead shrike on yucca stalk with seed pods

References

Paleontology and Geology

Bouc, K. (coordinator). 1994. *The Cellars of Time: Paleontology and Archeology in Nebraska. Nebraskaland Magazine*, Jan.–Feb., 1994, 72(1): 1–162. (Also published in *Nebraska History* 75(1), 162 pp.)

Graetz, J. L., R. A. Garrott, and S. R. Craven. 1995. *Faunal Survey of Agate Fossil Beds National Monument*. Omaha: National Park Service, Midwest Region. 43 pp.

Hunt, R. H., Jr. 1981. "Geology and vertebrate paleontology of the Agate Fossil Beds National Monument and surrounding region, Sioux County, Nebraska (1972–1978)." *National Geographic Society Research Reports* 13: 263–285.

Johnsgard, P. A. 2014a. "Secrets of the very long dead: Ashfall Fossil Beds State Historical Park." *Prairie Fire*, October, pp. 1, 3, 4.

Johnsgard, P. A. 2015a. "Secrets of the most sincerely dead: Agate Fossil Beds National Monument." *Prairie Fire*, November, pp. 15–17.

Keech, C. F., and R. Bentall. 1971. *Dunes on the Plains—The Sand Hills Region of Nebraska*. University of Nebraska Conservation and Survey Division, Resources Report 4. 18 pp.

Lugn, A. L. 1934. Part I: Outline of Pleistocene geology of Nebraska. The Geology and Mammalian Fauna of the Pleistocene of Nebraska. *University of Nebraska State Museum Bulletin* 41(1): 319–356.

Maher, H. D., Jr., G. F. Engelmann, and R. D. Shuster. 2003. *Roadside Geology of Nebraska*. Missoula, MT: Mountain Press.

Trimble, D. E. 1980. The Geologic Story of the Great Plains. *Geologic Survey Bulletin* 1493. Washington, DC: US Department of the Interior, US Geological Survey. 55 pp.

Voorhies, M. R. 1981. "Ancient ashfall creates a Pompeii of prehistoric animals, dwarfing the St. Helens eruption." *National Geographic* 159(1): 66–75.

Wright, H. E., Jr. 1970. "Vegetational history of the Great Plains." Pp. 157–172, in W. Dort, Jr. and J. K. Jones, Jr. (eds.), *Pleistocene and Recent Environments of the Central Great Plains*. Lawrence: University Press of Kansas.

Recent History and Native Americans

Brown, D. 1970. *Bury My Heart at Wounded Knee: An Indian History of the American West*. Henry Holt. 487 pp.

Colemam W. S. 2000. *Voices of Wounded Knee*. Lincoln: University of Nebraska Press. 474 pp.

DiSylvestro, R. 2005. *In the Shadow of Wounded Knee*. New York: Walker. 272 pp.

Hanson, J. A. 1983. *Northwest Nebraska's Indian People*. Chadron, NE: Chadron Centennial Committee.

Howard, J. H. 1965. The Ponca Tribe. *Bureau of American Ethnology Bulletin* 195. Washington, DC: Smithsonian Institution. 191 pp. (Reprinted 1995 and 2010 [2nd ed.], Lincoln: University of Nebraska Press.)

Hyde, G. E. 1937. *Red Cloud's Folk: A History of the Oglala Sioux*. Norman: University of Oklahoma Press. 331 pp.

Jensen, R. E., R. Paul, and J. Carter. 1991. *Eyewitness at Wounded Knee*. Lincoln: University of Nebraska Press. 232 pp.

Johnsgard, P. A. 2003a. *Lewis and Clark on the Great Plains: A Natural History*. Lincoln: University of Nebraska Press. 144 pp.

Johnsgard, P. A. 2008a. *Wind Through the Buffalo Grass: A Lakota Story Cycle*. Lincoln, NE: Plains Chronicles Press. 214 pp. https://digitalcommons.unl.edu/johnsgard/51/

Johnsgard, P. A. 2010a. "A place called Pahaku." *Prairie Fire*, June 2010, pp. 1, 19, 20, 23. (Reprinted 2014 in *Seasons of the Tallgrass Prairie: A Nebraska Year*, Lincoln: University of Nebraska Press, pp. 3–7.) https://digitalcommons.unl.edu/unpresssamples/282/

Lowie, R. H. 1954. *Indians of the Plains*. New York: McGraw-Hill. (Reprinted 1982, Lincoln: University of Nebraska Press.)

Mathiessen, P. 1993. *In the Spirit of Crazy Horse*. New York: Viking Press. 688 pp.

McGregor, J. H. 1940. *The Wounded Knee Massacre: From the Viewpoint of the Sioux*. Rapid City, SD: Fenske Printing Company.

Seymour, F. W. 1981. *Sitanka: The Full Story of Wounded Knee*. W. Hanover, MA: Christopher Publishing House.

Utley, H. J. 1963. *The Last Days of the Sioux Nation*. New Haven, CT: Yale University Press. 349 pp.

Nebraska Vertebrates

Ballinger, R. E., J. D. Lynch, and G. R. Smith. 2010. *Amphibians and Reptiles of Nebraska*. Oro Valley, AZ: Rusty Lizard Press and Lincoln: University of Nebraska Press.

Bouc, K. (ed.) 1987. The Fish Book. *NEBRASKAland Magazine* (special issue) 65(1): 1–132.

Genoways, H. H., J. D. Hoffman, P. W. Freeman, K. Geluso, R. A. Benedict, and J. J. Huebschman. 2008. Mammals of Nebraska: Checklist, Key, and Bibliography. *Bulletin of the University of Nebraska State Museum* 23. 92 pp.

Hudson, G. E. 1985. The Amphibians and Reptiles of Nebraska. *Nebraska Conservation Bulletin* 24. Lincoln: University of Nebraska Conservation and Survey Division. (First published 1942.) https://digitalcommons.unl.edu/conservationsurvey/359/

Johnsgard, P. A. 2005. *Prairie Dog Empire: A Saga of the Shortgrass Prairie*. Lincoln: University of Nebraska Press. 243 pp.

Johnsgard, P. A. 2013. *The Birds of Nebraska*. Rev. ed. Lincoln: University of Nebraska–Lincoln Digital Commons and Zea Books. 150 pp. https://digitalcommons.unl.edu/zeabook/17/

Johnsgard, P. A. 2020a. *Nebraska Wildlife: A Natural History*. Lincoln: University of Nebraska Press. 493 pp.

Jones, J. K. 1964. *Distribution and Taxonomy of Mammals of Nebraska*. University of Kansas Publications, Museum of Natural History 16(1): 1–356.

Morris, J., L. Morris, and L. Witt. 1974. *The Fishes of Nebraska*. Lincoln: Nebraska Game and Parks Commission. 98 pp.

Sharpe, R. S., W. R. Silcock, and J. G. Jorgensen. 2001. *The Birds of Nebraska*. Lincoln: University of Nebraska Press. 513 pp.

Biological Studies and Surveys, Nebraska and Adjoining States

Chapman, S. S., et al. 2001. *Ecoregions of Nebraska and Kansas* (color poster and map). Reston, VA: US Geological Survey.

Denison, E. 1994. *Missouri Wildflowers*. 4th ed. Jefferson City: Missouri Department of Conservation. 314 pp.

Ducey, J. E. 1988. *Nebraska Birds: Breeding Status and Distribution*. Omaha: Simmons-Boardman Books. 148 pp.

Haddock, M. J. 2005. *Wildflowers and Grasses of Kansas: A Field Guide*. Lawrence: University Press of Kansas. 374 pp.

Haddock, M. J., C. C. Freeman, and J. Bare. 2015. *Kansas Wildflowers and Weeds*. Lawrence: University Press of Kansas. 526 pp.

Johnsgard, P. A. 2001a. *The Nature of Nebraska: Ecology and Biodiversity*. Lincoln: University of Nebraska Press. 402 pp.

Johnsgard, P. A. 2009a. *A Nebraska Bird-Finding Guide*. Lincoln: University of Nebraska–Lincoln Digital Commons and Zea Books. 152 pp. https://digitalcommons.unl.edu/biosciornithology/51/ (See also https://digitalcommons.unl.edu/zeabook/5/)

Johnsgard, P. A. 2009b. "Nebraska's eight great natural wonders." *Nebraska Life*, November 2009, pp. 78–84.

Johnsgard, P. A. 2012a. *Nebraska's Wetlands: Their Wildlife and Ecology*. Water Survey Paper No. 78. Lincoln: School of Natural Resources, Conservation and Survey Division, University of Nebraska–Lincoln. 202 pp.

Johnsgard, P. A. 2014b. *Seasons of the Tallgrass Prairie: A Nebraska Year*. Lincoln: University of Nebraska Press. 171 pp.

Johnsgard, P. A. 2018a. *A Naturalist's Guide to the Great Plains*. Lincoln: University of Nebraska–Lincoln Digital Commons and Zea Books. 161 pp. https://digitalcommons.unl.edu/zeabook/63/

Jones, J. K., Jr. 1964. "Distribution and taxonomy of mammals of Nebraska." *University of Kansas Publications of the Museum of Natural History*, vol. 16: 1–356.

Knue, J. 1997. *Nebraska Wildlife Viewing Guide*. Helena, MT: Falcon Press. 96 pp.

LaGrange, T. G. 2005. *Guide to Nebraska Wetlands and Their Conservation Needs*. 2nd ed. Lincoln: Nebraska Game and Parks Commission. 57 pp. http://outdoornebraska.gov/nebraskawetlands/

Panella, M. J. 2010. *Nebraska's At-Risk Wildlife*. Lincoln: Nebraska Game and Parks Commission. 196 pp.

Schneider, R., M. Fritz, J. Jorgensen, S. Schainost, R. Simpson, G. Steinauer, and C. Rothe-Groleau. 2018. *Revision of the Tier 1 and 2 Lists of Species of Greatest Conservation Need, A Supplement to the Nebraska Natural Legacy Project State Wildlife Action Plan*. Lincoln: Nebraska Game and Parks Commission. 96 pp.

Schwartz, C. W., and E. R. Schwartz. 2016. *The Wild Mammals of Missouri*. 3rd ed. Columbia: University of Missouri Press, and Jefferson City: Missouri Department of Conservation. 396 pp.

Regional Plants and Prairie Ecology

Barth, R., and N. Ratzlaff. 2004. *Field Guide to Wildflowers: Fontenelle Forest and Neale Woods Nature Centers*. Bellevue, NE: Fontenelle Nature Association. 306 pp.

Barth, R., and N. Ratzlaff. 2007. *Field Guide to Trees, Shrubs, Woody Vines, Grasses, Sedges, and Rushes: Fontenelle Forest and Neale Woods Nature Centers*. Bellevue, NE: Fontenelle Nature Association. 218 pp.

Branson, F. A. 1952. "Native pastures of the dissected loess plains of central Nebraska." PhD diss., University of Nebraska–Lincoln. 120 pp.

Churchill, S. P., C. C. Freeman, and G. E. Kantak. 1988. "The vascular flora of the Niobrara Valley Preserve and adjacent areas in Nebraska." *Transactions of the Nebraska Academy of Sciences* 16: 1–15.

Farrar, J. 2011. *Field Guide to Wildflowers of Nebraska and the Great Plains*. 2nd ed. Iowa City: University of Iowa Press. 166 pp.

Hitchcock, A. S. 1935. *Manual of the Grasses of the United States*. US Department of Agriculture Publication No. 200. Washington, DC.

Hopkins, H. H. 1951. "Ecology of the native vegetation of the Loess Hills in central Nebraska." *Ecological Monographs* 21: 125–147.

Johnsgard, P. A. 2007a. *A Guide to the Tallgrass Prairies of Eastern Nebraska and Adjacent States*. Lincoln: University of Nebraska–Lincoln Digital Commons and Zea Books. 70 pp. https://digitalcommons.unl.edu/biosciornithology/39/

Johnsgard, P. A. 2009c. "Forbs and grasses and Cheshire cats: What is a tallgrass prairie?" *Prairie Fire*, December, pp. 3, 9.

Johnsgard, P. A. 2009d. "Autumn on the prairie: Nebraska's grasses." *Nebraska Life*, September/October, pp. 18–21.

Johnsgard, P. A. 2012b. "Spring Creek Prairie Audubon Center: An 800-acre schoolhouse." *Prairie Fire*, October 2012, pp. 18–20, 22.

Johnsgard, P. A. 2018b. *The Ecology of a Tallgrass Treasure: Audubon's Spring Creek Prairie*. Lincoln: University of Nebraska–Lincoln Digital Commons and Zea Books. 184 pp. https://digitalcommons.unl.edu/zeabook/66

Johnson, J. R., and G. E. Larson. 1999. *Grassland Plants of South Dakota and the Northern Great Plains*. South Dakota Agricultural Extension Station Publication B566 (rev.). South Dakota Sate University, Brookings.

Kantak, G. E. 1995. "Terrestrial plant communities of the middle Niobrara Valley, Nebraska." *Southwestern Naturalist* 40: 129–138.

Kantak, G. E., and S. P. Churchill. 1993. "The Niobrara Valley Preserve: Inventory of a biogeographical crossroads." *Transactions of the Nebraska Academy of Science* 20: 1–12.

Kaul, R., D. M. Sutherland, and S. B. Rolfsmeier. 2012. *The Flora of Nebraska*. 2nd ed. Lincoln: School of Natural Resources, University of Nebraska–Lincoln. 966 pp.

Kaul, R., G. E. Kantak, and S. P. Churchill. 1988. "The Niobrara River Valley, a postglacial migration corridor and refugium of forest plants and animals in the grasslands of central North America." *Botanical. Review* 54: 44–81.

Keeler, K., A. T. Harrison, and L. S. Vescio. 1980. "The flora and Sandhills prairie communities of Arapaho Prairie, Arthur County, Nebraska." *Prairie Naturalist* 12: 65–78.

Kottas, K. L. 2001. "Comparative floristic diversity of Spring Creek and Nine-mile prairies, Nebraska." *Transactions of the Nebraska Academy of Sciences and Affiliated Societies* 27: 31–59.

Küchler, A. W. 1964. *Potential Natural Vegetation of the Conterminous United States*. Special publication no. 36. New York: American Geographical Society.

Nagel, H. G. 1998. "The loess hills prairies of central Nebraska." Kearney: University of Nebraska at Kearney (*Platte Valley Review* 26:2).

Nagel, H. G., and O. A. Kolstad. 1987. "Comparison of plant species composition of Mormon Island Crane Meadows and Lillian Annette Rowe Sanctuary in central Nebraska." *Transactions of the Nebraska Academy of Sciences* 15: 37–48.

Nebraska Department of Agriculture. 1979. *Nebraska Weeds*. Lincoln: Nebraska Department of Agriculture. 247 pp.

Owensby, C. E. 1980. *Kansas Prairie Wildflowers*. Ames: Iowa State University Press.

Pool, R. J. 1914. "A study of the vegetation of the Sandhills of Nebraska." *University of Minnesota Botanical Studies* 4(3): 189–312.

Rothenberger, S. 1994. "Floristic analysis of the C. Bertrand Schulz and Marion Schulz Prairie, a mixed-grass prairie in south-central Nebraska." *Transactions of the Nebraska Academy of Sciences* 21: 21–30.

Rothenberger, S. 1998. "Vegetation of the Loess Hills." Pp. 63–73, in H. G. Nagel (ed.), *The Loess Hills Prairies of Central Nebraska* (*Platte Valley Review*). Kearney: University of Nebraska–Kearney. 205 pp.

Runkel, S. T., and D. M. Roosa. 1989. *Wildflowers of the Tallgrass Prairie*. Ames: Iowa State University Press.

Sheviak, C. J., and M. L. Bowles. 1986. "The prairie fringed orchids: A pollinator isolated pair." *Rhodora* 88: 167–190.

Smith, A. 1996. *Big Bluestem: Journey into the Tallgrass Prairie*. Tulsa, OK: Council Oak Books. 287 pp.

Steiger, T. L. 1930. "Structure of prairie vegetation." *Ecology* 11: 170–217.

Stubbendieck, J., and K. L. Kottas. 2005. *Common Grasses of Nebraska*. Lincoln: University of Nebraska–Lincoln, Institute of Agriculture and Natural Resources, Extension Circular EC 05-170. 121 pp. (includes 180 grasses, 7 sedges)

Stubbendieck, J., and K. L. Kottas. 2007. *Common Forbs and Shrubs of Nebraska*. Lincoln: University of Nebraska–Lincoln, Institute of Agriculture and Natural Resources, Extension Circular EC-118. 178 pp. (includes 144 forbs, 19 shrubs, 4 cacti)

van der Pijl, L., and C. H. Dodson. 1966. *Orchid Flowers: Their Pollination and Evolution*. Coral Gables: University of Miami Press.

Weaver, J. E. 1954. *North American Prairie*. Lincoln, NE: Johnsen Publishing.

Weaver, J. E. 1965. *Native Vegetation of Nebraska*. Lincoln: University of Nebraska Press.

Weaver, J. E. 1968. *Prairie Plants and Their Environment: A Fifty-Year Study in the Midwest*. Lincoln: University of Nebraska Press.

Weaver, J. E., and F. E. Clements. 1954. *Plant Ecology*. New York: McGraw-Hill.

State and Regional Studies

Bleed, A., and C. Flowerday, eds. 1998. *An Atlas of the Sand Hills*. 2nd ed. Resource Atlas No. 5b. Lincoln: Conservation and Survey Division, University of Nebraska–Lincoln. 260 pp.

Bogan, M. A., and C. A. Ramotnik. 1995. "The mammals." Pp. 140–186, in M. A. Bogan (ed.), *A Biological Survey of the Fort Niobrara and Valentine National Wildlife Refuges*, Fort Collins, CO: Midcontinent Ecological Science Center, National Biological Service, US Department of the Interior.

Brogie, M. A., and M. J. Mossman. 1983. "Spring and summer birds of the Niobrara Valley Preserve Area, Nebraska." *Nebraska Bird Review* 51: 44–51.

Freeman, P. W. 1990. "Mammals." Pp. 193–200, in A. Bleed and C. Flowerday (eds.), *An Atlas of the Sand Hills*, Resource Atlas No. 5a. Lincoln: Conservation and Survey Division, University of Nebraska–Lincoln. (35 species listed)

Johnsgard, P. A. 1979. *Birds of the Great Plains: Breeding Species and Their Distribution*. Lincoln: University of Nebraska Press. (See also the 2009 supplement and revised maps at https://digitalcommons.unl.edu/bioscibirdsgreatplains/1/.)

Johnsgard, P. A. 1995. *This Fragile Land: A Natural History of the Nebraska Sandhills*. Lincoln: University of Nebraska Press. 256 pp.

Johnsgard, P. A. 2007b. *A Guide to the Natural History of the Central Platte Valley of Nebraska*. Lincoln: University of

Nebraska–Lincoln Digital Commons and Zea Books. 156 pp. https://digitalcommons.unl.edu/biosciornithology/40/

Johnsgard, P. A. 2007c. *The Niobrara: A River Running through Time.* Lincoln: University of Nebraska Press. 373 pp.

Johnsgard, P. A. 2008b. *The Platte: Channels in Time.* Lincoln: University of Nebraska Press. 176 pp.

Johnsgard, P. A. 2015b. *Birding Nebraska's Central Platte Valley and Rainwater Basin.* Lincoln: University of Nebraska–Lincoln Digital Commons and Zea Books. 54 pp. https://digitalcommons.unl.edu/zeabook/36/

Johnsgard, P. A. 2018a. *A Naturalist's Guide to the Great Plains.* Lincoln: University of Nebraska–Lincoln Digital Commons and Zea Books. 161 pp. https://digitalcommons.unl.edu/zeabook/63/

Jones, S. R. 2000. *The Last Prairie: A Sandhills Journal.* New York: McGraw-Hill. 244 pp.

Kaul, R. 1998. "Plants." Pp. 127–142, in A. Bleed and C. Flowerday (eds.), *An Atlas of the Sand Hills*, 2nd ed., Resource Atlas No. 5b. Lincoln: Conservation and Survey Division, University of Nebraska–Lincoln.

Keech, C. F., and R. Bentall. 1971. *Dunes on the Plains: The Sand Hills Region of Nebraska.* Resources Report 4. Lincoln: Conservation and Survey Division, University of Nebraska. 18 pp.

Krapu, G. L., ed. 1981. *The Platte River Ecology Study: Special Research Report.* Jamestown, ND: US Geological Survey, Northern Prairie Wildlife Research Station. 186 pp. https://digitalcommons.unl.edu/usgsnpwrc/248/

LaGrange, T. 1997. *Guide to Nebraska Wetlands and their Conservation Needs.* Nebraska Game and Parks Commission. 34 pp.

McCarraher, D. B. 1977. *Nebraska's Sandhills Lakes.* Lincoln: Nebraska Game and Parks Commission. 67 pp.

Moul, F. 2006. *The National Grasslands: A Guide to America's Undiscovered Treasures.* Lincoln: University of Nebraska Press. 204 pp.

Novacek, J. M. 1989. "The water and wetland resources of the Nebraska Sandhills." Pp. 340–384, in A. G. van der Valk (ed.), *Northern Prairie Wetlands.* Ames: Iowa State University Press. 400 pp.

Oberholser, H. C., and W. L. McAtee. 1920. Waterfowl and Their Food Plants in the Sandhill Region of Nebraska. *Bulletin of the US Department of Agriculture* No. 794. Washington, DC: US Department of Agriculture. 79 pp.

Rosche, R. C. 1990. "Birding pristine Nebraska." *Winging It* 2(6): 1–2, 4–6.

State and National Bird Research

Baker, M. C., and J. T. Boylan. 1999. "Singing behavior, mating associations and reproductive success in a population of hybridizing lazuli and indigo buntings." *Condor* 181: 493–503.

Bicak, T. K. 1977. "Some eco-ethological aspects of a breeding population of long-billed curlews (*Numenius americanus*) in Nebraska." MS thesis, University of Nebraska at Omaha, Omaha, NE.

Boyle, W. J., and R. H. Bauer. 1994. "Birdfinding in forty national forests and grasslands." *Birding* (supplement) 26(2). 186 pp.

Brown, C. R., and M. B. Brown. 2001. "Birds of the Cedar Point Biological Station." Lincoln, NE: *Occasional Papers of the Cedar Point Biological Station*, No. 1. 36 pp.

Brown, C. R., M. B. Brown, P. A. Johnsgard, J. Kren, and W. C. Scharf. 1996. "Birds of the Cedar Point Biological Station area, Keith and Garden Counties, Nebraska: Seasonal occurrence and breeding data." *Transactions of the Nebraska Academy of Sciences* 29: 91–108.

Brown, M. B., S. J. Dinsmore, and C. R. Brown. 2012. *Birds of Southwestern Nebraska.* Lincoln: School of Natural Resources, Conservation and Survey Division, University of Nebraska–Lincoln. 152 pp.

Brown, M. B., and P. A. Johnsgard. 2013. *Birds of the Central Platte River Valley and Adjacent Counties.* Lincoln: University of Nebraska–Lincoln Digital Commons and Zea Books. 182 pp. http://digitalcommons.unl.edu/zeabook/15/

Currier, P. J., G. R. Lingle, and J. G. VanDerwalker. 1985. *Migratory Bird Habitat on the Platte and North Platte Rivers in Nebraska.* Grand Island, NE: Whooping Crane Habitat Maintenance Trust. 177 pp.

Ducey, J. E. 1988. *Nebraska Birds: Breeding Status and Distribution.* Omaha, NE: Simmons-Boardman Books.

Ducey, J. E. 1989. "Birds of the Niobrara River Valley." *Transactions of the Nebraska Academy of Science* 17: 37–60.

Faanes, C. E., and G. R. Lingle. 1995. *Breeding Birds of the Platte Valley of Nebraska.* US Geological Survey, Northern Prairie Wildlife Research Center. Jamestown, ND.

Farrar, J. (ed.) 1985. Birds of Nebraska. *NEBRASKAland Magazine* (special issue) 63(1): 1–146.

Farrar, J. 2004. "Birding Nebraska." *Nebraskaland Magazine* 82(1): 1–178.

Johnsgard, P. A. 1980. "Where have all the curlews gone?" *Natural History*, August, pp. 30–34.

Johnsgard, P. A. 2001b. *Prairie Birds: Fragile Splendor in the Great Plains.* Lawrence: University Press of Kansas. 331 pp.

Johnsgard, P. A. 2010b. "The drums of April." *Prairie Fire*, April 2010, pp. 12–13.

Johnsgard, P. A. 2014c. "The Hutton Niobrara Ranch Audubon Nature Sanctuary." *Prairie Fire*, July, pp. 12–14.

Johnsgard, P. A. 2015c. *Global Warming and Population Responses among Great Plains Birds.* Lincoln: University of Nebraska–Lincoln Digital Commons and Zea Books. 384 pp. https://digitalcommons.unl.edu/zeabook/26/

Johnsgard, P. A. 2016a. *The North American Grouse: Their Biology and Behavior.* Lincoln: University of Nebraska–Lincoln Digital Commons and Zea Books. 183 pp. http://digitalcommons.unl.edu/zeabook/41/

Johnsgard, P. A. 2016b. *The North American Geese: Their Biology and Behavior.* Lincoln: University of Nebraska–Lincoln Digital Commons and Zea Books. 159 pp. https://digitalcommons.unl.edu/zeabook/44/

Johnsgard, P. A. 2017a. *The North American Perching and Dabbling Ducks: Their Biology and Behavior.* Lincoln:

University of Nebraska–Lincoln Digital Commons and Zea Books. 228 pp. https://digitalcommons.unl.edu/zeabook/53/

Johnsgard, P. A. 2017b. *The North American Whistling-Ducks, Pochards, and Stifftails*. Lincoln: University of Nebraska–Lincoln Digital Commons and Zea Books. 188 pp. https://digitalcommons.unl.edu/zeabook/54/

Johnsgard, P. A. 2020b. *The North American Swans: Their Biology and Conservation*. Lincoln: University of Nebraska–Lincoln Digital Commons and Zea Books. 164 pp. https://digitalcommons.unl.edu/zeabook/89/

Johnsgard, P. A., and J. Kren. 2020. *The Birds of the Nebraska Sandhills*. Lincoln: University of Nebraska–Lincoln Digital Commons and Zea Books. 201 pp. https://digitalcommons.unl.edu/zeabook/96/

Johnsgard, P. A., and T. S. Shane. 2009. *Four Decades of Christmas Bird Counts in the Great Plains: Ornithological Evidence of a Changing Climate*. Lincoln: University of Nebraska–Lincoln Digital Commons and Zea Books. 201 pp. https://digitalcommons.unl.edu/bioscirnithology/46/

Johnson, D. H., ed. 2001–2004. *Effects of Management Practices on Grassland Birds*. Jamestown: USGS Northern Prairie Wildlife Research Center. (Nebraska species accounts include American bittern, Baird's sparrow, bobolink, Brewer's sparrow, burrowing owl, chestnut-collared longspur, clay-colored sparrow, dickcissel, eastern meadowlark, ferruginous hawk, field sparrow, golden eagle, grasshopper sparrow, greater prairie-chicken, greater sage-grouse, Henslow's sparrow, horned lark, lark bunting, lark sparrow, LeConte's sparrow, lesser prairie-chicken, loggerhead shrike, long-billed curlew, marbled godwit, McCown's (thick-billed) longspur, merlin, mountain plover, Nelson's sharp-tailed sparrow, northern harrier, prairie falcon, Savannah sparrow, sedge wren, short-eared owl, Sprague's pipit, Swainson's hawk, upland sandpiper, vesper sparrow, western meadowlark, willet, and Wilson's phalarope. These accounts are available online at https://pubs.er.usgs.gov/publication/pp1842 and most are also available by performing a title search [of the main title] at https://digitalcommons.unl.edu.)

Jones, J. O. 1990. *Where the Birds Are: A Guide to All 50 States and Canada*. New York: William Morrow.

Jorgensen, J. 2012. *Birds of the Rainwater Basin, Nebraska*. Lincoln: Nebraska Game and Parks Commission.

Kaufman, K. 2003. *City Birding*. New York: Stackpole Books.

Mollhoff, W. 2016. The Second Nebraska Breeding Bird Atlas. *Bulletin of the University of Nebraska State Museum* 29. 304 pp.

Short, L. L., Jr. 1965. Hybridization in the Flickers (*Colaptes*) of North America. *Bulletin of the American Museum of Natural History* 129: 311–428.

Sibley, C. G., and L. L. Short, Jr. 1964. "Hybridization in the orioles of the Great Plains." *Condor* 66: 130–150.

Sibley, C. G., and D. A. West. 1959. "Hybridization in the rufous-sided towhees of the Great Plains." *Auk* 76: 326–338.

West, D. A. 1962. "Hybridization in grosbeaks (*Pheucticus*) of the Great Plains." *Auk* 79: 399–424.

Zimmerman, J. L. 1993. *The Birds of Konza: The Avian Ecology of the Tallgrass Prairie*. University of Kansas Press, Lawrence. 186 pp.

Cranes

Baasch, G., D. Wright, A. J. Caven, and K. L. Metzger. 2017. *Evaluation of Nocturnal Roost and Diurnal Sites Used by Whooping Cranes in the Great Plains, United States*. US Geological Survey Open-File Report 2016-1209. 29 pp. https://doi.org/10.3133/ofr20161209

Dority, B., E. Thompson, S. Kaskie, and L. Tschauner. 2017. *The Economic Impact of the Annual Crane Migration on Central Nebraska*. Kearney: Bureau of Business and Technology, University of Nebraska at Kearney. 22 pp.

Gill, K., and P. A. Johnsgard. 2010. "The whooping cranes: Survivors against all odds." *Prairie Fire*, September. pp. 12, 13, 16, 22.

Johnsgard, P. A. 1981. *Those of the Gray Wind: The Sandhill Cranes*. New York: St. Martin's Press. 150 pp.

Johnsgard, P. A. 1983. *Cranes of the World*. Bloomington: Indiana University Press. 256 pp. (For a digital version, see https://digitalcommons.unl.edu/bioscicranes/.)

Johnsgard, P. A. 1991. *Crane Music: A Natural History of American Cranes*. Washington, DC: Smithsonian Institution Press. 136 pp.

Johnsgard, P. A. 2003b. "Great gathering on the Great Plains." *National Wildlife* 41(3): 20–29. https://digitalcommons.unl.edu/johnsgard/38/

Johnsgard, P. A. 2009e. "Nature notes: The wings of March." *Prairie Fire*, March 2009, pp. 1, 17, 18, 19.

Johnsgard, P. A. 2011. *Sandhill and Whooping Cranes: Ancient Voices over America's Wetlands*. Lincoln: University of Nebraska Press. 155 pp.

Johnsgard, P. A. 2015d. *A Chorus of Cranes: The Cranes of North America and the World*. Boulder: University Press of Colorado. 242 pp.

Johnsgard, P. A. 2020d. *The Lives, Lore, and Literature of Cranes: A Catechism for Crane Lovers*. Lincoln: University of Nebraska–Lincoln Digital Commons and Zea Books. 144 pp. https://digitalcommons.unl.edu/zeabook/93/

Jorgensen, J. G., and M. B. Brown. 2017. "Temporal migration shifts in the Aransas–Wood Buffalo population of whooping cranes (*Grus americana*) across North America." *Waterbirds* 40: 195–208.

Burrowing owl, defensive threat

REFERENCES

US and Regional Animal Monographs and Field Guides

Vertebrates (exclusive of birds; see previous sections)

Behler, J. L., and F. W. King. 1979. *The Audubon Society Field Guide to North American Reptiles and Amphibians*. A. A. Knopf, New York. 719 pp.

Conant, R., and J. Collins. 1998. *Reptiles and Amphibians of Eastern and Central North America*. Houghton Mifflin, Boston. 640 pp.

Jones, J. K., Jr., D. M. Armstrong, and J. R. Choate. 1985. *Guide to Mammals of the Plains States*. University of Nebraska Press, Lincoln. 371 pp.

Jones, J. K., Jr., D. M. Armstrong, R. S. Hoffmann, and C. Jones. 1983. *Mammals of the Northern Great Plains*. University of Nebraska Press, Lincoln. 379 pp.

Kays, R. W., and D. E. Wilson. 2002. *Mammals of North America*. Princeton University Press, Princeton, NJ. 818 pp.

Shaw, C. E., and S. Campbell. 1974. *Snakes of the American West*. A. A. Knopf, New York. 328 pp.

Smith, H., and R. D. Brodie, Jr. 2001. *Reptiles of North America: A Guide to Field Identification*. St. Martin's Press, New York. 240 pp.

Stebbens, R. C. 2005. *A Field Guide to Western Reptiles and Amphibians*. 2nd ed. Houghton Mifflin, Boston. 533 pp.

Stebbens, R. C., and N. W. Cohen. 1995. *A Natural History of Amphibians*. Princeton University Press, Princeton, NJ. 316 pp.

Tomelleri, J. R., and M. E. Eberle. 1990. *Fishes of the Central United States*. University Press of Kansas, Lawrence. 226 pp.

Whittaker, J. O., Jr. 1980. *National Audubon Society Field Guide to North American Mammals*. Rev. ed. A. A. Knopf, New York. 935 pp.

Wilson, D. E., and S. Ruff. 1999. *The Smithsonian Book of North American Mammals*. Smithsonian Institution Press, Washington, DC. 816 pp.

Invertebrates (Insects)

Abbott, J. C. 2005. *Dragonflies and Damselflies of Texas and the South-Central United States*. Princeton University Press, Princeton, NJ. 344 pp.

Brock, J. P., and K. Kaufman. 2003. *Kaufman Field Guide to Butterflies of North America*. Houghton Mifflin, Boston. 392 pp.

Capinera, J. L., R. D. Scott, and T. J. Walker. 2004. *Field Guide to Grasshoppers, Katydids and Crickets of the United States*. Cornell University Press, Ithaca, NY. 249 pp.

Dankert, N., D. Brust, H. Nagel, and S. M. Spomer. 2005. *Butterflies of Nebraska*. Kearney: University of Nebraska at Kearney. http://www.lopers.net/student_org/NebraskaInverts/butterfiles/home.htm (Version 5APR2005)

Dunkle, S. W. 2000. *Dragonflies through Binoculars: A Field Guide to Dragonflies of North America*. Oxford University Press, New York. 266 pp.

Eaton, E. R., and K. Kaufman. 2007. *Kaufman Field Guide to Insects of North America*. Houghton Mifflin, Boston.

Ferris, X. D., and E. M. Brown. 1981. *Butterflies of the Rocky Mountain States*. University of Oklahoma Press, Norman.

Glassberg, J. 1999. *Butterflies through Binoculars: The East: A Field Guide to the Butterflies of Eastern North America*. Oxford University Press, New York. 400 pp.

Glassberg, J. 2001. *Butterflies through Binoculars: The West: A Field Guide to the Butterflies of Western North America*. Oxford University Press, New York. 364 pp.

Heitzman, J. R., and J. E. Heitzman. 1996. *Butterflies and Moths of Missouri*. Missouri Department of Conservation, Jefferson City. 385 pp.

Howe, W. H. 1975. *The Butterflies of North America*. Doubleday, New York. 633 pp.

Marrone, G. M. 2002. *Field Guide to Butterflies of South Dakota*. South Dakota Department of Game, Fish & Parks, Pierre. 474 pp.

Milne, L., and M. Milne. 1989. *Field Guide to North American Insects and Spiders*. A. A. Knopf, New York. 992 pp.

Mitchell, R. T., and H. S. Zim. 2001. *Butterflies and Moths (A Golden Guide from St. Martin's Press)*. St. Martin's Press, New York. 160 pp.

Opler, P. A. 1999. *A Field Guide to the Western Butterflies*. Houghton Mifflin, Boston. 560 pp.

Paulson, D. 2009. *Dragonflies and Damselflies of the West*. Princeton University Press, Princeton, NJ. 534 pp.

Pyle, R. M. 1981. *The Audubon Society Field Guide to North American Butterflies*. Chanticleer Press, New York.

Schlicht., D., J. Downey, and J. Nekola. 2007. *Butterflies of Iowa*. University of Iowa Press, Iowa City. 400 pp.

Scott, J. A. 1986. *The Butterflies of North America: A Natural History and Field Guide*. Stanford University Press, Stanford, CA. 664 pp.

Williams, P. H., R. W. Thorp, and L. L. Richardson. 2014. *Bumble Bees of North America: An Identification Guide*. 208 pp.

Wilson, J., and O. J. Messinger. 2015. *The Bees in Your Backyard: A Guide to North America's Bees*. Princeton University Press, Princeton, NJ. 288 pp.

Long-billed curlew in flight

Index

Counties

Adams County 72-73, 126
Antelope County 20, 59-60, 117, 152
Arthur County 46, 107, 160

Banner County 34-36
Blaine County 45, 106
Boone County 61, 152
Box Butte County 32
Boyd County 23, 58
Brown County 41-43, 105
Brown Lake 46
Buffalo County 62-64, 66, 72, 121, 152
Burt County 80
Butler County 83, 157

Cass County 89, 134
Cedar County 59, 78, 152
Chase County 49, 51-52, 111
Cherry County 16, 39-42, 44, 54, 103, 148
Cheyenne County 37
Clay County 73-74, 123
Colfax County 80-81, 152
Cuming County 80
Custer County 46

Dakota County 78-79
Dawes County 29, 30, 31-32, 97
Dawson County 51, 110
Deuel County 38, 102
Diamond Bar Lake 46
Dixon County 77, 78, 127, 152
Dodge County 81, 128
Douglas County 83-84, 131, 152
Dundy County 51, 54

Fillmore County 69, 74-75, 124, 151, 153
Franklin County 25, 75, 125
Frontier County 52. 55, 112
Furnas County 55, 136, 151, 153

Gage County 92,
Garden County 20, 29, 37-38, 98, 102
Garfield County 45, 60
Gosper County 25, 51, 52-53, 56, 113
Grant County 43
Greeley County 61

Hall County 64-68, 122, 148, 153
Hamilton County 68-69, 123, 153

Harlan County 55, 115
Hayes County 52
Hitchcock County 54-55, 114
Holt County 58-59
Hooker County 45
Howard County 62, 148

Jefferson County 25, 91-92, 153
Johnson County 92, 137, 153-54

Kearney County 70-72, 125
Keith County 29, 46-49, 108
Keya Paha County 24, 41, 104
Kimball County 36, 100
Knox County 23, 59, 116, 154

Lancaster County 26, 82, 86-89, 130, 133, 148, 151, 154
Lincoln County 49-50, 109
Logan County 46
Loup County 45

Madison County 61, 118, 154
McPherson County 46
Merrick County 68, 119, 156
Morrill County 20, 36-37, 101

Nance County 24, 62, 119, 156
Nemaha County 92-93, 138, 151, 156
Nuckolls County 76

Otoe County 91, 135, 156

Pawnee County 21, 92, 93, 139, 151, 156
Perkins County 49
Phelps County 25, 53-54, 113
Pierce County 60, 118, 148
Platte County 61, 119, 156
Polk County 62

Red Willow County 52, 55
Richardson County 77, 93, 95, 138, 156
Rock County 40, 43

Saline County 91
Sarpy County 84-85, 91, 131
Saunders County 83, 130, 156-57
Scotts Bluff County 34, 99
Seward County 25, 85-86, 132, 148, 157
Sheridan County 20, 29, 32-34, 98
Sherman County 62, 120, 148

Sioux County 19, 29-31, 96, 158
Stanton County 79-80, 157

Thayer County 76, 157
Thomas County 40, 45
Thurston County 79

Valley County 60

Washington County 81-83, 129, 157
Wayne County 79, 157
Webster County 76
Wheeler County 58, 60

York County 69, 75

Described Sites

Abbreviations:
NWR, national wildlife refuge;
SRA, state recreation area;
WMA, wildlife management area;
WPA, wildlife production area

Agate Fossil Beds National Monument 19-20, 28, 30, 158
Alda Crane Viewing Site 19, 66
Alexandria Lakes SRA/WMA 91
Allwine Prairie Tract 152
American Game Marsh WMA 43
Amick Acres 66-68
Arbor Lake WMA 87, 89
Arbor Lodge State Historical Park 91
Arcadia Diversion Dam SRA 46
Arrowhead WMA 92
Ashfall Fossil Beds State Historical Park 20, 59, 158
Ash Grove WMA 75
Ash Hollow State Historical Park 37-38
Atkinson Lake SRA 58
Atlanta WPA 53-54
Audubon Society of Omaha Prairie Preserve, The 152-53
Ayr Lake 73

Bader Memorial Park Natural Area 68, 156
Ballards Marsh WMA 40
Barnett Park 55
Bartley Diversion Dam WMA 55
Bassway Strip WMA 63

INDEX

Basswood Ridge WMA 79
Bauermeister Prairie 84, 153
Bazile Creek WMA 59
Beaver Bend WMA 61
Berg Prairie East 156
Berg Prairie West 156
Big Alkali WMA 40
Big Indian Recreation Area 92
Birdwood Creek 50
Birdwood Lake WMA 50
Bitterns Call WMA 51
Bittersweet WMA 38
Black Island WMA 80
Bluebill Hawk WMA 75
Blue Hole WMA 63
Bluestem Lake SRA 86
Bluestem Prairie Preserve 153
Bluestem WPA 70
Bluewing WMA 74
Bobcat WMA 41
Bohemia Prairie WMA 59, 154
Boosalis Park 87
Bowman Lake SRA 62
Bowring Ranch State Historical Park 41
Bowwood WMA 93
Box Butte SRA 32
Box Elder Canyon WMA 50
Boyer Chute NWR 83, 157
Branched Oak SRA 85, 86, 154
Brauning WPA 75
Bridgeport saline marsh 36
Bridgeport SRA 36
Brown Lake 46
Brownville SRA 93
Bruce L. Anderson Recreation Area (Recharge Lake) 70
Buckskin Hills WMA 78, 152
Buffalo Creek WMA 34
Bulrush WMA 74
Burchard Lake WMA 93, 151, 156
Bur Oak WMA 85, 156

Calamus Reservoir SRA/WMA 45, 60
Cambridge Diversion Dam 55
Cedar Point Biological Station 49, 161
Chadron State Park 31-32
Chalco Hills Recreation Area 84
Chalkrock WMA 78
Champion Lake SRA 52
Chat Canyon WMA 41
Chester Island WMA 50
Chet and Jane Fleisbach WMA 36
Chimney Rock National Historic Site 17, 20, 36
Clarence and Ruth Fertig Tallgrass Prairie 152
Clark WPA 70
Clatonia Public Use Area 92
Clear Creek WMA 22, 38, 48
Clyde and Thelma Gewacke Prairie 153
Conestoga Lake SRA 86
Cornhusker WMA 64
Cottonmill Lake Public Use Area 63

Cottontail Lake 86
Cottonwood Lake SRA 41
Cottonwood–Steverson Lake WMA 40-41
Cottonwood WPA 53
Council Creek WMA 62
County Line WPA 69, 75
Courthouse Rock 36
Cozad WMA 51
Crane Trust 18, 56, 66, 67, 68, 153
Crane Trust Nature and Visitor Center 66
Crescent Lake NWR 20, 24, 29, 34, 37, 40
Crystal Lake Recreation Area 72-73
Cub Creek Recreation Area 41
Cuming City Cemetery 157
"Cupola, The" 21
Czechland Lake Recreation Area 83

Darr Strip WMA 51
Davis Creek Recreation Area 60, 61
Dead Timber SRA 81
Deep Well WMA 69
DeSoto NWR 77, 81-83, 157
Diamond Bar Lake 46
Diamond Lake WMA 92
DLD State Wayside Recreation Area 73
Dogwood WMA 51
Donald Whitney Memorial WMA 92
Dr. Bruce Cowgill WMA 68
Dry Lake 46

Eagle Scout Park 68
East Cozad WMA 51
East Hershey WMA 50
East Odessa SRA 63
East Sutherland WMA 49
East Willow Island WMA 51
Eckhardt Lagoon WPA 74
Elkhorn River 58, 59, 61, 79-81, 157
Elk Point Bend WMA 25, 78, 152
Elley WPA 52
Elm Creek WMA 76
Elmer Klapka Farm 156
Elwood Reservoir WMA 51, 52
Enders Reservoir SRA 51
Enders Reservoir WMA 51
Eugene T. Mahoney State Park 89

Facus Springs 36
Fontenelle Forest 11, 77, 84, 85, 153, 159
Fort Atkinson State Historical Park 20, 83, 157
Fort Hartsuff State Historical Park 60
Fort Kearny Hike-Bike Trail 70-72
Fort Kearny SRA 19, 72
Fort Kearny State Historical Park 72
Fort McPherson National Cemetery 50
Fort Niobrara NWR 21, 39-40, 43, 160
Fort Robinson State Park 21-22, 24, 30, 31
Four-Mile Creek WMA 95
Frank L. and Lillian Pokorny Memorial Prairie 152

Freeman Lakes WPA 85
Fremont Lakes SRA 81
Fremont Slough WMA 50
Frerichs WPA 70
Funk WPA 53

Gadwall WMA 69
Gallagher Canyon SRA 51
Gavins Point Dam 78
George Clayton Hall County Park 68
George Syas WMA 61
Gifford Point (Gifford Point WMA and Gifford Farm Education Center) 85
Gilbert-Baker WMA 30, 31
Gjerloff Prairie 153
Gleason WPA 70
Glenn Cunningham Lake 84
Glenvil WPA 74
Goldeneye WMA 38
Goldenrod WMA 38
Goose Lake WMA 58
Green Acres WPA 74
Greenhead WMA 74
Greenvale WMA 59, 154
Greenwing WMA 74
Griess WPA 75
Grove Lake WMA 59, 152

Hackberry Creek WMA 59
Hall County Park. *See* George Clayton Hall County Park
Hannon WPA 64
Hansen WPA 74
Harlan County Lake 55
Harms WPA 74
Harold W. Andersen WMA 62
Harvard WPA 56-58, 73
Hastings Museum 56, 73
Hayes Center WMA 52
Hedgefield Lake WMA 86
Henry Dieken Tallgrass Prairie 156
Hershey WMA 49
Hickory Ridge WMA 92
Hidden Marsh WMA 70
Holmes Lake Park 87
Holstein Hills 73
Homestead National Historical Park 22, 92, 153
Homestead Prairie 153
Hull Lake WMA 58
Hultine WPA 73
Hutton Niobrara Ranch Wildlife Sanctuary 43, 161

Imperial Reservoir 52
Indian Cave State Park 22, 77, 95, 156
Indian Creek WMA 76
Iron Horse Trail WMA 92, 93, 95
Ivan A. and Ivan F. Lamb Tallgrass Prairie 153-54

INDEX

J-2 Hydro Power Plant 52-53, 56
Jack Sinn Memorial WMA 83, 87
Jail Rock 36
James Ranch 30
Jeffrey Canyon WMA 49
Jeffrey Reservoir 49
Jensen Lagoon WPA 70
Jensen Prairie. *See* Audubon Society of Omaha Prairie Preserve, The
Johnson Lake SRA 51, 52
Johnson WPA 53
John W. and Louise Seier NWR 39-40, 43
Jones WPA 54
Joslyn Art Museum 11, 22

Keller Park SRA 41
Keller School Land WMA 41
Kenesaw WPA 72
Killdeer WMA 86
Killdeer WPA 70
Kilpatrick Lake 32
Kingsley Dam 48-49
Kinters Ford WMA 95
Kiowa WMA 34
Kirkpatrick Basin North WMA 70
Kirkpatrick Basin South WMA 70
Kissinger Basin WMA 74
Knott Tallgrass Prairie 156-57
Krause WPA 75

Lake Babcock Waterfowl Refuge 61
Lake Hastings 73
Lake Maloney SRA 49
Lake McConaughy SRA 22, 48
Lake Minatare SRA 34
Lake North 61
Lake Ogallala 48, 49
Lake Ogallala SRA 22, 48-49
Lake View Campground 49
Lake Yankton 78
Lange WPA 73-74
Larkspur WMA 83
Lewis and Clark Lake 59
Lewis and Clark Lake SRA 59
Lewis and Clark National Historic Trail Headquarters Visitor Center 21
Lewis and Clark Visitor Center 21, 78, 91
Lillian Annette Rowe Sanctuary and Iain Nicolson Audubon Center 18-19, 56, 57, 63, 66, 152, 160
Limestone Bluffs WMA 75
Lincoln Creek Prairie and Trail 153
Lincoln Saline Wetlands Nature Center 87, 154
Lindau WPA 70
Linder WPA 53
Little Blue River 73, 76
Little Blue WMA 76
Little Salt Fork Marsh Preserve 89
Loch Linda WMA 64
Lodgepole Creek 36

Long Lake SRA 43
Long Pine WMA 41
Lookingglass Creek WMA 61
Louis and Grace Bentzinger Tallgrass Prairie 154
Louisville Lakes SRA 89-90
Loup Junction WMA 62
Loup Lands WMA 62

Macon Lakes WPA 75
Madigan Prairie 83, 157
Mallard Haven WPA 58, 75
Margrave WMA 95
Marie Ratzlaff Prairie Preserve 153
Marshes near the Arthur County border 46
Marshes near the McPherson County border 46
Marsh Hawk WMA 75
Marsh Wren Saline Wetland 89
Martin's Reach WMA 64
Maskenthine Lake Recreation Area 80
Massie WPA 56-58, 74
Mayberry WMA 93
McMurtrey Marsh 74
Meadowlark Recreation Area 85
Meadowlark WPA 74
Medicine Creek Reservoir 52
Medicine Creek SRA/WMA 52
Meridian WMA 157
Merritt Reservoir WMA 40
Metcalf WMA 32
Middle Decatur Bend WMA 80
Midway Lake WMA 51
Milburn Dam WMA 45
Missouri National Recreational River 23, 25, 58, 59, 78
Missouri River Basin Lewis and Clark Visitor Center and Interpretive Trail 21, 91
Missouri River federal access areas 79
Moger WPA 74
Monroe Canyon 29, 31
MoPac East Recreational Trail 89
Mormon Island Crane Meadows 56, 68, 153, 160
Mormon Island SRA 64
Morphy WPA 75
Muskrat Run WMA 49

Neale Woods Nature Center 77, 84, 85, 153, 159
Nebraska National Forest, Bessey Ranger District 40, 45
Nebraska National Forest, Pine Ridge Ranger District 30, 31
Neligh Park 80
Nelson WPA 69
Nine Bridges Bridge 68
Nine Mile Creek WMA 34
Nine-Mile Prairie 87, 140, 142, 151, 154, 160
Niobrara State Park 23, 58, 59, 154

Niobrara Valley Preserve 24, 39, 41, 43, 159, 160
Northeast Sacramento WMA 72
North Lake Basin WMA 86
North Platte NWR 24, 34
North Platte sewage lagoons 50
North River WMA 49

Oak Glen WMA 85
Oak Lake Park 87
Oak Valley WMA 61, 154
Ogallala Strip WMA
Oglala National Grassland 24, 26, 27, 29, 30, 31
Olive Creek SRA 86
Oliver Reservoir SRA 36
Olson Nature Preserve 152
Omadi Bend WMA 79
Omaha Indian Reservation 24
Osage WMA 92
Oshkosh sewage lagoons 38

Papio D-4 Lake 84
Parshall Bridge WMA 58
Pawnee Lake SRA 86, 154
Pawnee Park 61
Pawnee Prairie WMA 93, 151, 156
Pelican Point SRA 80
Peterson WMA 30
Peterson WPA 52
Pibel Lake Recreation Area 60
Pine Glen WMA 41
Pine Ridge National Recreation Area 31
Pintail WMA 69
Pioneers Park 87, 89, 154
Pioneers Park Nature Center 87, 154
Platte River Road 19, 66
Platte River State Park 89
Platte WMA 50
Plum Creek WMA 51
Ponca Indian Reservation 25
Ponca State Park 23, 25, 77, 78, 152
Ponderosa WMA 32
Powder Horn WMA 81
Prairie-chicken lek 63-64, 73, 156
Prairie Corridor on Haines Branch 87, 89, 154
Prairie Dog WPA 70
Prairie Knoll WMA 93
Prairie Lake Recreation Area 72
Prairie Marsh WMA 76
Prairie Wolf WMA 62
Pressey WMA 46

Q2 Basin 69
Quadhamer Marsh WPA 75

Rainwater Basin 18, 19, 25-26, 53, 56, 58, 68, 69, 72, 73, 74, 85, 161, 162
Rakes Creek WMA 91
Randall W. Schilling WMA 91

INDEX

Rauscher WPA 75
Ravenna Lake SRA 63
Real WPA 75
Recharge Lake. *See* Bruce L. Anderson Recreation Area
Redbird WMA 58
Red Cedar Lake 83, 157
Red Fox WMA 79
Redington Gap road 36, 37
Redtail WMA 83
Red Willow Reservoir SRA/WMA 52, 54
Redwing WMA 59-60
Renquist Basin WMA 70
Richard Plautz Crane Viewing Site 19, 64, 66
Ritterbush Marsh WPA 75
Rock Creek Lake SRA 54
Rock Creek Station State Historical Park and SRA 91-92, 153
Rockford SRA 92
Rock Glen WMA 92, 153
Rolland WPA 75
Rose Creek WMA 153
Rulo Bluffs Preserve 26, 77, 95, 156

Sacramento-Wilcox WMA 54
Saline marsh near Bridgeport 36
Samuel R. McKelvie National Forest 40, 41
Sandhills marshes near Lakeside 32-34
Sandpiper WMA 75
Sandpiper (North Hultine) WPA 73
Sandy Channel SRA 63
Schlagel Creek WMA 40
Schramm Park SRA (and Schramm Education Center) 85
Scotia Canal WMA 60
Scotts Bluff National Monument 26, 27, 34, 35
Sherman Reservoir SRA/WMA 62
Shoemaker Island road 66
Shuck WPA 74
Sinninger Lagoon WPA 69
Sioux Strip WMA 79
Smartweed Marsh West WMA 76
Smartweed Marsh WMA 76
Smiley Canyon 31
Smith Falls State Park 40
Smith Lake WMA 32, 34, 37,
Smith WPA 56, 58, 74

Soldier Creek Wilderness 30
Southeast Sacramento WMA 55
South Sacramento WMA 55
South Twin Lake WMA 41
Sowbelly Canyon 29, 30-31
Spencer Dam WMA 59
Spikerush WMA 69, 70
Spring Creek Prairie Audubon Center 26, 87, 88, 89, 90, 140, 154, 160
Springer WPA 69
Stagecoach Lake SRA 86
Standing Bear Lake 84
Stolley Prairie 153
Storm Prairie 156-57
Stuhr Museum of the Prairie Pioneer 56, 68
Summit Reservoir SRA 80
Sunny Hollow WMA 62, 156
Sutherland Reservoir SRA 49
Swan Creek WMA 91
Swanson Reservoir and WMA 54-55

Table Rock WMA 93, 156
Tamora WPA 85
Taylor Ranch road 64-66
Teal WMA 86
Theesen WPA 74
Thomas Creek WMA 41
Thompson-Barnes WMA 157
Timber Point 83
Toadstool Geological Park 24, 26, 30
Triple Creek WMA 91
Tri-state corner 36
Troester WPA 69
Twin Lakes WMA: in Rock County, 43; in Seward County, 85, 157
Twin Oaks WMA 92
Two Rivers SRA/WMA 84

Union Pacific SRA 63
University of Nebraska State Museum 19, 27
University of Nebraska State Museum Trailside 22

Valentine NWR 40, 43
Verdon Lake SRA 95
Victoria Springs SRA 46
Victor Lakes WPA 52

Waco Basin WPA 69
Wagon Train Lake SRA 86
Walgren Lake WMA 32
Walnut Creek Public Use Area 91
Wapiti WMA 50
War Axe SRA 63
Wehrspann Lake. *See* Chalco Hills Recreation Area
Weis Lagoon 75
Wellfleet WMA 50
Weseman WPA 72
West Brady WMA 50
West Cozad WMA 51
West Sacramento WMA 54
Whitefront WMA 74
Whitetail WMA 80-81
Whitewater Lake 46
Whitney Lake WMA 32
Wildcat Creek Tallgrass Prairie 153
Wildcat Hills 11, 27, 29, 34, 37
Wildcat Hills Nature Center 27, 34
Wildcat Hills SRA 34, 36
Wilderness Park (Cuming County) 80
Wilderness Park (Lancaster County) 87-89, 154
Wildwood Lake WMA 87
Wilkinson WMA 61, 156
Wilkins WPA 75
Willa Cather Memorial Prairie 76
Willow Creek SRA 60
Willow Island WMA 51
Willow Lake WMA 43
Wilson Creek WMA 91
Windmill SRA 63
Winnebago Indian Reservation 24
Wiseman WMA 78, 152
Wolf-Wildcat WMA 92
Wood Duck WMA 79, 157
Wyuka Cemetery 89

Yankee Hill Lake WMA 86
Yellowbanks WMA 61
Youngson WPA 70
Yutan Prairie 156-57

Zorinsky Lake Park 84

IN MEMORIAM

Paul A. Johnsgard

June 28, 1931 – May 28, 2021

Books on Nebraska and the Great Plains by Paul A. Johnsgard

The Platte: Channels in Time. 1984, 2008. University of Nebraska Press. 176 pp.

This Fragile Land: A Natural History of the Nebraska Sandhills. 1995. University of Nebraska Press. 256 pp.

The Nature of Nebraska: Ecology and Biodiversity. 2001. University of Nebraska Press. 402 pp.

Prairie Birds: Fragile Splendor in the Great Plains. 2001. University of Kansas Press. 331 pp.

Great Wildlife of the Great Plains. 2003. University Press of Kansas. 309 pp.

Lewis and Clark on the Great Plains: A Natural History. 2003. University of Nebraska Press. 143 pp.

Prairie Dog Empire: A Saga of the Shortgrass Prairie. 2005. University of Nebraska Press. 243 pp.

The Niobrara: A River Running Through Time. 2007. University of Nebraska Press. 375 pp.

Wind Through the Buffalo Grass: A Lakota Story Cycle. 2008. Plains Chronicles Press. 214 pp.

Birds of the Great Plains: Breeding Species and Their Distribution: New Expanded Edition (2009). 2009. UNL Digital Commons. 530 pp.

A Nebraska Bird-Finding Guide. 2011. Zea Books, UNL Digital Commons. 167 pp.

Nebraska's Wetlands: Their Wildlife and Ecology. 2012. Nebraska Water Survey Paper No. 78, Conservation and Survey Division, School of Natural Resources, Institute of Agriculture and Natural Resources, University of Nebraska–Lincoln. UNL Digital Commons. 200 pp.

Wetland Birds of the Central Plains: South Dakota, Nebraska, and Kansas. 2012. Zea Books, UNL Digital Commons. 275 pp.

Wings over the Great Plains: Bird Migrations in the Central Flyway. 2012. Zea Books, UNL Digital Commons. 249 pp.

The Birds of Nebraska, Revised Edition 2013. 2013. Zea Books, UNL Digital Commons. 146 pp.

Seasons of the Tallgrass Prairie: A Nebraska Year. 2014. University of Nebraska Press. 171 pp.

At Home and at Large in the Great Plains: Essays and Memories. 2015. Zea Books, UNL Digital Commons. 169 pp.

Birding Nebraska's Central Platte Valley and Rainwater Basin. 2015. Zea Books, UNL Digital Commons. 54 pp.

Global Warming and Population Responses among Great Plains Birds. 2015. Zea Books, UNL Digital Commons. 384 pp.

The Birds of Nebraska. (2nd digital ed.) 2018. Zea Books, UNL Digital Commons. 307 pp.

Ecology of a Tallgrass Treasure: Audubon's Spring Creek Prairie. 2018. Zea Books, UNL Digital Commons. 183 pp.

A Naturalist's Guide to the Great Plains. 2018. Zea Books, UNL Digital Commons. 161 pp.

Audubon's Lillian Annette Rowe Sanctuary: A Refuge, a River, and a Migration. 2020. Prairie Chronicles Press. 204 pp.

Wildlife of Nebraska: A Natural History. 2020. University of Nebraska Press. 528 pp.

Coauthored Books

Birds of the Central Platte River Valley and Adjacent Counties, with Mary Bomberger Brown. 2013. Zea Books, UNL Digital Commons. 182 pp.

Natural Treasures of the Great Plains: An Ecological Perspective, with Tom Lynch and Jack Philips (coeditor, author, and illustrator). 2015. Prairie Chronicles Press. 216 pp.

The Birds of the Nebraska Sandhills, with Josef Kren. 2020. Zea Books, UNL Digital Commons. 201 pp.

www.ingramcontent.com/pod-product-compliance
Lightning Source LLC
Chambersburg PA
CBHW081233170426
43198CB00017B/2747